GW00646547

200 Modern Brilliancies

Kevin Wicker

Arco Publishing, Inc. New York

Published 1981 by Arco Publishing, Inc.
219 Park Avenue South, New York, N.Y. 10003

ISBN 0-668-05214-7
Library of Congress Catalog Card Number: 80-54188

Printed in Great Britain

Contents by Opening

Introduction

The material in this book consists of 200 decisive chess games, each of 24 moves or less, and each accompanied by a diagram and notes. This is very much a book that the reader should use constructively; every diagram appears at a critical point in the game, normally where a sacrifice is conceived or executed, and it's well worth trying to work out the next move. Don't waste it - this kind of practice is invaluable towards sharpening up your own practical play.

Since all the games are short, they are obviously critical for the student of opening theory - although I have avoided extensive 'theoretical' annotations because (a) space forbids and (b) serious opening specialists will already know far more than I can say. The games are however arranged in order of openings - starting at 1 e4, going through 1 d4, and finishing with various 'flank' openings. A list of contents by openings is on page 5.

The reader will notice that nearly a third of the material covers the Sicilian Defence. This is not due to any preference on my part (I don't play it!) but to the relative weight and quality of material available - it seems that a small slip by Black in the Sicilian is especially prone to violent punishment.

Many of the players will be well-known to you: Spassky, Tal, Korchnoi, Larsen, Timman etc., and many strangers are here too. I've simply selected what to me are the most engaging brevities of the last ten years. Particularly attractive are the games of Planinc (look at game 175!), Walter Browne, and the two wins by Ljubojevic - but each to his own favourites. I will just exhort you, once again, to have a bash at the diagrams - with pen and paper if you like. It really is worth it.

Some acknowledgements are in order. First, to the players in this book - winners and losers alike - without whom...! To John Nicholson, who helped me considerably with research; of course, to Bob Wade, even though he refused to show me his games from Malta; and Paul Lamford, for enthusiastic editorial assistance. Also Cary Groves for helping with the proofreading.

KJW
London, July 1980

Symbols

!	Good move
!!	Very strong move
?	Weak move
??	Bad blunder
!?	Interesting
?!	Dubious
+	Check
TN	Theoretical Novelty
1-0	White won
0-1	Black won
½:½	Draw

200 Modern Brilliancies

Game 1: Centre Counter

Modern chess is a tough, competitive affair; why? The answer, I believe, has a lot to do with the example of the champions. And here was a champion indeed.

Fischer-Addison
Palma de Mallorca 1970

1 e4 d5!? 2 ed ♕xd5 3 ♘c3 ♕d8 4 d4 ♘f6 5 ♗c4 ♗f5 6 ♕f3!

A strong move which envisages the speculative sacrifice of a pawn for rapid development of his ♕-side. First Black must attend to the threat against b7.

6...♕c8 7 ♗g5! ♗xc2 8 ♖c1 ♗g6 9 ♘ge2 ♘bd7 10 0-0 e6 11 ♗xf6 gf

On 11...♘xf6 12 d5! Black can offer to return the pawn with 12...♗d6!? 13 de 0-0, although here too White can complicate by 13 ♗b5+ ♔e7 14 de fe 15 ♖e1. Instead, he tries to close the position at the cost of a weakened pawn structure. 12 d5 e5 13 ♗b5 ♗e7 14 ♘g3 a6 15 ♗d3 ♕d8

Now castling is suspect in view of the weakness on f5 and the possibility of h4-h5 for White.
16 h4! h5 17 ♗f5 ♘b6 (1)

18 ♘ce4!
A subtle pawn offer purely to open lines which Black can hardly decline - he's running short of alternatives.
18...♘xd5 19 ♖fd1 c6 20 ♘c3! ♕b6 21 ♖xd5! cd 22 ♘xd5 ♕xb2

No better was 22...♕d8 23 ♗xg6 fg 24 ♘c7+ ♔f7 25 ♕b3+! with ♘e6+ to follow.
23 ♖b1 ♕xa2 24 ♖xb7 1-0

There is no defence, i.e. 24...♗d8 25 ♗xg6 fg 26 ♘xf6+ ♗xf6 27 ♕xf6.

Game 2: Centre Counter

Mengarini-Schiller
New York 1980

1 e4 d5 2 ed ♕xd5 3 ♘c3 ♕d6 (?! 3
...♕a5) 4 d4 c6 5 ♗c4 ♘f6 6 ♘ge2!
♗g4 7 f3 ♗h5 (7...♗f5!?) 8 ♗f4
♕d8 9 ♗e5

Better 9 ♕d2 followed by either
0-0 or 0-0-0, according to Blumenfeld.

9...♘bd7 10 ♘f4 e6 11 ♕e2 (11
♘xh5 ♘xh5 threat ...♘xe5 and ...
♕h4+) 11...♕a5 12 g4?! ♗g6 13
h4? *(2)*

Interesting, and even better a
move before, was 13 ♗xf6 followed
by ♘xe6 with an attack. The text
looks crushing (13...h6 14 ♘xg6)
but allows an effective counter-
attack.

13...♗b4! 14 h5

On 14 ♕e3 Blumenfeld gives 14...
♘d5! 15 ♘xd5 cd 16 ♗b3 ♖c8! 17
♔d2 ♘xe5 18 de d4! 19 ♕xd4 ♖d8,
or here 17 ♗xg7 ♖g8 18 ♗e5
♗xc3+ 19 bc ♖xc3 20 ♕d2 ♖e3+!
21 ♔d1 ♕xd2+ 22 ♔xd2 ♖xf3.

Unclear is 14 0-0!?

14...♘xe5! 15 de ♗xc3+ 16 bc
♕xc3+ 17 ♔f2 0-0-0 18 hg

Neither 18 ♖ad1? ♗xc2 19 ef
♗xd1 20 ♖xd1 ♖xd1, nor 18 ♔g3?
♖d2 19 ♕f1 ♘e4+ 20 ♔h4 ♖f2
were helpful. Black's reply is a
'desperado' sac.

18...♘xg4+! 19 fg ♖d2 20 gf ♖xe2+
21 ♗xe2 ♕xe5 22 ♔f3? (Necessary
was 22 ♘d3, though Black's better.)
22...♖f8 23 ♗c4 ♖xf7 0-1

Game 3: Latvian Gambit

Atars-Tomson
Corres Theme Tournament 1973

1 e4 e5 2 ♘f3 f5?!

This eccentric opening is the
private preserve of correspondence
players and - Latvians, although to
my knowledge Tal hasn't played it
recently.

3 ♗c4 fe

Siegers-Purins, corres 1971, introduced 3...b5!? with the idea 4
♗xb5?! fe 5 ♘xe5 ♕g5. The game
went 4 ♗xg8 (4 ♗b3!?) 4...♖xg8 5
♕e2 ♕e7 6 ♕xb5?! (6 ♘c3!?) 6...
♘c6! 7 ♕d5 fe! 8 ♘xe5? ♕xe5 9
♕xg8 ♘b4! 10 ♕b3 ♘d3+!! 11 ♔e2
♗a6 12 c4 ♕d4 0-1 (13 ♖f1 ♗xc4).

4 ♘xe5 ♕g5

On 4...d5 Milić gives 5 ♕h5+ g6 6
♘xg6 ♘f6 7 ♕e5+ ♗e7 8 ♗b5+! c6
9 ♘xe7 ♕xe7 10 ♕xe7+ ♔xe7 11
♗e2 with a pawn up.

5 d4! ♕xg2 6 ♕h5+ g6 7 ♗f7+ ♔d8
8 ♗xg6! ♕xh1+ 9 ♔e2 c6 10 ♘c3
♔c7 *(3)*

This line looks like a dead duck.
Also rapid is 10...♘f6 11 ♕h4 ♗e7
12 ♗g5! ♕xa1 13 ♗xf6 ♗xf6 14
♕xf6+ ♔c7 15 ♘c4! b6 16 ♕e5+
d6 17 ♘b5+! 1-0, Purins-Englitls,
corres 1971.

11 ♗f4! ♕xa1 12 ♘xd7+! ♔xd7
Or 12...♗d6 (12...♔d8 13 ♕e5!)
13 ♘b5+! ♔xd7 (13...cb 14 ♕c5+!)
14 ♘xd6 hg 15 ♕xh8 threat ♕h3+.
13 ♕f5+ ♔d8 14 ♕xf8+ ♔d7 15
♕e8 mate

Game 4: Falkbeer Counter-Gambit

Murei-Nikitinikh
Zenit Ch (USSR Sporting Soc)
1971

1 e4 e5 2 f4!? d5!?
This move is a strategically
desirable reponse to the King's

Gambit, but must now be considered suspect at this point; it works
best after 2...ef 3 ♗c4 d5! (cf. game
6). On 2...ef 3 ♘f3 Fischer's plan
...d6, ...g5 is interesting (cf. game
5).

3 ed e4 4 d3 ed (4...♘f6) 5 ♗xd3
♕xd5?! (5...♘f6) 6 ♘c3! ♕e6+ (6
...♕xg2?? 7 ♗e4!) 7 ♘ge2 ♘h6?!
After this he's in trouble. 7...♘f6
should be tried.
8 f5! ♘xf5 9 0-0 ♘e3 10 ♗xe3
♕xe3+ 11 ♔h1 ♗d6 12 ♘f4! 0-0 13
♕h5 g6 *(4)*
On 13...h6 14 ♘g6!? looks
promising; 14...fg 15 ♕xg6 or 14
...♖e8 15 ♖xf7 ♔xf7? 16 ♘e5+
♔e7 17 ♘d5+. Or 13...f5? 14 ♗c4+
♔h8 15 ♘g6 mate.

14 Nxg6! fg 15 ♗xg6! hg 16 ♕xg6+
♔h8 17 ♘d5 ♖xf1+
On 17...♕e8 18 ♖xf8+ ♕xf8 19
♘f6! ♗f5! (19...♕g7 20 ♕h5+) 20
♕xf5 ♕h6 21 ♕c8+ ♗f8 (22...♕f8
23 ♕h3+ ♔g7 24 ♖f1 ♕xf6 25
♖xf6 ♔xf6 26 ♕f3+ and 27 ♕xb7)
22 ♖f1! is decisive.
18 ♖xf1 ♕e2 19 ♕h6+ ♔g8 20
♘f6+ 1-0

Game 5: King's Gambit Accepted

Day-Morović
Buenos Aires Olympiad 1978

1 e4 e5 2 f4 ef 3 ♘f3 d6!? 4 d4 g5
5 h4 g4 6 ♘g1!
Not 6 ♘g5?! f6 7 ♘h3 gh 8 ♕h5+
♔d7 9 ♗xf4 ♕e8! This game
suggests a definition of a 'positional
advantage'; your own moves are
easy and natural, but the opponent's
aren't. Here the centre pawns sit
like purring pussycats while Black
rushes around barking madly...
6...♗h6 7 ♘e2 ♕f6 8 ♘bc3 c6
A game Day-Berry, Calgory 1975,
went 8...♘e7 9 ♕d2 ♘bc6 10 g3 fg
11 ♕xh6 ♕f2+ 12 ♔d1 g2 13 ♗xg2
♕xg2 14 ♖g1 ♕f3 15 ♗g5! g3 16
♖xg3 ♕f1+ 17 ♔d2 ♕xa1 18 ♘d5
and White won.
9 g3 f3 10 ♘f4 ♕e7(?!) 11 ♔f2!
♘d7 12 ♗c4 b5 *(5)*
Hubris, but what else?

13 ♗xb5!
Not 13 ♗b3?! b4 14 ♘b1 ♘gf6!
13...♗xf4

This looks poor, but the
immediate 13...cb allows 14 ♘fd5
♕d8 15 ♗xh6 ♘xh6 16 ♕d2 ♘g8
17 ♘xb5 ♘df6 18 ♕f4! and the
rooks join in soon.
14 ♗xf4 cb 15 ♘xb5 ♘gf6 16
♘xd6+ ♔d8
No good is 16...♕xd6? 17 ♗xd6
♘xe4+ 18 ♔g1 ♘xd6 (18...f2+) 19
♕e1+, i.e. 19...♔f8 20 ♕b4! or 19
...♔d8 20 ♕a5+ ♘b6 21 ♕e5.
17 ♖e1! ♘h5 18 ♘f5 ♕b4 19 ♗d6!
♕xb2 20 ♖ab1 ♕xa2 21 ♕d2 ♘hf6
(What else?) 22 ♕c3! ♖g8 23 ♖a1
♕e6 24 d5! 1-0

Game 6: King's Gambit Accepted

Black was programmed by
Professor Grünblatt in Massachusetts
but the computer does badly
despite playing a 'rusty' opponent.

Fischer-Computer
1977

1 e4 e5 2 f4 ef 3 ♗c4 d5! (Best) 4
♗xd5 ♘f6 5 ♘c3 ♗b4 6 ♘f3 0-0?
Black can solve most of his
problems by 6...♗xc3 7 dc c6 8
♗c4 ♕xd1+. Perhaps the computer
can't 'judge' the merit of giving up
two bishops to displace the White
king?
7 0-0 ♘xd5?!
Tempo loss, though theory - 7...
♗xc3 8 dc c6 9 ♗c4 ♕xd1 10 ♖xd1
♘xe4 11 ♗xf4, Blackburne-Pillsbury,
Hastings 1895! - also favours White.

8 ♘xd5 ♗d6 9 d4 g5 *(6)*

Otherwise it'll simply be a pawn down.

10 ♘xg5! ♕xg5 11 e5 ♗h3 (11... ♗e7 12 ♗xf4 ♕h4 13 g3) **12 ♖f2 ♗xe5 13 de c6**

Allows ♘c7, but White has better. **14 ♗xf4 ♕g7 15 ♘f6+ ♔h8 16 ♕h5** (threat ♗h6) **16...♖d8 17 ♕xh3 ♘a6 18 ♖f3 ♕g6 19 ♖c1 ♔g7 20 ♖g3 ♖h8 21 ♕h6 mate**

Game 7: Vienna Game

Berg-Dobosz
Esbjerg II 1979

1 e4 e5 2 ♘c3 ♘f6 3 f4 d5!

Best. 3...ef? 4 e5 ♕e7 5 ♕e2 forces 5...♘g8.

4 fe ♘xe4 5 ♘f3 (5 d3!?) **5...♗g4 6 ♕e2 ♘c5?**

Correct was 6...♘xc3 7 dc with a minimal space advantage for White. The text plans to blockade with ... ♘e6, but it won't hold up.

7 d4 ♗xf3 (7...♘e6 8 ♕b5+!?) **8 ♕xf3 ♘e6 9 ♗e3 c6 10 ♗d3 ♗e7 11 0-0 0-0 12 ♕h3 g6** *(7)*

Black's play has been virtually forced.

13 ♖xf7! ♖xf7 (13...♔xf7!?) **14 ♕xe6 ♗g5**

Or 14...♕e8 15 ♖f1 ♘a6 16 ♗xa6 ba 17 ♖xf7 ♕xf7 18 ♕xc6 with a material plus.

15 ♗xg5 ♕xg5 16 ♘e4! ♕e7 (16... de 17 ♗c4) **17 ♘f6+ ♔h8 18 ♕c8+ ♖f8 19 ♕h3 ♕g7** (else ♗xg6) **20 ♖f1 h6**

Berg gives 20...♘a6 21 ♖f4 ♘b4 22 ♘xh7! and wins.

21 ♖f3 ♘a6 22 ♖g3 g5 23 ♕f5 ♘b4 (?! but 23...♖f7 24 h4) **24 ♖xg5! 1-0**

Game 8: Scotch Game

Botterill-Thomas
British Ch, Clacton 1974

1 e4 e5 2 ♘f3 ♘c6 3 d4!? ed 4 ♘xd4

Interesting is 4 c3 - the Göring Gambit. Casa-Teschner, Lugano 1980, continued 4...dc 5 ♗c4 cb 6 ♗xb2 d5? (6...d6; 6...♗b4+) 7 ed ♘ce7 8 0-0 ♘f5 9 ♗b5+! ♗d7 10 ♗xd7+ ♕xd7 11 ♘e5 ♕b5 12 ♘c3! ♕a6 (12...♕xb2 13 ♕a4+) 13 ♖e1 ♘ge7 14 ♕f3! h5 15 a4! ♖h6 16 ♘b5 ♖c8 17 ♖ac1 c6 18 d6 ♖xd6 19 ♘xd6+ ♘xd6 20 ♗a3 c5 21 ♗xc5 ♖xc5 22 ♖xc5 1-0.
4...♗c5 5 ♘b3 ♗b6 6 a4!? a6 7 ♘c3 ♘ge7 (7...d6) 8 ♗g5 0-0?! 9 ♘d5! ♗a7? *(8)*

Loses instantly! Here (and preferably on move 8), ...f6 was called for.

10 ♘f6+!! gf 11 ♗xf6 ♕e8 12 ♕h5 ♘d8 13 ♕h6 ♘e6 14 0-0-0!
Not 14 ♗c4 d5! 15 ♗xd5 (15 ed ♘f5) 15...♘xd5 16 ed ♘d4+ 17 ♔f1 ♕e2+ 18 ♔g1 ♘f3+! winning for Black. This keeps him trussed up.
14...♗xf2 15 ♖d3 ♘g6 16 ♖h3 ♗h4 17 ♖xh4 ♘xh4 18 ♕xh4 1-0
The threat is e5, ♗d3, ♕xh7 mate (Barden and Harding); but simply 19 ♕g3+ is a bigger threat, and 18... h5 19 ♕xh5 ♘g7 20 ♕g5 mates.

Game 9: Scotch Game

The winner of this game, Jean Hébert, also won the event.

Hébert-Biyiasas
Canadian Closed Ch 1978

1 e4 e5 2 ♘f3 ♘c6 3 d4!? ed 4 ♘xd4 ♕h4!? (unnatural) 5 ♘b5!? ♕xe4+?! (5...♗c5!?) 6 ♗e2 ♕d8 7 0-0 a6 8 ♘1c3 ♕e5? *(9)*
Hébert suggests 8...♕e8 - an amazing royal position after 8 moves! - 9 ♘d4; but not 9 ♘xc7? ♔xc7 10 ♘d5+ ♔b8 11 ♘b6 d6! justifying Black's provocation.

9 ♘d5! ♘f6
He's lost after this; the king and surrounding black squares are too weak. The test was 9...ab 10 ♗f4 ♕xb2 11 ♗xc7+ ♔e8 12 ♘b6 ♕a3 13 ♖e1 ♗e7 14 ♗xb5 ♔f8 15 ♘xa8 ♕xa8 16 ♗d6! ♕a5 17 ♗xc6 bc 18 ♗xe7+ ♘xe7 19 ♕d6 ♕g5 20 ♕c7! and wins.
10 ♘bxc7 ♘d4 11 ♗f3! ♘xd5 12 ♘xd5 ♘e6 13 ♖e1 ♕d4 14 ♕e2
Also good is 14 ♗e3! ♕xd1 15

♗b6+ ♔e8 16 ♘c7+ ♔e7 17 ♖axd1
♖b8 18 ♗a7 picking off the rook.
14...♗d6 15 ♗e3 ♕xb2 16 ♖ab1
(also 16 ♘b6!) 16...♕xa2 17 ♘c3
♕a3 18 ♖b3 ♗xh2+ (18...♕a5 19
♗b6+) 19 ♔xh2 ♕d6+ 20 ♔g1 1-0

Game 10: 3 Knights Opening

Szmetan-Frey
Bogota 1977

1 e4 e5 2 ♘f3 ♘c6 3 ♘c3 g6
'Inferior', in the classical sense, to
3...♘f6, in that it fails to contest
the centre.
4 d4! ed 5 ♘d5!? ♗g7 6 ♗g5 ♘ce7
An alternative was the hedge-
hoggish 6...f6 7 ♗h4 ♘ce7, but not
6...♘ge7? 7 ♘xd4! ♗xd4 8 ♕xd4!
♘xd4 9 ♘f6+ ♔f8 10 ♗h6 mate!
**7 ♘xd4 c6 8 ♘xe7 ♘xe7 9 ♕d2 h6
10 ♗h4 d5 11 0-0-0!? g5**
Or 11...de 12 ♘b5!? ♕xd2+ 13
♖xd2 cb 14 ♗xb5+ ♗d7 (forced)
and White is better.
12 ♗g3 de(?!) 13 ♕e3 ♕d5? *(10)*

Walking into a trap. Szmetan

intended 13...♕b6 14 ♗d6! with an
unclear position.
**14 ♘b5! ♗xb2+!? 15 ♔xb2 ♕xd1
16 ♘c7+ ♔d8 17 ♗d3!**
This move, gaining the use of the
a1-h8 diagonal with tempo, is what
you should have seen in the
diagram position. Black is defenceless now.
**17...♕xh1 18 ♕d4+ ♘d5 19 ♕xh8+
♔e7 20 ♕e8+ ♔f6 21 ♕e5+ ♔g6 22
♗xe4+ f5 23 ♕e8+ 1-0**
Finely executed by the enterprising young Argentinian.

Game 11: 4 Knights Opening

Bellon-Wagman
Cirella Diamonte 1976/7

**1 e4 e5 2 ♘f3 ♘c6 3 ♘c3 ♘f6 4 d4
ed 5 ♘d5!? ♘xe4 6 ♕e2 f5 7 ♗f4!?
d6 8 0-0-0 ♘e5?**
A bishop move, or ...♘e7, was
better than this, which just provides
another target.
9 ♖xd4 c6 10 ♘xe5 de *(11)*

11 ♖xe4! ♗d6?!

Better than 11...fe? 12 ♕h5+ ♚d7 13 ♕f5+ ♚e8 14 ♕xe5+ ♗e7 (14...♚d7 15 g3! cd 16 ♗b5 mate) 15 ♕xg7 ♖f8 16 ♘c7+ ♚d7 17 ♕d4+. But Black could still have had a game of sorts after 11...cd 12 ♖xe5+ ♚f7.

12 ♖xe5+! ♚f7

Or 12...♗xe5 13 ♕xe5+ ♚f7 14 ♘c7 ♖b8 15 ♗c4+ ♚g6 16 ♖d1 plan ♖d6+. Now White finishes efficiently - a win in this game clinched a GM title. Hence the rush!

13 ♘c7! ♕xc7 14 ♕h5+ 1-0

It's mate after 14...♚f6 15 ♗g5+!, or 14...g6 15 ♗c4+ ♚f6 16 ♗g5+! etc.

11 ♗xg5+! ♘xg5 12 f4 ♚e6 13 fg ♕g7 14 ♘c3

Black can't last; his king position is intolerable.

14...♘b6 15 ♖f6+! ♚d7 16 ♖af1 ♚e8 17 ♖f7! ♕xf7 18 ♖xf7 ♚xf7 19 g6+ ♚e6 20 ♕e1+! 1-0

Game 12: Petroff's Defence

Gurgenidze-Bellin
Tbilisi-Sukhumi 1977

1 e4 e5 2 ♘f3 ♘f6 3 d4 ♘xe4 4 ♗d3 d5 5 ♘xe5 ♘d7 6 ♘xf7!?

Peaceable! 6...♚xf7 7 ♕h5+ ♚e7 (7...g6 8 ♕xd5+, or 7...♚g8?? 8 ♕xd5 mate) 8 ♕e2! ♚f7 9 ♕h5+ with a draw. Black, however, plays for more a la I.Zaitsev-Karpov, Leningrad 1966; but Gurgenidze refutes it over the board.

6...♚e7!? 7 ♕e2!

New and good; if 7...♕xf7 8 f3 favours White.

7...♚xf7 8 ♕h5+ ♚f6 9 0-0 ♚f7

Otherwise White drives the knight from e4 and follows up with ♗g5+.

10 ♕h4+ g5 (12)

Game 13: Ruy Lopez, Steinitz

The winner of this game is an ex-Canadian of Estonian descent living in Aix-en-Provence.

Bessenay-Puhm
France 1976

1 e4 e5 2 ♘f3 ♘c6 3 ♗b5 d6 4 d4 ♗d7 5 ♘c3 ed!?

Compulsory after 5...♘f6 6 ♗xc6 ♗xc6 7 ♕d3 anyway, so Black plays for an active K-bishop.

6 ♘xd4 g6 7 ♗e3 ♗g7 8 ♕d2 ♘f6 9 f3 0-0 10 ♗xc6 bc 11 0-0-0?!

Lends point to the Black strategy; he should eliminate the 'long' bishop by 11 ♗h6!, as 11...♘xe4? 12 ♘xe4 ♕h4+ 13 g3 ♕xh6 fails to

14 ♘f6+! ♔h8 15 ♕xh6 ♗xh6 16
♘xd7.

11...♖e8! 12 ♗h6 ♗h8 13 h4 ♕b8!
14 h5 ♕b4 15 a3?!

Bozić suggests 15 hg fg 16 ♘ce2.

15...♕b7 16 ♖de1 c5! 17 ♘de2
♖ab8 18 ♘d1?! (13)

Essential was 18 b3, but 18...c4 is
very strong.

18...♘xe4!! 19 fe ♗xb2+ 20 ♘xb2
♕xb2+ 21 ♔d1 ♕a1+ 22 ♘c1 (22
♔c1 ♖b1) 22...♗g4+ 23 ♖e2 ♖xe4
24 ♗e3 ♖b1! 0-1

The rout is complete; 25 ♕d3
♖xc1+ 26 ♗xc1 ♗xe2+; or 25 ♖e1
♕e5 26 ♗f2 ♖xc1+.

Game 14: Ruy Lopez, Steinitz Deferred

A typical correspondence melée
in obscure theory. Even the resign-
nation is deep - but, it seems, the
rising cost of postage ensures an
honest assessment of one's chances!

Cipollini-Gubnitsky
World Cup Corres II 1977

1 e4 e5 2 ♘f3 ♘c6 3 ♗b5 a6 4 ♗a4
d6!? 5 0-0 ♗g4 6 h3 h5 7 d4!?

To control g5 and threaten
Black's bishop.

7...b5!? 8 ♗b3 ♘xd4 9 hg hg 10
♘g5

Also possible is 10 ♗xf7+ ♔xf7
11 ♘g5+ followed by c3 and ♕xg4,
but not 10 ♘xd4?? ♕h4 11 f3 g3.

10...♘h6 11 f4 d5! 12 ♗xd5 ♗c5
13 ♗e3

Not 13 ♗xa8? ♘e2+ 14 ♔h1/2
♕xg5! 15 fg ♘g8 mate.

13...♕d6! 14 b4 ♗b6 15 ♖e1
(New - Trajković. 15 c4) 15...
0-0-0!? 16 ♕d2 ♘hf5! 17 ♘xf7 (14)

Otherwise the h-file decides;
Gubnitsky gives 17 ef ♕h6 18 ♘h3
♖xd5 19 fe ♘xf5! 20 ♗xb6 ♕xb6+
winning. The game is prettier.

17...♘xe3!! 18 ♘xd6+ ♖xd6 19
♖xe3

No better is 19 ♕xe3 ef 20 ♕xf4
♘e2+ 21 ♔f1 ♘xf4 and ... ♖h1
mate, or 19 fe ♘xd5! 20 exd6 ♘e2+
21 ♔f1 ♘g3 mate!

19...ef 0-1!

A correct decision. 20 ♘c3 fe 21
♕e1 ♖dh6, or 20 ♖d3 ♘f3+ 21 ♔f1

&xd2+ 22 &xd2 f3! and mates, or
20 c3!? fe 21 ♕xd4 &xd4 22 cd c6!
23 &b3 &dh6 24 &f1 &h1+ 25 &e2
&8h2 26 &xe3 &xg2 and White is
helpless.

Game 15: Ruy Lopez, Schliemann

Thomas-Bosković
USA 1975

1 e4 e5 2 &f3 &c6 3 &b5 f5!? 4
&c3 fe 5 &xe4 d5

Hult-End, Stockholm 1971/2,
went 5...&f6!? 6 ♕e2 &e7 7 &eg5?
(7 &xf6+ gf 8 d4 e4 9 &h4 - West-
inen) 7...&d6! 8 &xe5 0-0 9 &xc6
bc 10 &xc6 &b8 11 &e6 &xe6 12
♕xe6+ &h8 13 ♕h3 &b6! 14 &a4
&b4 15 b3 &e4+ 16 &f1 &g4 17 f3
♕f6! 18 c3 ♕e7 19 &b2 &e5 20
&g1 &h4 21 ♕g3 &xf3+ 0-1.

6 &xe5 de 7 &xc6 ♕g5 (7...♕d5!?)
8 ♕e2 &f6 9 &xa7+?

More apposite is 9 f4! attending
to defence and development.

9...&d7 10 &xd7+ *(15)*

10...&xd7! 11 ♕xe4+ &d8!

An improvement on 11...&e7 12
♕xb7 0-0 13 0-0, although 13...
&d6 gives Black an attack then too.
The text traps White's knight, and
is forcing.

12 ♕xb7 &xa7! 13 ♕xa7 ♕xg2 14
&f1 &c5 15 ♕a6

A painful way to go, but forced.
Black has protected a8 and b8 and
prepared ...&e8+ with superb
economy.

15...&e8+ 16 ♕e2 (16 &d1? ♕f3+)
16...&xe2+ 17 &xe2 ♕e4+! 18 &d1
♕f3+ 19 &e1 &f6 20 d3 &g4 21
&g5+ &d7 22 &h4 &xh2 23 &g1
♕f7! 0-1

Game 16: Ruy Lopez, Schliemann

He may be the best, but he takes
his time - so this is the champ's
only successful appearance here
(but cf. game 64).

Karpov-Tseitlin
39th USSR Ch, Leningrad
1971

1 e4 e5 2 &f3 &c6 3 &b5 f5!? 4
&c3 &d4 5 &a4 &f6 6 &xe5 fe 7
0-0 &c5 8 &xe4!?

Preferable, according to Yudovich,
was the simple 8 d3! when White is
slightly better.

8...&xe4 9 ♕h5+ g6 10 &xg6 &f6?!

Better is 10...♕g5! making a
contest of two pieces versus rook
and two pawns.

11 ♕e5+! ♗e7 12 ♘xh8 b5 (not 12 ...♘e6?? 13 ♕xe6!) 13 ♕xd4 ba 14 ♖e1 ♔f8 15 d3 ♖b8 16 ♕e5!

Threat 17 ♗h6+ ♔g8 18 ♕xe7. 16...♘g8 17 ♕h5 ♔g7 18 ♘f7 ♕e8 *(16)*

19 ♗h6+! ♘xh6 20 ♕xh6+ ♔xf7 21 ♕xh7+ ♔f8 22 ♖e3 ♖b6 23 ♖g3! 1-0

Game 17: Ruy Lopez, 3...♗e7

Kupreichik-Planinc
Sombor 1971

1 e4 e5 2 ♘f3 ♘c6 3 ♗b5 ♗e7!?
Typical Planinc, the economical and straightforward development.
4 0-0 ♘f6 5 ♖e1 d6 6 c3 0-0 7 d4 ♗d7 8 h3 ♖e8

Instead 8...♘xd4?! 9 ♘xd4! ed 10 ♗xd7 ♕xd7 11 cd gives White a space advantage. 8...♕e8!? threat 9...♘xd4 was possible.
9 ♘bd2 ♗f8 10 ♘c4!? ed 11 cd

d5?!
Hoping for 12 ed?! ♖xe1+ 13 ♕xe1 ♘b4 with an isolated ♕-pawn for a target, but he finds that Kupreichik isn't so meek!
12 ♗b3!? de *(17)*

13 ♗xf7+! ♔xf7 14 ♕b3+ ♔g6?
According to Marić Black can save himself by 14...♗e6! 15 ♘g5+ ♔g8 16 ♘xe6 ♘a5! 17 ♘xd8+ ♘xb3 18 ab ♖exd8 19 ♘xe4 ♖xd4.
15 ♘h4+ ♔h5 16 ♘xe4! ♖xe4
Or 16...♘xe4 17 ♕f3+ ♔xh4 18 ♖xe4+ ♖xe4 19 ♕xe4+ ♔h5 20 ♕xh7 mate.
17 ♖xe4 g5 18 ♕f7+ ♔h6 19 ♘f5+! 1-0

Game 18: Ruy Lopez, Berlin

Faibisovich-Lomaya
USSR Team Ch, Groznii 1969

1 e4 e5 2 ♘f3 ♘c6 3 ♗b5 ♘f6 4 0-0 ♘xe4 5 ♖e1 ♘d6 6 ♘xe5 ♗e7 (Not

6...♘xb5?? 7 ♘xc6+)   7 ♗d3!?
♘xe5 8 ♖xe5 0-0 9 ♘c3 c6

Not a bad idea if followed up
correctly.

10 b3 ♘e8 11 ♗b2 d5 12 ♕h5
g6? *(18)*

Necessary was 12...♘f6; White
was hoping for this one!

13 ♘xd5!!

Very pretty. Now on 13...gh
comes 14 ♘xe7+! ♔g7 15 ♖h5+ f6
(or 15...♘f6) 16 ♖xh7 mate, but
not 14 ♗xh7+? (deduct 5 points)
14...♔h8!; and if 13...cd White still
gives up his queen by 14 ♕xh7+!
♔xh7 15 ♖h5+ ♔g8 16 ♖h8
mate.

13...♕xd5 14 ♕h6!

Not 14 ♖xd5? gh; this wins
material, as 14...♕d6 15 ♕xh7+!
still works. The rest is less
exciting.

14...♗e6 15 ♖xd5 cd 16 ♖e1 ♗f6

Otherwise 17 ♖xe6! fe 18 ♗xg6
wins.

17 ♗a3 ♗g7 18 ♕f4 ♖c8 19 h4 ♘c7
20 ♗xf8 ♗xf8 21 h5 ♗e7 22 ♕d4
b6 23 ♕a4 1-0

Game 19: Ruy Lopez, Berlin

D.Waterman-Samo
Mechanics Institute Marathon
California 1974

1 e4 e5 2 ♘f3 ♘c6 3 ♗b5 ♘f6 4
♕e2!? d6 5 d4 ♗d7 6 ♗xc6 ♗xc6 7
♘c3 ♕e7?!

With what (effective) development
plan? He should probably make
concessions, e.g. 7...ed 8 ♘xd4 ♗e7;
then 9 ♘xc6 bc 10 e5(?!) won't
hurt - 10...de 11 ♕xe5 0-0.

8 0-0! 0-0-0?!

No good is 8...ed 9 ♘xd4 ♗xe4?
10 ♘xe4 ♘xe4 11 ♖e1 d5 12 f3
♘d6 13 ♕d1.

9 d5! ♗d7 10 a4 g6 11 ♗e3 ♔b8 12
♕c4 ♘g4?! (12...♗c8) 13 ♘b5 ♗xb5

On 13...♘xe3 Waterman gives 14
♕xc7+ ♔a8 15 ♕a5! ♗xb5 16 ab
b6 17 ♕xb6 ♘g4 18 ♕c6+ ♔b8 19
b6! ♕b7 20 ♖xa7 ♕xc6 21 dc
winning. 17...♘xf1 is better but
still fails to the same trick.

14 ♗xa7+! ♔xa7 15 ab+ ♔b8 (15...
♔b6? 16 ♖a6+!) 16 ♖a3 ♔c8? *(19)*

17 ♕c6!! 1-0

Splat! Black should have tried 16 ...♘f6, i.e. 17 ♖fa1 ♔c8 18 ♕c6? bc 19 bc ♘d7!, but 17 b6 works: 17... ♔c8 18 ♖a8+ ♔d7 19 ♕b5+ c6 20 dc+ etc.

Game 20: Ruy Lopez, Classical

Padevsky-Mesing
Vrnjačka Banja 1973

1 e4 e5 2 ♘f3 ♘c6 3 ♗b5 ♗c5!? 4 c3 f5!? 5 d4 fe 6 ♘fd2

A cautionary note for would-be Blacks: 6 ♗xc6 ef?! (6...dc - game 21) 7 ♗xf3 ed 8 0-0! favours White. Torre-Tatai, Haifa Ol 1976, went 8 ...♘f6 9 ♖e1+ ♗e7 10 ♗g5 c6? 11 ♗xf6 gf 12 ♗h5+ ♔f8 13 ♕xd4 ♖g8 14 ♘d2 d5 15 ♖e2 ♗h3 16 g3 ♔g7 17 ♗g4! ♗xg4 18 ♕xg4+ ♔h8 19 ♕e6! ♖g7 20 ♖ae1 ♕f8 21 ♘b3 ♗d8 22 ♘d4 ♖e7 23 ♕d6! 1-0.

6...♗e7!? 7 d5 *(20a)*

20a
B

7...♘f6! (7...♘b8 8 ♕h5+) **8 dc bc 9 ♗e2?! d5 10 ♘b3 c5 11 ♗g5**

Here 11 ♗b5+ ♔f7 does no harm; in view of the cramping centre White could try 11 ♗e3!? so that if 11...d4 12 ♘xd4!? is possible. 11... c4!?

11...0-0 12 ♘1d2 a5!

Not 12...c4? 13 ♘xc4! Now White should try 13 c4 c6 14 cd cd 15 ♖c1 ♕b6, according to Mesing.

13 a4 ♕e8! 14 ♘f1? ♕g6! 15 h4

Or 15 ♗xf6 ♕xf6 16 f3 ef 17 ♕xd5+ ♗e6 18 ♕xf3 ♗xb3.

15...h6 16 ♗h5!? ♘xh5 17 ♗xe7 *(20b)*

20b
B

17...♘f4!! 18 ♗xf8 ♗g4! 19 ♕c2

On 19 f3 ef 20 gf ♘d3+! 21 ♔d2 (21 ♔e2? ♕e4+!) 21...♖xf8! 22 fg ♖f2+ 23 ♕e2 ♖xe2+ 24 ♔xe2 ♕e4+ 25 ♔d2 ♕xh1 26 ♔xd3 c4+ Black is well ahead.

19...♗xg2+! 20 ♔d2 ♖xf8 21 ♔c1 ♘e1! 0-1

Game 21: Ruy Lopez, Classical

Gutierrez-L.Bronstein
Buenos Aires Olympiad 1978

1 e4 e5 2 ♘f3 ♘c6 3 ♗b5 ♗c5 4 c3 f5 5 ♗xc6 dc 6 ♘xe5 ♗d6

Hoping for 7 ♕h5+? g6 8 ♘xg6 ♘f6 9 ♕h4 ♖g8 10 e5 ♖xg6 11 ef ♗e6 with a tremendous attack for Black.

7 d4 fe 8 ♕h5+ g6 9 ♘xg6?

Leading to horrible difficulties, as Black develops activity on the g-file. Much more sensible was 9 ♕e2.

9...♘f6 10 ♕h4 ♖g8 11 ♘e5 ♗xe5 12 de ♕d3! 13 h3

No good is 13 ♘d2 ♗g4 14 f3 ef 15 gf ♕e3+ 16 ♔d1 ♗xf3+, or here 16 ♔f1 ♗f5! Black's next threatens both ...♗c4 and ...0-0-0.

13...♗e6! 14 ♘d2 0-0-0! 15 ♕h6 *(21)*

Otherwise there comes ...e3 followed by ...♖xg2.

15...♘d5! 16 ♕xe6+ ♔b8 17 ♕f5 ♘e3!

An eloquent quiet move leading to a forcing finish as 18 ♕xe4? loses immediately to 18...♘c2+ 19 ♔d1 ♕xe4.

18 fe ♕xe3+ 19 ♔d1 ♖xg2 20 ♔c2 ♖8xd2+ 21 ♗xd2 ♕xd2+ 23 ♔b3 ♕xb2+ 24 ♔c4 ♕b5+ 0-1.

Game 22: Ruy Lopez, Classical

Hesse-Beyen
Corres Olympiad Prelims 1974

1 e4 e5 2 ♘f3 ♘c6 3 ♗b5 ♗c5 4 c3 ♘f6 5 d4

Kavalek-Spassky, Solingen 1977, varied with 5 0-0 0-0 6 d4 ♗b6 7 ♖e1 d6 8 ♗g5 h6 9 ♗h4 ed 10 ♗xc6 dc! 11 ♘xc3 bc 12 ♕a4 ♕d7! 13 ♗xf6 gf 14 h3?! (better 14 ♖ad1 planning e5) 14...♔h8! 15 ♘e2 ♖g8 16 ♘f4 ♗b7 with better chances for Black. The finish was 17 ♘h4 ♖ae8 18 ♘f5 ♔h7 19 ♕c2 ♖e5 20 ♕d2 c5! 21 ♘d5? ♖xf5! 22 ef ♕xf5 23 ♖ed1 c4 24 ♔h1 ♖g5 0-1.

5...ed 6 e5!? ♘e4 7 0-0 d5 8 exd6ep 0-0 9 dc ♕xc7 10 cd *(22)*

10...♘xd4!?

Not 10...♖d8? 11 ♕c2 winning a piece, and on 10...♗d6 11 ♘c3 it's not clear that Black has enough for his pawn. This sacrifice leads to a lot of play.

11 ♘xd4 ♕b6 12 ♗d3 ♘xf2! 13 ♖xf2 ♗xd4 14 ♕f3?!

Beyen gives 14 ♕c2 ♖d8 15 ♗f1 (not 15 ♗xh7+ ♔h8 threatening ... ♗xf2+ and ...♖d1+) 15...♖d5! 16 ♘c3 ♖f5 17 ♘d1 ♗d7 18 ♗d3 ♖e8 19 ♔f1 ♖fe5 20 ♗d2 ♕h6! 21 ♕c4! ♕d6 equal/unclear.

14...♗g4! 15 ♕xg4 ♗xf2+ 16 ♔f1 ♖fe8 17 ♗d2 ♖ad8

Were White's king on h1 Black could win immediately with 17... ♕xb2 with the main threat of 18... ♕c1+. Here it is sensitive on the diagonal f1-a6, e.g. 18 ♗xh7+ ♔xh7 19 ♕f5+ ♔g8 20 ♕xf2 ♕b5+ 21 ♔g1 ♖e2. No better is 18 ♗c3 ♗d4!

18 ♕f5 ♖xd3! 19 ♕xd3 ♗g1! 20 ♕f3

Longer but still hopeless is 20 ♕g3 ♗d4 21 ♕d3 ♕f6+ 22 ♕f3 ♕a6+, or 20 ♗e1 ♗xh2 21 ♗f2 ♕xb2 22 ♗d4 ♕c1+ 23 ♔f2 ♕e1+ 24 ♔f3 ♕g3 mate.

20...♗xh2 0-1

Game 23: Ruy Lopez, Exchange

Piotrowski-J.Sokolow
12th Polish Corres Ch 1971

1 e4 e5 2 ♘f3 ♘c6 3 ♗b5 a6 4 ♗xc6 dc 5 0-0 ♗g4!? 6 h3 h5 (6... ♗xf3?!) 7 d3 ♕f6 8 ♘bd2

All theory; Black innovates next move. Of course 8 hg? hg 9 ♘e1 ♕h4 10 f4 ♗c5+ loses miserably; interesting is 8 ♗e3!? ♗xf3 9 ♕xf3 ♕xf3 10 gf ♗d6! with a little-practiced position. Instead, Bohm-

Hernandez, Amsterdam II 1979, concluded in just 5 moves - 8 ♗e3!? ♘e7!? 9 ♘bd2 ♘g6 10 hg? hg 11 ♘g5 ♘f4 12 ♕xg4 ♕xg5! 0-1 (13 ♕f3 ♕xg2+!).

8...b5!? 9 ♖e1 (9 ♘b3!? - Pytel) 9... ♗c5 10 c3 ♖d8 11 ♕c2 ♘e7 12 b4 ♗a7 13 ♗b2 ♘g6 14 d4

At last; just in time to fall into a combination!

14...♘f4 15 h4

Not 15 ♘xe5 ♗xh3! 16 gh?! ♕g5+.

15...♘g6 16 de ♕f4! 17 ♘d4 (23)

17...♘xh4!! 18 g3 ♖xd4!

Sublime. This wins 2 pieces for a rook, so White resorts to desperate measures; 19 gf ♖xd2 20 ♕c1 ♖xf2! 21 ♖e3 (21 ♔h1 ♘f3!) 21... ♖e2 is easy.

19 cd ♕xd2! 20 ♕xc6+ ♗d7 21 ♕a8+ ♔e7 22 ♕xh8 ♘f3+ 23 ♔h1 ♕xf2 24 ♕xh5 ♗g4! 0-1

Game 24: Alekhine's Defence

Remember the old maxim about not moving one's queen about too much in the opening!?

Casper-Heckert
¼-final, E.German Ch
Benhausen/Thür 1975

1 e4 ♘f6 2 ♘c3 d5 3 e5 d4 4 ef dc
5 d4!? cb 6 fg ba♕ 7 gh♕ ♕xa2?!

It was safer to simplify by 7...
♕c3+ 8 ♕d2 ♕xd2+, but this is
much more fun!

8 ♘f3 ♗f5 9 ♘e5! ♕a5+

Not 9...♕xc2 10 ♕xc2 ♗xc2 11
♗h6 ♘d7, when Black meets 12
♘xd7 by 12...♔xd7!, but 12 ♗xf8
♘xf8 13 ♗b5+ c6 14 ♘xc6 wins.
And on 9...♗xc2 10 ♕d2 the threat
of ♗c4 is very strong.

10 ♗d2 ♕ad5 11 ♗c4 ♕e4+ 12 ♗e3
e6

An entertaining possibility was 12
...♗g6 13 ♕xh7! ♕xe5 14 ♗xf7+.

13 0-0 ♕dh4? (24)

This one comes under fire too.
But Black stood badly, e.g. 13...
♕xc2 14 ♕xc2 ♗xc2 15 d5! ed 16
♗c5 ♘d7 17 ♗b5 c6 18 ♘xc6 with
a crushing attack. Something must
give.

14 ♗d3 ♕d5 15 ♗xf5 ef 16 ♖e1!
♘d7 17 ♘f3 ♕h5 18 ♗g5+ ♕e4 19
♕d2 f6 20 ♗xf6 ♕xe1+ 21 ♕xe1+
♔f7 22 ♘g5+ ♔g6 23 ♕g8+ 1-0

Game 25: Alekhine's Defence

Planinc-Kovačević
33rd Yugoslav Ch, Belgrade 1978

1 e4 ♘f6 2 ♘c3 d5 3 e5 ♘fd7 4
♘xd5 ♘xe5 5 ♗e3 c5 6 b3 ♘bc6

More solid is 6...♘ec6! 7 ♗b2 e5.
Clearly White's thrice-moved knight
is well placed while Black's knight
is exposed to attack.

7 ♗b2 a6 8 f4 ♘d7 9 ♘f3 ♘f6 10
♗c4! e6 11 f5 b5 (25)

12 fe!

The only sensible move, though
by no means clear. White gets only
a pawn for his piece but the
position is very open.

12...bc 13 ef+ ♔xf7 14 ♘g5+ ♔g6

Or 14...♔g8 15 ♕f3 with various
threats; White plans to castle,
capture on f6 and bring his knights
in via e4, d5.

15 ♕f3! ♔xg5?!

Kovačević prefers 15...♘d4 16

♕xa8 ♔xg5, which has the merit of blocking the b2-f6 diagonal.
16 ♕xc6 ♗d7 17 ♕f3 h5 18 0-0 cb 19 ♖ae1! ♔g6 20 ♘d5 ♖h6?!

White's activity seems to outweigh the piece after 20...♘xd5 21 ♕f7+ ♔h6 22 ♖e5 ♗g4 23 ♖xd5 ♕e8 24 ♕f4+ ♔h7 25 h3 as well, but the text looks easier.
21 ♘xf6 gf 22 ♗xf6 ♔c8 23 ♗b2 ♗f5 24 ♖e8! 1-0

Game 26: Alekhine's Defence

Bellon-Kovačević
Karlovac 1979

1 ♘c3 ♘f6 2 e4 d5 3 e5 ♘fd7 (3... d4!? - game 24) 4 e6!? fe 5 d4 g6?!

Kovačević doesn't seem to have much luck with this opening! White's pawn sac is speculative but dangerous; here 5...♘f6! 6 ♘f3 g6 was accurate.
6 h4! ♘f6 7 h5! ♘xh5 8 ♖xh5 gh 9 ♕xh5+ ♔d7 10 ♘f3 ♗g7 11 ♗h6! ♗f6 *(26)*

And not 11...♗xh6?? 12 ♘e5+ ♔d6 13 ♘b5 mate!

12 ♘xd5!! ed?

According to Kovačević 12...c6 13 ♘f4 ♕c7 was unclear - although White obviously has excellent compensation for the exchange.
13 ♕xd5+ ♔e8 14 ♕h5+ ♔d7 15 0-0-0 c6

Or 15...♕g8 (15...♕e8?? 16 ♕d5 mate!) 16 ♘e5+ ♔d8 17 ♘f7+ ♔d7 18 ♗c4 e6 19 ♗xe6+! ♕xe6 20 ♖e1+ ♔d7 21 ♕d5 mate.
16 ♗f4! ♕g8 17 ♘e5+ ♔d8

Or 17...♗xe5 18 de+ ♔c7 (18... ♔e6 19 ♗c4 mate) 19 e6+ ♔b6 20 ♗e3+ and mate next move.
18 ♘f7+ ♔d7 19 ♕f5+! ♔e8 20 ♕xc8+ ♔xf7 21 ♗c4+ 1-0

Game 27: Alekhine's Defence

Utkin-Grants
Corres 1971

1 e4 ♘f6 2 e5 ♘d5 3 d4 d6 4 ♘f3 de (4...g6!?) 5 ♘xe5 ♘d7?!

Only for those who prefer to defend. 5...e6; 5...♗f5.
6 ♘xf7!? ♔xf7 7 ♕h5+ ♔e6 8 g3! ♘7f6 9 ♗h3+ ♔d6 10 ♕e5+ ♔c6 11 ♗g2 b5!?

Or 11...♕d6 12 c4; possibly 11... e6 12 c4 is a sensible way to return the material.
12 a4! b4 13 c4 bc 14 bc ♗a6 15 ♘d2 e6 16 c4 ♗d6 *(27)*

Black's last real hope was to return the piece with 16...♗xc4 as the immediate 17 ♕xe6+ ♔b7! 18 ♘xc4 fails to 18...♗b4+ 19 ♗d2 (19 ♔d1 ♖e8!) 19...♖e8! and White's initiative is insufficient.

17 ♕xe6!! Rb8

The point is 17...♖e8 18 cd+ with the variations a) 18...♔b7 19 ♖b1+ ♗b5 20 ♖xb5+ ♔a6 21 ♗f1! ♖xe6+ 22 de with the threat ♖b8+ or ♘b3! followed by ♖b8; b) 18...♔b6 19 a5+! ♔b5 20 ♗f1+ ♔b4 21 ♗a3+ ♔c3 (21...♔xa5 22 ♗c5 mate) 22 ♖c1+ ♔xd4 23 ♘b3 mate.

18 0-0 ♕g8 19 cd+ ♔b7 20 ♖e1 ♔a8 21 ♗a3 1-0

Game 28: Alekhine's Defence

**Nigmadzianov-Kaplin
USSR 1977**

1 e4 ♘f6 2 e5 ♘d5 3 d4 d6 4 ♘f3 ♗g4 5 ♗e2 c6?!

More thematic is 5...e6 leaving c6 free for the Q-knight.

6 c4 ♘b6 7 ♘bd2 ♘8d7 8 ♘g5! ♗xe2 9 e6! f6 (9...♗xd1?? 10 ef mate) 10 ♕xe2 fg 11 ♘e4!

Insisting on a piece sac which ties up the whole Black position, since 11...h6?? 12 ♕h5+ mates, and 11...♕c7 12 ♘xg5 0-0-0 13 ♘f7 costs

the exchange.

11...♘f6 12 ♘xg5 ♕c7 13 ♘f7 ♖g8 14 g4! h6 15 h4 d5

Unattractive is 15...g5 16 hg hg 17 ♗xg5 ♖xg5 18 ♘xg5 0-0-0 19 ♘f7 ♖e8 20 g5 ♘g8 with material equality and continued pressure for White. In the game Black's last chance appears to be 16...♘c4, which isn't quite clear; missing this he allows a pretty finish.

16 c5 ♘c8? 17 g5 ♘e4 18 gh gh 19 ♕h5 ♘f6 (28)

20 ♘d6+ ♔d8 21 ♕e8+! 1-0

Game 29: Alekhine's Defence

**Erler-T.Espig
E.German Ch, Dinglestädt 1971**

1 e4 ♘f6 2 e5 ♘d5 3 c4 ♘b6 4 c5

This patch of theoretical jungle has a pawn sacrifice lurking in the undergrowth.

4...♘d5 5 ♗c4 e6 6 ♘c3

Here it is. The alternative, 6 d4 d6, doesn't give White anything.

6...♘xc3 7 dc ♘c6 8 ♗f4 ♗xc5 9

♕g4 g5!?

Not 9...0-0? 10 ♗h6; instead 9... ♖g8?!, 9...♔f8?!, 9...g6 or 9...♗f8 all leave White with active play for his pawn after 10 0-0-0.

10 ♗xg5 ♖g8 11 ♘h3

Hennings gives 11 f4 ♘xe5 12 ♕h4 ♖xg5 13 fg ♘xc4 14 ♕xc4 ♕xg5 15 ♘e2 d6! as slightly better for Black.

11...♗e7 12 f4 ♘xe5 13 fe ♗xg5 14 ♕h5 ♖g7 15 0-0 b6? *(29)*

In view of what follows 15...h6 was called for. Boleslavsky's analysis gives 16 ♖ae1 here - spot the improvement!

29
W

16 ♖xf7! ♗e3+

Forced; 16...♖xf7 17 ♘xg5 ♕e7 18 ♖f1 wins a piece.

17 ♖f2+! ♔e7 18 ♕f3! ♗xf2+ 19 ♘xf2 ♗a6 20 ♕f6+! ♔e8 21 ♕xg7 ♗xc4 22 ♘e4 ♕e7 23 ♘f6+ 1-0

Game 30: Alekhine's Defence

An example of what can happen when White gets three quarters of the board to play with. Rellstab is

one of the oldest active masters in the world: here, very active!

Rellstab-Berding
W.Germany 1975

1 e4 ♘f6 2 e5 ♘d5 3 c4 ♘b6 4 d4 d6 5 f4 de 6 fe ♘c6 7 ♗e3 ♗f5 8 ♘c3 e6 9 ♘f3 ♗e7 (all theory; 9... ♗g4!? 10 ♕d2, 9...♕d7 10 d5!?) 10 d5!? ed 11 cd ♘b4 12 ♘d4 ♗d7

On 12...♗g6 13 ♗b5+ ♔f8 14 0-0 White is better, and on 12...♗c8 Keene gives 13 d6! ed 14 ♗b5+ ♗d7 15 e6!? winning.

13 e6 ♗c8?!

Williams-Cafferty, British Ch, Blackpool 1971, went 13...fe 14 de ♗c6 15 ♕g4 ♗h4+ 16 g3! ♗xh1 17 0-0-0 ♗f6? (17...♕f6 18 ♗e2 - Keene) 18 ♘f5 ♘6d5 19 ♘xg7+ ♗xg7 20 ♕h5+! ♔e7 21 ♗c5+ ♔xe6 22 ♗h3+ 1-0.

14 ♗b5+ ♔f8 15 0-0 ♗f6 16 ♕h5 ♕e7 17 ♖xf6! ♕xf6 (17...gf 18 ♗h6+) 18 ♖f1 ♕g6 19 ♖xf7+ ♔g8 *(30)*

Now comes a pretty finish.

30
W

20 ♗h6! gh

On 20...♛xh5 would follow 21 ♖xg7+ ♚f8 22 e7 mate.
21 ♘f5! ♘6xd5 22 ♕g4! 1-0

Game 31: French, Advanced

Zaitsev-Pokojowczyk
Sochi 1976

1 e4 e6 2 d4 d5 3 e5 c5 4 c3 ♘c6 5 ♘f3 ♛b6 6 a3

Threat of 7 b4!, which would resolve the tension and cramp Black.

6...c4 (6...a5! - Zaitsev) 7 ♘bd2 ♘a5 8 g3 ♗d7 9 ♗h3 f6?!

Hubristic; e6 is weak. 9...h6!? (to prepare ...0-0-0).

10 ef gf 11 0-0 0-0-0 12 ♖e1 ♗g7 13 ♖b1! ♚b8 *(31)*

Intending a tactical defence against White's next, which fails, as would 13...♘e7 14 b3 cb 15 ♘xb3 ♗a4? 16 ♖xe6. It is an interesting exercise to try and work out (write them down!) all the variations Zaitsev must have calculated now.

31
W

14 b4! cb 15 ♘xb3 ♘xb3

Now 15...♗a4 fails to 16 ♖xe6 ♗xb3 17 ♕f1 ♗c4 18 ♗f4+ ♚a8 19 ♕e1! winning Black's queen. No better is 17...♘c6 18 ♗f4+ ♚a8 19 ♘d2, regaining the piece with an enormous attack.

16 ♖xb3!

Less effective is 16 ♕xb3 permitting exchanges. Now Black should acquiesce in the defence 16...♕c6 17 ♗f4+ ♚a8 18 ♕e2 ♖e8 19 ♖eb1, but instead he falls into a trap.

16...♗a4? 17 ♖xb6! ♗xd1 18 ♖bxe6! ♗xf3 19 ♗f4+ ♚a8 20 ♗c7!

The first point. 20 ♖e8? ♘h6 gets nowhere, but now on 20...♖c8 (20...♖f8? 21 ♖e8+) 21 ♖e8 ♘e7 22 ♖8xe7 ♖cg8 23 ♗e6 is a killer.

20...♘h6 21 ♗xd8 ♖xd8 22 ♖e8 1-0

The second point is revealed after 22...♖b8 23 ♖xb8+ ♚xb8 24 ♖e7! picking up the unfortunate bishop.

Game 32: French, Advanced

Provost-Materi
Canadian Junior Ch, Toronto 1978

1 e4 e6 2 d4 d5 3 e5 c5 4 c3 ♘c6 5 ♘f3 ♛b6 6 ♗d3 ♗d7?!

Known to be inferior since Nimzowitsch. 6...cd 7 cd ♗d7 8 0-0!? is the Milner-Barry gambit.

7 dc! ♗xc5 8 ♕e2 (8 0-0) 8...a5!? 9 b3!? ♘ge7 10 0-0 h6 11 ♘bd2 g5?!

Energetic-looking but loosening. He should try 11...♕c7, both pressuring White's e-pawn and

giving the bishop a retreat (e.g.
♗-a7-b8!?).

12 ♗b2 ♘f5 13 b4! (opening lines)
13...g4 14 ♗xf5 ef

Worse is 14...gf 15 ♘xf3 ♗xf2+?!
16 ♕xf2 ♕xf2+ 17 ♖xf2 ef 18 b5
and Black's pawn structure is
rotten. Now White opens up some
black squares.

**15 e6! ♗xe6 16 ♘e5 ♘xe5 17 ♕xe5
0-0-0 18 bc ♕xb2** *(32)*

19 ♖ab1! ♕a3

If 19...♕xd2 20 c6! leaves Black
defenceless; 20...bc 21 ♖b8+ ♔d7
22 ♖b7+ mates. The text intends
20 c6 ♕d6 with some chances.

**20 ♖xb7! ♔xb7 21 ♖b1+ ♔a8 22
♕c7! ♖b8**

Very elegant play answers 22...
♖d7: 23 ♕c6+ ♔a7 24 ♕b6+ ♔a8
25 ♕a6+ ♖a7 26 ♕c6+!

23 ♖b6! 1-0

Game 33: French, Advance

Hedman-Romanishin
Cienfuegos 1977

1 e4 e6 2 d4 d5 3 e5 b6!? 4 c3 ♕d7

Not 4...♗a6?? 5 ♗xa6 ♘xa6 6
♕a4+. Also Black is waiting for a
move of White's K-bishop before
offering to swap.

5 ♘f3 ♘e7 6 ♗d3 (6 a4!?; 6 h4!?)
6...♗a6 7 ♗xa6 ♘xa6 8 ♕d3 (?!; 8
a4!) **8...♘b8 9 ♘bd2 ♘bc6! 10 0-0
♘g6 11 ♖e1 f6! 12 ef gf**

In contrast to game 31, a well-
conceived bid for the initiative, as
Black's king is safe; 13 ♕a6 is met
by 13...♗d6 and 14...0-0. 13 ♕e2!?
looks more testing than White's
next though.

**13 ♘f1 0-0-0 14 ♕a6+ ♔b8 15 a4
e5! 16 a5 e4 17 ♘3d2 ♖g8 18
b4?** *(33)*

An oversight, but Black's attack is
already the more dangerous.

**18...♗xb4! 19 ab cb 20 cb ♘xb4 21
♕a4**

Disastrous would be 21 ♕e2 ♘f4
22 ♕d1 ♕h3!, or 21 ♕a3 ♘c2.

**21...♕xa4 22 ♖xa4 ♘d3 23 ♖d1
♘gf4 0-1**

The main threat is 24...♖xg2+/
♘e2+ 25 ♔h1 ♘xf2 mate, and on
24 ♘g3 ♘xc1 25 ♖xc1 ♖xg3! Black
simplifies to a won ending.

Game 34: French, Exchange

Tatai-Korchnoi
Beersheva 1978

1 e4 e6 2 d4 d5 3 ed ed 4 ♗d3 c5!?

Typical Korchnoi - accepting an isolated pawn to create complications. But a French player must prove that 3 ed doesn't just draw! 5 ♘f3 ♘c6 6 ♕e2+?!

Angling for a Q-swap but losing tempo to a black rook later on. 6...♗e7! 7 dc ♘f6 8 h3?!

To stop ...♗g4, but the pawn becomes an object of attack. He can't hold the c-pawn, i.e. 8 ♘bd2(a3) 0-0 9 ♘b3(b4) ♖e8 10 0-0 ♗xc5, or 10 ♗e3 ♗g4 with the threat of ...d4. 8...0-0 9 0-0 ♗xc5 10 c3 ♖e8 11 ♕c2 ♕d6! 12 ♘bd2? *(34)*

Unwisely blocking the queen's defence of f2; 12 ♔h1!?

12...♕g3! (threat ...♗xh3) 13 ♗f5 ♖e2! 14 ♘d4 ♘xd4 0-1

After 15 cd ♗xd4 16 ♗xc8 ♖xf2 17 ♖xf2 ♕xf2+ 18 ♔h2 ♗e5+! 19 ♔h1 ♕e1+ it's even mate.

Game 35: French, MacCutcheon

Shabanov-Mnatsakanian
½-final 39th USSR Ch.
Daugavpils 1971

1 e4 e6 2 d4 d5 3 ♘c3 ♘f6!? 4 ♗g5 ♗b4 5 e5 h6 6 ♗d2 ♗xc3 7 bc ♘e4 8 ♕g4 ♔f8?!

Theory advocates 8...g6 here, and 9 h4 instead of White's next. 9 ♗d3!? ♘xd2 10 ♔xd2 c5 11 ♘f3 ♕a5 12 h4! ♘c6 13 ♕f4 b6? *(35)*

Black plans ♗-a6xd3 opening up White's king, but White gets there first because ...b6 cuts off the queen from his defence. Better was 13...cd.

14 ♘g5! hg

No good is 14...♘d8 15 ♘xf7! ♘xf7 16 ♗g6. 15 hg ♖xh1 (15...♖g8 16 g6) 16 g6! ♔e7

On 16...f5 17 ef! ♖xa1 18 ♕d6+ mates, while 16...♘d8 17 ♖xh1 transposes to the game. 17 ♖xh1 ♘d8 18 ♖h7 cd 19 gf dc+ 20 ♔d1 ♘xf7 21 ♖xg7 1-0

Game 36: French, Winawer

Nilsson-Sorensen
Aalborg 1979

1 e4 e6 2 d4 d5 3 ♘c3 ♝b4 4 e5 c5
5 a3 cd?

Better is 5 ...♝xc3+, or even 5...
♝a5!? The text wins a pawn but
Black will be bereft of central or
Q-side counterplay, always a bad
sign in the French.
6 ab dc 7 ♘f3 ♛c7 8 ♜a3!? cb 9
♝xb2 ♘d7 10 ♜c3 ♛b8 11 ♝e2
♘e7

And not 11...♘xe5? 12 ♘xe5
♛xe5 13 ♜xc8+.
12 ♛d2 0-0 13 ♝e3 ♘f5?! 14 ♜a3
♘b6 15 g4 ♘e7 16 ♝d3! ♘c4?! *(36)*

36
W

17 ♝xh7+!!
An elaboration on the theme of
the greek gift; an efficient check
takes 2 moves in the follow-up, and
all White's Q-side is en pris mean-
while. But it seems to work.
17...♚xh7 18 ♛g5 ♘g6
Not the most tenacious, though
other lines lose too, i.e. a) 18...
a) 18...♘xa3 19 ♛h5+ ♚g8 20 ♘g5

♜d8 21 ♛xf7+ ♚h8 22 ♛xe7 ♝d7
23 ♛f7! ♜c8 (forced) 24 ♜g1! and
♜-g3-h3 mate can't be stopped.
b) 18...♘g8!? 19 ♛h4+! ♘h6 20 g5!
♜g8 (or, e.g., 20...♘xa3 21 gh g6 22
♘g5+! ♚g8 23 ♘xe6! fe 24 ♛e7
♜f7 25 ♛e8+ ♚h7 26 ♛xf7+ ♚xh6
27 ♝c1+ etc.) 21 g6+!! ♚xg6 (21...
fg 22 ♘g5+ ♚h8 23 ♘f7+ ♚h7 24
♜h3 wins) 22 ♜g1+ ♚h7 23 ♘g5+
♚g6 (23...♚h8 24 ♘xf7+ ♚h7 25
♜h3 is easy.) 24 ♘e4+ ♚h7 25
♘f6+! gf 26 ♛xh6+! ♚xh6 27 ♜h3
mate. Here 25...♚h8 is also met by
26 ♛xh6+! and 27 ♜xg8 mate.
Which goes to show that such
sacrifices must be, in part, intuitive!
19 ♛h5+ ♚g8 20 ♘g5 ♜e8 21 ♜f3!
♘gxe5 22 ♜xf7! 1-0

Game 37: French, Modern Winawer

Ladisic-Roos
Bagneux 1976

1 e4 e6 2 d4 d5 3 ♘c3 ♝b4 4 e5
♛d7!? 5 a3 ♝xc3+ 6 bc b6 7 ♘f3?!
More testing is 7 ♛g4! f5 8 ♛g3
♝a6 9 ♝xa6 ♘xa6 10 ♘e2! Now
Black is happy; he could also play
7...♝a6 or 7...♘e7!?
7...♝b7!? 8 a4 ♘c6 9 ♝d3 ♘ge7 10
0-0 h6 11 ♛e2 a6!? 12 ♝e3?!
An aimless looking move. Now
Black develops unpleasant ♛-side
pressure. Better is 12 ♝a3 planning
♝xe7 with equality.
12...♘a5 13 ♘d2 ♛c6! 14 ♘b3 ♘c4

Not 14...♕xc3 15 ♗d2 ♕c6 16
♘/♗xa5 and White stands well.
15 ♗c1 g6 16 f3 ♘f5 17 ♔h1?!

White's last two moves also look
planless. Black now sets up a threat
which his opponent overlooks.
17...h5 18 a5 h4 19 ab cb 20 ♗g5
♕d7! 21 ♘d2? (37)

So that on 21...b5 22 ♘b3 he
gains c5 for the knight. 21 ♗f6 was
essential, however, when Black
must rely on the Q-side for his
advantage.

21...♘g3+! 22 hg hg+ 23 ♔g1 ♕c8!
0-1

The threat is 24...♖h1+ 25 ♔xh1
♕h8+, mating, and 24 ♗f6 ♕g8
doesn't help.

Game 38: French, Tarrasch

Jansa-Marović
Madonna di Campiglio 1974

1 e4 e6 2 d4 d5 3 ♘d2 b6!? 4 ♘gf3
♘f6 5 ♗d3 de

Cedes the centre, but 5...♗a6 6
♗xa6 ♘xa6 7 ed!? gives White a
slight edge in useful development.
6 ♘xe4 ♗b7 7 ♕e2 ♗e7 8 ♗f4
♘bd7 9 0-0-0 ♘d5?

A bad plan, to gain the bishop
pair, but deserting his king.
10 ♗d2 ♘b4 11 ♗xb4 ♗xb4 12 ♘e5
0-0 13 ♘xd7 ♕xd7 (38)

14 ♘f6+! gf 15 ♗xh7+! ♔h8
This is obviously a better chance
than 15...♔xh7 16 ♕h5+, 17 ♕g4+,
and 18 ♖d3.
16 ♕h5 ♔g7
Or 16...♖fb8 17 ♗e4+ ♔g7 18
♕h7+ ♔f8 19 ♗xb7 winning the
exchange.
17 ♕g4+ ♔h8 18 d5!
And not 18 ♖d3? ♕d5 19 ♖h3
♕g5 20 ♕xg5 fg 21 ♗e4+ ♔g7
when Black escapes. The text is
unanswerable, i.e. 18...f5 19 ♗xf5
ef 20 ♕h5+ ♔g7 21 ♕g5+ ♔h7 22
♖d3 f4 23 ♖g3! fg 24 hg mate. Or
18...♕a4 19 c3! ♕xa2 20 ♗b1! and
21 ♖d3.
18...♖fd8 19 ♖d3 ♗xd5 20 ♗f5
♗xg2 21 ♕xg2 1-0

Game 39: French, Tarrasch

Tal-Uhlmann
Moscow 1971

1 e4 e6 2 d4 d5 3 ♘d2 c5 (best!) 4
♘gf3 ♘c6 5 ♗b5!? de 6 ♘xe4 ♗d7
7 ♗g5!? ♕a5+

On 7...♕b6 Tal intended 8 ♕e2
cd 9 0-0-0.

8 ♘c3 cd 9 ♘xd4 ♗b4?! 10 0-0
♗xc3 11 bc ♕xc3? *(39)*

But it was already getting tricky,
i.e. 11...a6 12 ♗xc6 ♗xc6 13 ♘xc6
♕xg5 14 ♕d6! ♘e7 15 ♖fd1 ♘xc6
(15...bc?? 16 ♕d7+ ♔f8 17 ♕d8+)
16 ♕d7+ ♔f8 17 ♕xb7 with clear
advantage - Tal; or here 14...♘h6
15 f4! ♘f5 16 ♕c7 ♕f6 17 ♕xb7
0-0 18 ♖f3 - Uhlmann.

39
W

12 ♘f5! ef 13 ♖e1+ ♗e6 14 ♕d6 a6
On 14...♘f6 15 ♖ad1! (15 ♗d2
♘e4!? 16 ♖xe4 ♕xa1+) 15...h6 (15
...♘e4?? 16 ♕e7 mate) 16 ♗xf6 gf
17 ♖xe6+ fe 18 ♕xe6+ ♔f8 19 ♖d7
♕a1+ 20 ♗f1 wins.

15 ♗d2 ♕xc2 16 ♗b4!
And not 16 ♖ac1? ♕xc1 17 ♖xc1
ab 18 ♖xc6 ♖d8!

16...ab 17 ♕f8+ ♔d7 18 ♖ed1+!
"So-called accuracy to the end" is
Tal's sinister comment to this move.
The point is clear on move 21.
18...♔c7 19 ♕xa8 1-0
A dignified resignation, in view of
19...♘f6 20 ♕xh8 ♘e4 21 ♗e1! etc.

Game 40: French, Tarrasch

Bebchuk-Bronstein
Moscow Spartakiade 1974

1 e4 e6 2 d4 d5 3 ♘d2 c5 4 ed ed 5
♘gf3 c4!?
Quaint. Bronstein now suggests 6
♗e2, but White's choice looks
correct to me.
6 b3 cb (6...c3? 7 ♘b1 and ♕d3) 7
ab ♗b4 8 ♗b5+ ♗d7 9 ♕e2+
Cf. the comment to White's 6th
in game 34.
9...♘e7 10 0-0
Very poor is 10 ♗xd7+ ♕xd7 11
♘e5 ♕e6! 12 ♕b5+ ♘c6 13 ♕xb7
0-0 giving Black a huge lead in
development.
10...0-0 11 ♗a3 ♗xa3 12 ♖xa3
♘bc6 13 c4?! (More solid is 13 c3.)
13...♖e8 14 ♕d3 ♘g6! 15 cd ♘b4
16 ♕c4 a5 17 ♖d1
Otherwise 17...♖c8 traps the
queen.
17...♘f4 18 ♗xd7 ♕xd7 19 ♘e5? *(40)*
Black is already a lot better and
19 ♖3a1 or 19 ♕f1 was necessary.
The rest is easy, once you've seen
it.

19...♖xe5! 20 de ♕g4 21 ♕f1
♘h3+! 22 ♔h1 ♕xd1 23 ♕xd1
♘xf2+ 24 ♔g1 ♘xd1 0-1

Game 41: French, Tarrasch

Ghizdavu-Padevsky
Varna 1973

1 e4 e6 2 d4 d5 3 ♘d2 c5 4 ed
♕xd5?! 5 ♘gf3 cd 6 ♗c4 ♕d6 7 0-0
♘c6 8 ♘b3 a6

Hanging on to the pawn is very
risky, e.g. 8...e5 9 ♘g5!? ♘h6 10 f4
with the initiative. 8...♘f6 has been
tried.

9 ♘bxd4 ♘xd4 10 ♘xd4 ♘f6 11
b3!? ♗e7 12 ♗b2 b5?! 13 ♕f3!
♖b8 14 ♗d3 ♗b7 15 ♕h3 ♘d5

Not 15...0-0? 16 ♘xb5! ab 17
♗xf6 winning two pawns.

16 ♖ad1 ♕f4?!

On 16...♕f4 17 ♕g4 ♗xg2 things
get complicated. Ciric gives 18
♘xb5!? (18 ♘xe6!?) 18...ab 19
♗xb5+ ♖xb5 20 ♖xd6 ♗xd6 21
♕xg7 ♖f8 22 ♖d1 ♖d5 23 ♖xd5

♗xd5 24 ♗e5 with slightly the
better chances for White in view of
his connected passed pawns; Black
comes off worse in the game, however.

17 g3 ♕c7 *(41)*

18 ♘xe6! fe 19 ♗xg7 ♗f6

Black also loses after 19...♖g8 20
♕xh7 ♔d7 22 c4 ♘b6/b4 23 ♗f5+!
20 ♗xh8 ♗xh8 21 ♕xe6+ ♔f8 22
♗e4 ♘c3 23 ♖d7! ♘e2+ 24 ♔h1 1-0

On 24...♗xe4+ 25 f3! ♕xd7 26
fe+ wins.

Game 42: Modern Defence, Averbakh

A.Rodriguez-Rakić
Vrnjacka Banja 1977

1 e4 g6 2 d4 ♗g7 3 c4 d6 4 ♘c3
♘d7

Avoiding 4...♘f6 - the King's
Indian, and 4...♘c6?! 5 d5 favours
White. 4...e5 is playable but can be
boring for Black, e.g. 5 de de 6
♕xd8+ ♔xd8 7 f4! ♘d7 8 ♘f3 c6 9

♗e2 f6 10 0-0 ♘h6 11 fe ♘xe5 12
♘xe5 fe 13 ♗g5+ ♔e8 14 ♖ad1
♘f7 15 ♗e3 ♗f8 16 c5 ♗e7?
(correct ♘-d8-e6) 17 ♘b5! cb 18
♗xb5+ ♔f8 19 ♗h6+ 1-0, Ivkov-
Kagan, Rio de Janeiro 1979.

5 ♘f3 e5 6 ♗e2 ♘h6 (6...c6 7 0-0
♘h6 - Ermenkov) 7 h4!? ed 8
♘xd4 ♘c5 9 h5 c6 10 ♗f4 ♕e7?!
11 ♗f3 g5?! *(42)*

Such moves never seem to work.

12 ♘xc6!! bc

Or 12...♕d7 13 ♗xd6 ♕xc6 14 e5
followed by ♘d5 and great carnage
in the ranks.

13 ♗xd6 ♕b7 14 ♗xc5 ♕xb2 15
0-0! ♕xc3

Not 15...♗xc3 16 ♕d6. Now 16
♕d6 can be met by 16...♕f6! 17
♕xf6 ♗xf6 18 e5 ♗e7 19 ♗xc6+
♗d7 with advantage to Black.

16 e5! ♗d7 17 ♗xc6!! ♖d8

Forced; 17...♗xc6 18 ♕d6, or 17
...0-0-0 18 ♕a4. The finish is both
elegant and convincing:

18 ♕d6 ♗f8 19 ♗xd7+ ♖xd7 20
♕b8+ ♖d8 21 ♕b5+ ♖d7 22 ♖ad1
♗xc5 23 ♕xd7+ ♔f8 24 ♕d8+ 1-0

Game 43: Modern Defence, Austrian Attack

Ree-van Baarle
Dutch Ch, Leeuwarden 1971

1 e4 g6 2 d4 ♗g7 3 c3 d6 4 f4 ♘f6
5 ♗d3 0-0 6 ♘f3 c5 7 dc!? dc 8 0-0
♘c6 9 e5 ♘d5 10 ♗e4

White stands well, according to
Sokolov. Now 10...e6?! leaves
Black cramped; 10...♘c7 deprives
his queen of a square; 10...♗e6!?
(preparing ...f6) 11 ♘g5!? seems to
maintain White's pressure.

10...♘b6 11 ♘a3 ♕c7 12 ♗e3 a6 13
♕e2

Not 13 ♗xc5? ♘xe5 solving all
Black's problems. Black's next fails
to combat the pressure on the g1-a7
diagonal; 13...♗g4!? or 13...f6!?
were worth considering.

13...♖d8?! 14 ♕f2 ♘d7 15 ♘g5!
h6? *(43)*

16 ♘xf7! ♔xf7 17 e6+ ♔xe6

On 17...♔g8 18 ed White wins a
pawn and keeps up his attack.

18 f5+ ♔f7 19 fg+ ♔g8 20 ♕f7+
♔h8 21 ♗xh6! ♖g8

Or 21...♕e5 22 ♖f5 ♖f8 23
♗xg7+ ♕xg7 24 ♖h5+.
**22 ♗xg7+ ♖xg7 23 ♕e8+ ♖g8 24
g7+! 1-0**

Game 44: Modern Defence,
Austrian Attack

Mike ±eo is a talented amatuer
and in this game, which won a
brilliancy prize in the 'Evening
Standard' weekend congress, he
pulls off a dream combination.

Yeo—Erdal-Smith
London 1979

**1 e4 g6 2 d4 ♗g7 3 ♘c3 d6 4 f4 a6
5 ♘f3 (5 a4!? b6) 5...b5 6 ♗d3
♗b7 7 0-0 ♘d7?! 8 e5 b4?!**

Also strong for White is 8...c5 9
♘g5! threat e6, e.g. 9...♘h6 10 f5!
cd 11 fg dc? (11...♘xe5) 12 gf+
♘xf7 13 ♘xf7 ♕b6+ 14 ♔h1 ♕c6
15 ♕g4 0-0 16 ♗xh7+! ♔xh7 17
♘g5+ ♔g8 18 ♕e6+ ♖f7 19 ♕xf7+
1-0, I.Zaitsev-Adamski, Polanica
Zdroj 1971.
9 ♘e4 d5?! 10 ♘eg5 e6 (44)

**11 f5!! gf 12 ♘xf7! ♔xf7 13 ♘g5+
♔e7 14 ♘xe6!**

An exquisite double knight sac,
which Black must accept.
**14...♔xe6 15 ♗xf5+ ♔e7 16 ♗g5+
♘df6**

On 16...♗f6 17 ef+ ♘dxf6 Black
remains too exposed, e.g. 18 ♕h5!?
♗c8 19 ♖ae1+ ♔f8 20 ♗h6+ ♘xh6
21 ♕xh6+ ♔f7 22 ♗xh7 ♖xh7 23
♕xh7+ ♔f8 24 ♕h8+ etc.
**17 ♕e1! ♔f7 18 ♗e6+!! ♔g6 19
♕g3 ♘e4 20 ♗f7 mate**

Game 45: Modern Defence,
Classical

Grünfeld-Soltis
Lone Pine 1979

**1 e4 g6 2 d4 ♗g7 3 ♘c3 d6 4 ♘f3
a6 5 ♗e2 b5 6 0-0 ♗b7 7 ♗g5!**

A good developing move with
considerable nuisance value. Now
on 7...b4 8 ♘d5; interesting is 7...
♘f6!? 8 e5.
**7...♘d7 8 ♖e1 h6 9 ♗h4 ♘b6 10 a3
c5?!**

Another opportunity for ...♘f6
gone.
11 e5! cd 12 ♕xd4 de 13 ♕e3 ♕c7?

Now 13...♘f6 was essential. This
simply puts his queen in the firing
line, committing him (psychologically) to the next highly undesirable
move.
**14 ♗g3! f6?! 15 ♘h4! ♔f7 16 ♕d3
f5 (45)**

Forced. 16...g5? 17 ♗h5+. The
text requires White to display a

little imagination.

45
W

17 ♘xg6! ♛d7

On 17...♚xg6 18 ♗h5+! ♚f6 (18 ...♚xh5, 18...♚h7 19 ♛xf5 mate) 19 ♗xe5+ is easy.

18 ♗h5 ♛xd3 19 ♘f4+! 1-0

Game 46: Modern Defence

An impressive game combining attack and defence; the variation at move 20 is very pleasing.

Georgiev-Hazai
Sofia 1979

1 e4 g6 2 d4 ♗g7 3 ♘c3 d6 4 ♗e3 a6 5 h4!?

After Black's ...h5 the position resembles a Sämisch King's Indian where Black has more Q-side counterplay with White's c-pawn still at home.

5...♘f6 6 f3 h5! 7 ♛d2 b5 8 0-0-0 ♘bd7 9 e5!? (9 ♔b1 was more circumspect.) **9...b4! 10 ♘e4 ♘d5 11 ♘g5 ♘7b6 12 e6?! ♗xe6 13 ♘xe6 fe 14 ♘h3**

Necessary; 14 ♗d3? ♘xe3 15 ♗xg6+ ♚d7 16 ♛xe3 ♗h6 17 f4 ♘d5 is much better for Black.

14...♛d7 15 ♛d3 ♛a4! 16 ♚b1

Not 16 ♛xg6+ ♚d7! 17 ♛xg7? ♜ag8, or here 17 ♘g5 ♗f6 with threats.

16...♚d7 17 ♘g5 ♜hb8 18 ♛e4 *(46)*

46
B

18...♘c3+!! 19 bc bc 20 ♚a1

Black earns his !! for 20 ♛xe6+ ♚c6 21 d5+ ♘xd5+ 22 ♚a1 ♛xc2! 23 ♛xd5+ ♚d7 24 ♛e6+ ♚d8 25 ♛g8+ ♗f8! 26 ♘e6+ (26 ♛xf8+ ♚d7) 26...♚e8 27 ♛xf8+ ♚d7 28 ♘c5+ ♚c6 and wins.

20...♘d5 21 ♘xe6 ♛a3 22 ♘c5+ ♚d8 0-1

After 23 ♘e6+ ♚c8 24 ♗c1 Black crowns his attack with 24...♛b2+! 25 ♗xb2 cb+ 26 ♚b1 ♘c3 mate!

Game 47: Pirc Defence

Modesty did not forbid, but I must confess that luck played a generous part in this game, which won a brilliancy prize in the Surrey weekend congress.

Wicker-Gilliam
London 1975

1 e4 d6 2 d4 ♘f6 3 ♘c3 g6 4 ♗g5!? c6 5 ♕d2

For those who wanted to see Tal in action, not Wicker, I offer 5 ♘f3 ♗g7 6 ♕d2 ♗g4 7 0-0-0 h6 8 ♗e3 b5 9 ♗d3 a6 10 ♖de1!? ♘fd7 11 e5 d5? (11...♗xf3 12 ed ♗g4 13 de ♕a5 is critical.) 12 ♘h4 c5 13 ♘xg6! fg 14 ♗xg6+ ♔f8 15 ♘xd5 ♘c6 16 f3 ♗e6 17 ♘f4 ♗g8 18 ♕d3?! (better 18 ♗h5!) 18...e6 19 ♕e4 ♘e7 20 ♖d1! ♕b8 21 ♘h5 ♘d5 22 dc ♕xe5 23 ♗d4 ♕g5+ 24 f4 1-0 Tal-Bronstein, USSR 1973.

5...b5!? 6 ♗d3 a5!? 7 ♘f3 ♗a6 8 0-0-0 b4 9 ♘a4 ♗b5!

A considerable improvement on 9 ...h6? 10 ♗xf6 ef 11 e5! ♗xd3 12 ♕xd3 ♗g7 13 e6!, Fuller-Gilliam, 2 rounds earlier.

10 e5!? ♘d5! *(47)*

Not 10...♘fd7 11 ed!; now however, 11 c4 ♗xa4 or 11 b3 ♗xa4 12 ba ♘c3 are unattractive, so White tries a radical solution.

11 ♗xb5!? cb 12 ♘c5! h6!?

The complications after 12...dc 13 dc h6 14 ♗f6!? are incalculable. **13 e6!** dc (13...f5!? - Basman; 14 ♘h4!?) **14 ♘e5! f5?!**

A little better is 14...fe (14...f6? 15 ♕d3) 15 ♕d3 ♖g8 16 ♕f3! ♘f6 (16...♖g7 17 ♗xh6) 17 ♕xa8 hg 18 dc and White is on top.

15 dc ♗g7 (15...hg 16 ♘f7) **16 ♘f7 ♕c8?!** (16...♕c7) **17 ♕xd5 ♘c6 18 ♘d6+! 1-0**

Prettiest is 18...ed 19 cd ♕b7 20 d7+ ♔f8 21 d8♕+! ♘xd8 22 ♕xd8+ ♖xd8 23 ♖xd8 mate.

Game 48: Pirc Defence

Regan-Shamkovich
USA 1976

1 e4 ♘f6 2 ♘c3 d6 3 d4 g6 4 ♗c4 ♗g7 5 ♕e2 ♘c6! 6 e5 *(48)*

Instead 6 ♘f3 ♗g4 7 ♗e3 e5 is very comfortable for Black. Shamkovich claims to innovate now; 6... ♘xd4 7 ef! ♘xe2 8 fg ♖g8 9 ♘gxe2 gives White a lively game.

6...♘h5!? 7 g4!? (wins a piece) **7...**

&xd4 8 &d1 &xg4! 9 &xd4 &f5 10 &d5 0-0 11 &xb7 &xe5

Chances are about equal; it's hard to condemn White for pawn-grabbing because it's not clear what else he should do.

12 &d5 &b8 13 &xa7 e6 14 &f3 &h4! 15 &ge2

Very dangerous is 15 &xc7 &d4 16 &d1 &bc8(xc2).

15...c5 16 &h6?!

To castle long, but he loses the two bishops and the f-pawn. Shamkovich gives 16 &g3 &c4! 17 &d2 &xg3 18 hg &xc2 with advantage.

16...&g7! 17 &xg7 &xg7 18 0-0-0 &xf2 19 &hf1 &e3+ 20 &d2 (forced) 20...&xb2! 21 &xb2 &xd2 22 &c1 &e3! 23 &b7 (23 &h1 &xe2, or 23 &f1 &h3) 23...d5 0-1

Game 49: Pirc Defence, Classical

Tal-Petrosian
USSR Cup (Teams) Moscow 1974

1 e4 g6 2 d4 &g7 3 &c3 d6 4 &f3 &f6 5 &e2 0-0 6 0-0 &c6 7 d5 &b8 8 &e1 e5

This would be fine if Tal were the kind of player to accept a blocked position when he's ahead in development. Perhaps 8...c6 isn't too bad; but the whole game isn't much of an advert for the plan &-c6-b8.

9 de &xe6 10 &f4 h6 11 &d4 &d7 12 &d2 &h7 13 e5! de 14 &xe5 &e4?

The pawn sacrifice 14...&c6 15 &xc6 &xc6 (15...bc?!) 16 &xd8 and 17 &xc7 would at least slow things down. Black grabs the important black-square bishop but White's "knight centre" is very strong.

15 &xe4 &xe5 16 &f3! &g7

Better than 16...&xb2?! when 17 &ad1 leaves White with even more of an initiative.

17 &ad1 &c8 18 &c4 &e8 *(49)*

Succumbs to a neat little attack. 18...&g4!? - Tal.

49 W

19 &eg5+! hg

Refusing didn't help: 19...&g8 20 &e6! or 19...&h8 20 &f4 hg 21 &xg5 &h6 22 &xf7+!

20 &xg5+ &g8 21 &f4 &d7 22 &xd7! &xd7 23 &xf7+! 1-0

Not 23 &h4? &e8. Now, however, 23...&xf7 24 &xf7+ &h8 25 &e4 &g4 26 &xg6 &f5 (26...&g8 27 &h7+ &f8 28 &f4+) 27 &f7+ &g8 28 &h6+ is just torture.

Game 50: Pirc Defence, Classical

Kostro-Kaiszauri
Sweden 1974

1 e4 d6 2 d4 ♘f6 3 ♘c3 g6 4 ♘f3 ♗g7 5 h3 0-0 6 ♗e2 e5 7 de?!

It's hard to find more than a promise of equality in this move, as Black is set to play ...c6 controlling the key square, d5, and ♘-d7-c5-e6 aiming at the key squares d4 and f4.

7...de 8 0-0 ♘bd7 9 ♗e3 ♕e7 10 ♘d2 ♘c5 11 ♗c4 c6 12 a4 ♖d8 13 ♕b1?!

Artificial, but the natural 13 ♕e2 offers a target for ♘-e6-d4/f4.

13...♘h5! 14 b4 ♘e6 15 ♖e1 ♘hf4 16 ♔h2?!

Preferable, though unpleasant, was 16 ♗xe6. According to Pytel Black could sacrifice here with 16...♘xg2 17 ♔xg2 ♘f4+, though Black's choice is even stronger.

16...♘g5! 17 ♗d3 *(50)*

He's lost, since 17 ♗xf4 ef gives Black a monster K-bishop, and 17 h4 ♖xd2! 18 ♗xd2 ♘f3+ 19 gf ♕xh4+ leads to mate.

17...♗xh3! 18 gh ♕e6! 19 ♗f1 ♖xd2! 20 ♗xd2 ♘f3+ 21 ♔h1 ♘xh3 22 ♗e3
Or 22 ♗g2 ♘xf2 mate!
22...♕g4 23 ♘e2 ♘hg1! 0-1

Game 51: Pirc Defence, Byrne System

Scandinavian names are shared by lots of people - Vikings had many sons! - and White here is Swedish, not the better known Icelander. Black, the same winner as the last game, is an expatriate Georgian.

Olafsson-Kaiszauri
Sweden 1974

1 e4 d6 2 d4 ♘f6 3 ♘c3 g6 4 ♗g5 ♗g7 5 f4 h6 6 ♗h4 c5 7 e5 ♘h5 8 dc ♘xf4!?

New, according to Sokolov. It involves a risky-looking pawn sac with the objectives of rapid development and opening the h8/a1 diagonal.

9 ed g5 10 ♗f2 ♘c6 11 ♕d2??

A better plan would be g3, ♗g2 retaining the option of short castling. White's king comes to grief on the Q-side.

11...ed 12 cd 0-0 13 0-0-0 ♕a5! 14 g3 *(51)*

Winning a piece by 14 d7? ♗xd7 15 ♕xd7 rebounds after 15...♗xc3 16 bc ♕xa2 threatening ...♖d8 and ...♕a1.

50
B

14...Ɗb4!

Threat is 15...Ɗxc3 16 bc (16
♕xc3 Ɗxa2+) and Black has ♕-a3+
xa2+-a1 mate.

**15 Ɗc4 Ɗe6! 16 Ɗd4 Ɗxc4 17
Ɗxg7 Ɗxa2**

And not 17...♔xg7? 18 ♕d4+.
Now 18 ♕d4 Ɗe6 or 18 ♕e3 ♖fe8
doesn't seem to help.

**18 Ɗxf8 Ɗb3! 19 cb ♕a1+ 20 Ɗb1
♖c8+ 21 ♔c3 ♖xc3+ 0-1**

In view of 22 bc Ɗbd3+ 23 ♔d2
(23 ♖xd3 Ɗxd3+ 24 ♔d2 ♕b2+ 25
♔xd3 ♕xb1+ and 26...♔xf8) 23...
♕b2+ 24 ♔e3 ♕f2+ 25 ♔e4 Ɗc5+
mating soon.

Game 52: Pirc Defence,
Austrian Attack

**Suetin-Zhidkov
USSR 1972**

**1 e4 g6 2 d4 Ɗg7 3 Ɗc3 d6 4 f4
Ɗf6 5 Ɗf3 0-0 6 Ɗd3 Ɗc6 7 e5 de 8
fe Ɗd5 (8...Ɗh5!?) 9 Ɗxd5 ♕xd5**

10 c3 Ɗe6!

More apposite than 10...Ɗg4 11
h3 Ɗxf3 12 ♕xf3 with a big centre
and two bishops for the ending;
now White can't win a piece, i.e. 11
c4?! (weakening) 11...♕d7 12 d5
Ɗb4 13 Ɗb1 Ɗg4 with good play.
11 ♕e2 ♖ad8 12 Ɗg5? *(52)*

Better was 12 0-0.

**12...Ɗxd4!! 13 cd ♕xd4 14 Ɗxe6
fe 15 Ɗc4 Ɗxe5**

The Black rooks hold White's
king in a straight jacket, and the
black squares are dropping off. If
now 16 Ɗe3 ♕h4+ 17 Ɗf2 (17 g3
Ɗxg3+) 17...♖xf2! 18 ♕xf2 ♕xc4
is winning, or 17 Ɗxe6+ ♔h8 18
Ɗe3 ♕b4+ 19 Ɗd2 ♕h4+ 20 ♔d1
Ɗxb2 21 ♖b1 Ɗc3.
16 g3 ♖f2! 17 ♕xf2? ♕d1 mate.

White's 17th was not best - but he
was losing, e.g. 17 ♕e3 ♕xc4 18
♕xe5 (18 ♕xf2 ♕e4+; 18 ♔xf2
Ɗd4) 18...♖f5 19 ♕e2 ♕b4+ 20
Ɗd2 ♕xb2 21 ♖d1 ♖e5 22 Ɗe3
♕c3+ 23 ♔f2 ♖f8+, or 17 Ɗxe6+
♔h8 18 ♕e3 ♖xh2! 19 ♖xh2 (19
♕xd4 ♖xh1+) 19...♕d1+ 20 ♔f2
♖f8+ 21 ♔g2 ♕f1 mate.

Game 53: Pirc Defence, Austrian Attack

I have a fixed image of the way they play chess in Poland; each move, played with a bang and a flourish in a desperate time-scramble, is a brilliant sacrifice...

Borkowski-Balcerowski
Poland 1979

1 e4 d6 2 d4 g6 3 f4 ♗g7 4 ♘c3 ♘f6 5 ♘f3 0-0 6 ♗d3 ♘a6 7 e5 ♘d7 8 h4

Dubious according to Filipowicz, who recommends 8 ♘e4! Now Black hits back in the centre.

8...de 9 fe c5! 10 h5 cd 11 hg hg 12 e6?! dc! 13 ef+ ♖xf7 14 ♗xg6 *(53)*

Hoping for 14...cb? 15 ♗xf7+ ♔xf7 16 ♘g5+! ♔f8 17 ♘e6+ ♔g8 18 ♘xd8 ba♕ 19 ♕d5+, but Black has better.

53
B

14...♖xf3! 15 ♕d5+! (15 ♕xf3 ♘e5) 15...e6! 16 ♕xe6+ ♔f8 17 gf ♘e5!

And not 17...♕e7? 18 ♖h8+!! ♗xh8 19 ♘h6+ ♗g7 20 ♗xg7+ ♕xg7 21 ♕e8 mate. Now it just fails:

18 ♖h8+!? ♗xh8 19 ♘h6+ ♗g7 20 ♕xe5 ♕d2+! 21 ♗xd2 cd+ 22 ♔xd2 0-1

Game 54: Pirc Defence, Austrian Attack

Perecz-Hever
Hungary 1974

1 e4 d6 2 d4 ♘f6 3 ♘c3 g6 4 f4 ♗g7 5 ♘f3 0-0 6 e5 ♘fd7 7 h4 c5 8 h5 cd 9 hg!?

Blunt. The safe continuation is 9 ♕xd4 de 10 ♕f2, but this attack is obviously critical and rather unpleasant to face.

9...dc 10 gf+ ♖xf7 11 ♗c4 e6?

With the idea 12 ♗xe6? ♘xe5!, but preferable, according to Florian, is 11...♘f8.

12 ♘g5 ♘xe5 13 ♕h5!

Not 13 fe? cb! 14 ♕h5 ♕xg5! when Black wins. Now Black, in turn, should avoid 13...♕a5 14 fe ♕xe5+ 15 ♗e2 ♕f5 16 g4 ♕g3+ 17 ♔d1 ♖d5+ 18 ♗d3 ♖xd3+ 19 cd ♕xd3+ 20 ♔e1 ♕g3+ 21 ♔e2 when the checks run out.

13...h6 14 fe hg

Careless would be 14...cb? 15 ♕xf7+ followed by ♖xh6+ and mate. Now White has a simplifying combination which regains his piece and keeps Black tied down.

15 ♕h7+ ♔f8 16 ♕h8+! ♗xh8 17 ♖xh8+ ♔g7 18 ♖xd8 ♖c7

Here or next move ...♘c6 was preferable.

19 ♗d3 cb? 20 ♗xb2 d5 21 ♗a3! ♗d7

He seems to be lost, e.g. 21...♘c6 22 ♖e8 ♔f7 (22...♖xe5? 23 ♗b2) 23 ♖h8; 21...♘d7 22 ♗d6; 21...♘a6 22 ♗f8+ ♔f7 23 ♔d2.

22 ♗f8+ ♔f7 23 ♔d2 ♖c8 *(54)*

24 ♗h7!! 1-0

Because of 24...♖xd8 25 ♖f1+ ♔e8 26 ♗g6 mate.

Game 55: Pirc Defence, Chinese Attack

With a billion population, China could produce quite a few surprises by its advent in the world chess arena - despite Donner's incredulity, expressed a couple of days before this game, that a western GM could lose to a chinese...

**Liu Wen Che-Donner
Buenos Aires Olympiad 1978**

1 e4 d6 2 d4 ♘f6 3 ♘c3 g6 4 ♗e2 ♗g7 5 g4!?

This is the Chinese attack (cf. 1 d4 ♘f6 2 g4?!). Byrne and Mednis call it "new" and then go on to cite a Russian game which continued 5 ...♘a6 and subsequently became obscure; a desirable reaction is 5... c5 striving to open the centre up quickly. Donner's reply looks like culture shock.

5...h6?! 6 h3 c5 7 d5 0-0?! 8 h4!

This means trouble.

8...e6 9 g5 hg 10 hg ♘e8?

Better to play ...♘h7, ...♖e8 and ...♘f8. Now Wen Che systematically plods onto the h-file with his queen, after which he is winning. And how!

11 ♕d3 ed 12 ♘xd5 ♘c6 13 ♕g3 ♗e6 14 ♕h4 f5 15 ♕h7+ ♔f7 *(55)*

16 ♕xg6+!! ♔xg6 17 ♗h5+ ♔h7 18 ♗f7+ ♗h6 19 g6+! ♔g7

Or 19...♔h8 20 ♖xh6+ ♔g7 21 ♖h7 mate.

20 ♗xh6+ 1-0

Quite a combination for an untitled player of any race.

Game 56: Caro-Kann, Closed

Planinc-Ciric
Yugoslavia 1970

1 e4 c6 2 d3!? d5 3 ♘d2 g6

On 3...♕c7 a caveman might
attempt to emulate Grefe-Denker,
Lone Pine 1979: 4 f4?! ♕xf4 5
♘gf3 ♘f6? 6 ♘b3 ♕c7 7 e5 ♘g4 8
d4 ♗f5?! 9 ♘h4! ♗d7 10 ♗e2 ♘h6
11 ♗xh6 gh 12 0-0 ♘a6?! 13 ♗xa6
ba 14 ♘c5 e6 15 ♕h5! ♗c8 16 ♖f6
♗xc5 17 dc ♖b8 18 ♖af1 ♖f8 19
♕xh6 ♕xe5 (19...♖xb2 20 ♕xh7
♖xa2 21 ♘g6; not 21 ♖xf7 ♕xf7
22 ♖xf7 ♖a1+) 20 ♕xh7 ♖xb2 21
♖xf7 ♖xf7 22 ♕g8+ 1-0.

4 ♘gf3 ♗g7 5 g3 e5

Maric dislikes this move enough
to award a ?, which looks a bit
harsh, even if the plan 5...♗g4 and
...e6 was better.

6 ♗g2 ♘e7 7 0-0 0-0 8 c3 de

Maybe 8...h6 and if 9 ♖e1 ♕c7,
planning ...♗e6, was better. Even 8
...f5 comes into consideration,
though it's a bit loose.

9 ♘xe4!? b6?! 10 ♖e1 h6 11 ♘ed2!

Good and hard to find; now both
knights converge on d6. If Black
replies 11...♕c7 12 ♘c4 ♘d7 13 d4!
creates problems.

**11...♕xd3 12 ♘xe5 ♕d6 13 ♘ec4!
♕c7 14 ♘e4 ♘d5 15 ♘cd6 ♗e6 16
c4 ♘e7** *(56)*

White has stoked up enough
horsepower for a winning attack
and demonstrates convincingly that
nearly every Black piece is misplaced.

17 ♗xh6! ♗xh6 18 ♘f6+ ♔h8 (18...
♔g7?? 19 ♘fe8+) **19 ♕d4 c5 20
♕h4**

Not 20 ♕c3? ♕xd6 21 ♘e8+
♕d4.

**20...♘g8 21 ♘xg8 ♔xg8 22 ♘b5
♕d8 23 ♕xh6 ♘d7 24 ♖xe6 1-0**

Game 57: Caro-Kann, Closed

A game by Russia's currently
most prodigious prodigy.

Dolmatov-Kasparov
USSR 1978

**1 e4 c6 2 d3 e5!? 3 g3 g6 4 d4
♘f6!? 5 ♘c3?!**

Better is 5 de ♕a5+ 6 ♘d2 ♘xe4
(Gufeld) 7 ♕e2 ♘xd2 8 ♗xd2.

**5...♕a5! 6 ♗g2 d6 7 ♘e2 ♗g7 8 de
de 9 ♕d6!? ♘a6 10 0-0 ♗e6 11 ♖d1
♘b4!**

Eschewing queen swaps via ...♖d8
or ...♕c5. Now Gufeld gives 12
♕d2 0-0 in Black's favour, since the

combination 13 a3 ☖fd8 14 ab? ♕xa1 15 ♕xd8+ ☖xd8 16 ☖xd8+ ♗f8 17 ♗h6 is illegal.

12 ♗e3 ♘xc2 13 b4!? ♘xb4 14 ♗c5 ♗f8! 15 ♕xe5 *(57)*

Or 15 ♗xb4?! ♕xb4.

15...♘g4!

Clearer than 15...♗e7 16 ♘d5!? or 15...♗xc5 16 ♕xf6 because Black gets the initiative and all the black squares.

16 ♕xh8 ♕xc5 17 ☖f1

Or 17 ♕d4 ♘c2 18 ♕xc5 ♗xc5 19 ☖ac1 ♘xf2!

17...0-0-0! 18 ♕xh7

Or 18 h3 ♘xf2! 19 ☖xf2 ♕xf2+! 20 ♔xf2 ♗c5+ with two sound extra pawns.

18...♘d3 19 ♘d1 ♕e5! 20 ☖b1 ♗c5 21 h3 ♘gxf2 22 ♘xf2 ☖h8! 0-1

Game 58: Caro-Kann, Panov

**Tseitlin-Krutyansky
USSR 1971**

1 e4 c6 2 d4 d5 3 ed!? cd 4 c4!?
Another plan is 4 ♗d3!? ♘c6 5 c3

intending ♗f4, h3, ♘f3 etc.
4...♘f6 5 ♘c3 ♘c6 6 ♗g5 dc?! 7 ♗xc4 a6

Sensible, but the follow-up isn't.

8 ♘f3 b5?! 9 d5!? ♘a5 10 ♗e2 ♗b7 *(58a)*

11 ♘xb5! ♘xd5

On 11...ab 12 ♗xb5+ ♘d7 White can choose between 13 ♘e5!? with an attack or 13 b4 regaining the piece.

12 ♘bd4 f6 13 ♕a4+ ♕d7!? 14 ♕xa5 e5 (threat ....♗b4) 15 ♗d2 ed 16 0-0 ♗d6 17 ♗c4! ♘e7 18 ☖fe1! ♗xf3 19 gf ♕h3 *(58b)*

The counterplay just isn't there.

20 ☖xe7+!! ♔xe7 (20...♗xe7 21

♕d5!) 21 ♖e1+ ♔f8 22 ♗f4!

Decisive; 22...♗xf4 23 ♕b4+ or 22...♕d7 23 ♕d5 ♖d8 24 ♗xd6+ 22...g6 23 ♕d5! 1-0

Game 59: Caro-Kann, Panov

Martin-Bellon
Las Palmas 1977

1 e4 c6 2 d4 d5 3 ed cd 4 c4 ♘f6 5 ♘c3 ♘c6 6 ♗g5 ♕a5!? (6...dc?! - game 58. Now 7 ♗xf6!?) 7 ♘f3 ♗g4 8 ♕b3!? 0-0-0 9 ♗xf6 gf 10 cd ♘b4

Or 10...♗xf3 11 gf ♘xd4?? 12 ♕c4+.

Now White should reply 11 ♘d2 intending ♘-c4-e3, and on 11...♗xd5 12 ♘xd5 intending 13 ♖c1+ ♔b8?! 14 ♕g3+.

11 ♗c4?! ♔b8 12 a3?! e6!? 13 de fe 14 0-0?! (Still 14 ♘d2!?) 14... ♗xf3 15 ab ♖g8!

Very strong. The threat is ... ♖xg2+-g3 mate.

16 g3 ♕h5 17 ♖fc1?!

White seems to have all sorts of counterplay after 17 ♗xe6; Djurašević gives 17...♖xd4 18 ♘b5 (18 ♗xg8?? ♕h3) 18...♖xb4 19 ♕c3 ♖xg3+!? 20 fg ♗c5+ 21 ♖f2 ♖xb5 with advantage to Black, but what about 22 ♔f1!? The answer must be that 22...♗c6 23 ♕xf6 a6 gives Black a safe king and White's is unsafe. Black seems unable to do better, e.g. 18...♖h4 19 ♖xa7!? with the threat ♖a8+, or 19...♗c5? 20 ♗xg8 (20...♕h3 21 ♕xf3). The

text gives Black a useful tempo.
17...♖xd4 18 ♘b5

There was a threat of 18...♕xh2+!! 19 ♔xh2 ♖h4+ 20 gh ♗d6+ 21 ♔h3 ♗g2 mate.
18...♖d2 19 ♕e3 *(59)*

19...♖xg3+! 20 fg ♕xh2+ 21 ♔f1 ♕h1+ 22 ♕g1 ♗g2+! 23 ♔e1 ♕xg1+ 24 ♔xd2 ♗h6+ 0-1

Game 60: Caro-Kann, Panov

Larsen-Pomar
Spain 1978

1 e4 c6 2 d4 d5 3 ed cd 4 c4 ♘f6 5 ♘c3 e6 6 ♘f3 ♗e7 7 cd ♘xd5 8 ♗d3 0-0 9 0-0 b6?! 10 ♘xd5! ed 11 ♘e5

Preparing a grandmasterly exploit-ation of Black's weakened white squares on the Q-side.

11...♗a6 12 ♗xa6 ♘xa6 13 ♕a4 ♕c8?

To avoid ♘-c6xe7, but 13...♘c7 was necessary.

14 ♗f4 ♕b7 15 ♕c6! ♖ab8

On 15...♕xc6 16 ♘xc6 White

intends to play a3 and double his rooks on the c-file while Black's knight and Q-rook remain tied down. **16 ♖fc1 ♘b4?! 17 ♕d7!**

Another star move since 17... ♕xd7? 18 ♘xd7 ♖bd8 (18...♘d3? 19 ♘xb8) 19 ♘xf8 ♘d3 20 ♖c7 costs the exchange, while 17...♖fd8 18 ♕f5! gives a direct attack as in the game.

17...♘a6 18 ♖c3! ♗f6 19 ♕f5! ♖fe8

Larsen mentions 19...♗xe5 20 ♗xe5 ♖bc8 21 ♕f6!

20 ♖h3 h6 *(60)*

21 ♗xh6! ♕c8

Rejecting 21...♗xe5 22 ♗g5! f6 (22...♗f6 23 ♗xf6) 23 de fg 24 ♕h7+ ♔f8 25 ♖f3+ ♔e7 26 ♕xg7+ ♔d8 27 ♖f7 ♕c6 (27...♖e7 28 ♕f8+ ♖e8 29 ♕d6+) 28 ♕xg5+ ♔c8 29 ♖c1 ♘c5 30 b4, but the text loses sooner.

22 ♘d7! ♖e6 23 ♗xg7! 1-0

Game 61: Caro-Kann

Spassky-Larsen
Bugojno 1978

1 e4 c6 2 d4 d5 3 ♘c3 de 4 ♘xe4

♗f5 5 ♘g3 ♗g6 6 ♘f3 ♘d7 7 ♗d3 ♕a5+?!

Normal, natural, and better is 7...e6.

8 ♗d2 ♕c7 9 ♗xg6 hg 10 ♕e2 e6 11 ♘e4!?

Intending g3 and ♗f4. 11 c4!? was an alternative, with ♘c3 to follow. Now Blackstock suggests 11...♘gf6!?

11...0-0-0 12 g3 c5?!

This can't be wise, but on 12... ♘gf6 13 ♘eg5! ♘h6 14 ♘e5 Black appears to be in trouble. His position is already very difficult.

13 ♗f4 ♕c6 14 0-0-0 c4 15 ♘c3 ♘h6

Still 15...♘gf6 16 ♘g5 is good, and 15...♘b6 to prevent White's next is crushed by 16 ♘e5 (16... ♕c7 17 ♘xg6).

16 d5! ed 17 ♖xd5 ♗c5 18 ♖hd1 f6 *(61)*

No good is 18...♖he8 19 ♖xd7! ♕xd7 20 ♖xd7 ♖xe2 21 ♖c7+ and wins, and White threatened 19 ♘e5 ♘xe5 20 ♕xe5.

19 ♖d6! ♗xd6 20 ♖xd6 ♕c5 21 ♖d5! 1-0

On 21...♛b4 22 ♗d6(♖b5) and 23 ♛xc4+; or 21...♛c6 22 ♘b5! assassinates the black royal family.

Game 62: Caro-Kann

Nona Gaprindashvili, although no longer Women's World Champion, continues to prove herself at GM level in men's chess, often quite savagely.

Gaprindashvili-Nikolac
Wijk aan Zee 1979

1 e4 c6 2 d4 d5 3 ♘d2 de 4 ♘xe4 ♗f5 5 ♘g3 ♗g6 6 h4 h6

The alternative 6...h5 competes for space but weakens g5.

7 h5 ♗h7 8 ♘f3 ♘d7 9 ♗d3 ♗xd3 10 ♛xd3 e6 11 ♗f4!? ♛a5+ 12 c3!? (New? - 12 ♗d2) 12...♘gf6 13 a4 c5 14 0-0 ♖c8(?!) 15 ♖fe1 c4(?!) 16 ♛c2 ♗e7

On 16...♘xh5 17 ♘xh5 ♛xh5 18 ♛e4! b6 (18...♛d5?? 19 ♛xd5) 19 ♛b7 is hard to meet (19...♖d8 20 ♗c7).

17 ♘e5 0-0

Gaprindashvili gives 17...♘d5 18 ♘xf7! ♚xf7 19 ♛g6+ ♚f8 20 ♛xe6 ♘7b6 21 ♖e5 ♖c6 22 ♛xe7+!, or 17...♘xe5 18 ♖xe5 ♘d5 19 ♘f5! ef 20 ♛xf5 ♖d8 21 ♖ae1 ♖d7 22 ♛g4.

18 ♘f5! ♖fe8? *(62)*

Or 18...ef 19 ♘xd7 ♘xd7 20 ♖xe7 with advantage. Best is 18... ♛d8.

62
W

19 ♘xg7!! ♚xg7 20 ♗xh6+! ♚xh6 (20...♚g8 21 ♖e3) 21 ♘xf7+ ♚xh5 22 g4+! ♚h4

Or:

a) 22...♘xg4 23 ♛h7+ ♘h6 24 ♛xh6+ ♚g4 25 ♖e4+ ♚f5 26 ♖f4 mate;

b) 22...♛xg4 23 ♛g6+ ♚f4 (23... ♚h4 24 ♚g2!) 24 ♛g3+ ♚f5 25 ♘h6 mate.

23 f3! ♘xg4

On 23...♛c7 24 ♖e5! ♘xg4 25 ♖h5+! wins.

24 ♖e4! 1-0

Game 63: Caro-Kann

Browne-Bellon
Las Palmas 1970

1 e4 c6 2 d4 d5 3 ♘d2 de 4 ♘xe4 ♘f6 5 ♘xf6+ gf (5...ef!? cf games 64-5) 6 ♗e2 ♗f5 7 ♘f3 ♛c7 8 0-0 e6 9 c4 ♘d7 10 ♗e3 ♗d6

Possible 10...0-0-0. Now Browne produces one of his ferocious TN's.

11 c5! ♗e7 12 ♘d2!

To prevent ...♗-e4-d5. It also rules out ...0-0.

12...0-0? 13 f4!

The threat is g4 and f5. Black could try to grovel with 13...h6 14 g4 ♗h7 15 f5, but by retreating at once hopes to answer 14 g4 with 14 ...h5!?, e.g. 15 gh ♗f5 16 ♗g4 ♗xg4 17 ♕xg4+ ♔h8 intending ...♖g8, ... f5, ...♘-f6-d5. Browne stops this! **13...♗g6!? 14 f5! ♗xf5 15 ♖xf5! ef 16 ♗d3 ♖fe8 17 ♗xf5 ♘f8 18 ♘e4 ♔h8 19 ♕h5 ♘g6 20 ♖f1 ♖g8 21 ♖f3 ♕a5?? (63)**

It was necessary to return the exchange by 21...♖g7 22 ♗h6 ♖ag8 and not 22...♖7g8 23 ♖h3 threatening 24 ♗f8! ♘xf8 25 ♕xh7+! ♘xh7 26 ♖xh7 mate. White is better, but the text falls for a real 'sucker punch':

22 ♕xh7+! 1-0

Game 64: Caro-Kann

Spassky-Pfleger
Munich 1979

1 e4 c6 2 d4 d5 3 ♘c3 de 4 ♘xe4 ♘d7 5 ♗c4

I'll cheat and sneak in a win by the World Champion here, though it's too long: 5 ♘f3 ♘gf6 6 ♘xf6+ ♘xf6 7 ♘e5 ♗f5?! (7...♗e6) 8 c3 e6 9 g4 ♗g6 10 h4 h5 11 g5 ♘d5 12 ♘xg6 fg 13 ♕c2 ♔f7 14 ♖h3 ♘e7 15 ♗c4 ♘f5 16 ♖f3 ♕d7 17 ♖xf5+! gf 18 ♕xf5+ ♔e7 19 ♕e4 ♖e8 20 ♗f4 ♔d8 21 ♕e5 ♖g8 22 0-0-0 g6 23 ♖e1 ♗g7 24 ♕b8+ ♔e7 25 ♖xe6+! 1-0 (25...♕xe6 26 ♕c7+ ♕d7 27 ♗d6 mate!) Karpov-Hort, Bugojno 1978.

5...♘gf6 6 ♘xf6+ ef!? 7 ♘e2 ♘b6 8 ♗b3 ♗d6 9 c4 ♗c7 10 ♗f4 0-0 11 ♗xc7 ♕xc7 12 c5?!

This is O.K. while White controls d5, and of course 12...♘d5? 13 ♗xd5 gives him a simple advantage, but Black should equalise now. **12...♘d7 13 0-0 b6?**

Stean gives 13...♖d8! 14 ♕c2 (else ...♘xc5) 14...♘f8 intending ... ♗e6 with equality. **14 cb ab 15 ♖e1 ♗b7 16 ♘g3 ♖fe8 (64)**

17 ♗xf7+!! ♔xf7 18 ♕h5+ g6

To stop ♘f5, e.g. 18...♔f8 19 ♕xh7 ♕f4 20 ♘f5 ♕g5 21 ♕h8+

♣f7 22 ♞d6+ wins.
19 ♛xh7+ ♣f8 20 h4! 1-0
Amazingly simple - Black has no
defence against 21 h5 gh 22 ♞f5.

Game 65: Caro-Kann

Sznapik-Lechtynsky
Dečin 1979

**1 e4 c6 2 d4 d5 3 ♞c3 de 4 ♞xe4
♞f6 5 ♞xf6+ ef 6 ♝c4 ♛e7+!**
Recommended by Bronstein and
Keene. 6...♝d6?! 7 ♛e2+! ♛e7 8
♛xe7+ is a simplification White
seeks in order to exploit his Q-side
pawn majority.
**7 ♛e2 ♝e6 8 ♝b3 ♞a6! 9 ♝e3
♝xb3 10 ab ♛e6 11 ♞f3 ♝d6 12
0-0 0-0 13 ♜fd1 ♜fe8 14 ♛d2 (14
♛c4!?) 14...♞b4! 15 c4**
Strategically ill-motivated (backward doubled b-pawns); 15 c3 ♞d5
16 ♜e1 and if 16...♞xe3 17 ♜xe3
♛xb3 18 ♜xe8+ ♜xe8 19 ♜xa7
may be preferable. The text pre-
pares a tactic which backfires.
**15...a5! 16 d5? (16 ♞e1!) 16...cd
17 cd ♛f5 18 ♝b6** *(65)*

Lechtynsky points out 18...♝f4
19 ♝e3 is equal, but prefers to lure
White into a pit of his own digging.
18...♜a6! 19 ♝xa5? ♜ea8 20 ♝xb4
Entertaining is 20 ♜e1 ♜xa5?? 21
♜xa5 ♜xa5 22 ♜e8+ ♝f8 23 ♜xf8+
♣xf8 24 ♛xb4+ ♣g8 25 ♛xa5
♛b1+ 26 ♛e1; but the calm 20...
♛d7 wins simply.
**20...♜xa1 (20...♝xb4? 21 ♜xa6) 21
♝xd6 ♜xd1+ 22 ♛xd1 ♛xd5! 0-1**

Game 66: Caro-Kann

Schneider-Philgren
Rilton Cup 1979/80

**1 e4 c6 2 d4 d5 3 ♞d2 de 4 ♞xe4
♞d7 5 ♝c4 ♞gf6 6 ♞g5!?**
This avoidance of exchanges
involves White in some convolutions
but he hopes to emphasise Black's
lack of space as a result.
6...e6 7 ♛e2 ♞b6 8 ♝b3 h6
Not 8...♛xd4? 9 ♞1f3 (intending
♞e5) 9...♛g4 10 ♞xf7! or 9...♝b4+
10 c3 ♝xc3+ 11 ♣f1! wins.
9 ♞5f3 a5?!
Since Black intends ...c5 he can
do without this.
**10 a4 c5 11 ♝e3 ♛c7 12 ♞e5!
♞bd7?!**
This hardly sets about solving
Black's development problems. A
more realistic try would be 12...
♝d6 so that if 13 dc ♝xe5 14 cb
♛e7 frees Black's game.
**13 ♞gf3 ♝e7 14 0-0 0-0 15 ♜fe1
b6?** *(66)*
Instead 15...♞xe5 would avoid
White's next.

16 ♘xf7!! ♖xf7

Or 16...♔xf7 17 ♗xe6+! ♔e8 (17
...♔xe6 18 ♗f4+) 18 ♕d3 with a
big attack.

17 ♗f4! ♕xf4 18 ♕xe6

Threatens both ♕xf7+ and ♕xe7,
so Black arranges an expensive Q-
swap.

**18...c4 19 ♗xc4 ♘e5 20 ♕xe5 ♗d6
21 ♕xf4 ♗xf4 22 ♖e7! ♗a6 23
♗xf7+ ♔f8 24 ♖ae1 1-0**

Game 67: Sicilian, Alapin

Should this be renamed, not the
Morra Game but the Murray
(Chandler) variation?; the young
New Zealand master plays it all the
time.

**Chandler-Jacoby
Hamburg 1980**

1 e4 c5 2 c3 d5

To 'exploit' White's inability to
play ♘c3. Another way is 2...♘f6!?
3 e5 ♘d5 with a centre square
compensating(?) White's space.

3 ed ♕xd5 4 d4 ♘c6

Castro-Sigurjonsson, Esbjerg 1979
deserves mention and a diagram: 4
...♘f6 5 ♘f3 ♗g4 6 ♗e2 e6 7 h3
♗h5 8 0-0 ♘c6 9 ♗e3 cd 10 cd ♗e7
11 ♘c3 ♕d6!? 12 ♕d2 0-0 13 ♖fd1
♖fd8 14 ♖ac1 ♖ac8 15 a3 ♕b8 16
b4 ♗xf3 17 ♗xf3 ♘xd4!? 18 ♗xd4
e5 19 ♘d5! ♘xd5 20 ♖xc8 ♕xc8
21 ♗xe5 ♘xb4? *(67a)*

22 ♕xd8+!! ♖xd8 23 ♗xb7! 1-0.
**5 ♘f3 ♗g4 6 ♗e2 cd 7 cd e6 8 ♘c3
♕d7 9 0-0 ♘f6 10 h3 ♗h5?!**

In view of White's reply 10...♗xf3
11 ♗xf3 ♘xd4 12 ♗xb7 ♕xb7 13
♕xd4 ♗e7 looks better.

11 ♘e5! ♗xe5?!

On 11...♗xe2 12 ♘xd7 ♗xd1 13
♘xf6+ gf 14 ♖xd1 - threat d5 - is a
small, safe plus; 12 ♕xe2!? compli-
cates, i.e. 12...♘xd4? 13 ♕e3! ♕d6
14 ♖d1 ♘f5 15 ♕e2.

12 de ♗xe2

Not 12...♕xd1 13 ♗xd1! ♗xd1
14 ♖xd1 ♘d7 15 ♘b5.

**13 ♕xe2 ♘d5 14 ♘xd5 ♕xd5 15
♖d1 ♕a5 16 ♗g5! ♗e7** (16...h6 17
♕d3!) **17 ♗xe7 ♔xe7** *(67b)*

67b
W

18 ♕g4! ♕xe5 19 ♕b4+ ♔f6 (19...
♔e8) 20 ♖d7 ♖hf8 21 ♖e1! ♕b8
22 ♕h4+! ♔g6 23 ♕g4+ ♔f6 24
♖xf7+ 1-0

Game 68: Sicilian, Nimzowitsch

Gurgenidze-Mnatsakanian Tbilisi 1977

1 e4 c5 2 ♘f3 ♘f6!? 3 e5 ♘d5 4
♘c3 e6 5 ♘e4 ♘c6 6 c4 ♘b6 7 b4!

An enterprising 'positional' pawn
offer.

7...♘xb4 8 ♗b2 ♗e7

Georgadze recommends 8...d5! 9
ed f5 (9...♗xd6 10 ♗xg7 ♖g8 11
♘f6+) 10 ♘xc5 ♗xd6 11 ♘b3 0-0!
12 c5 ♘a4 13 ♗xg7 ♔xg7 14 cd
♕xd6 15 d4 with a small plus for
White. Jekabson-Shabalov, USSR
1978, showed why it's unwise for
Black to castle in this line - 8...♕c7
9 a4 a5 10 ♖a3 ♕c6 11 ♕b1 h6 12
♗e2 ♗e7 13 0-0 0-0? 14 ♘f6+ ♗xf6
15 ef d6 16 fg ♖e8 17 ♘g5! f5 18
♖h3 e5 19 ♖xh6 ♔xg7 20 ♖h7+

♕g6 21 f4! ♗d7 22 ♘h5+ 1-0.
9 h4! h6 10 a4! a5 11 ♖a3! ♕c7 12
♖h3! ♕c6 (68)

68
W

13 ♕b1!

White plans to complete his
development then win by ♖g3 - so
the odd pawn doesn't matter.

13...♘xa4 14 ♗a1 ♘b6 15 ♗e2 a4
(15...♘xc4?! 16 ♗xc4 b5) 16
♔f1!? ♖a5 17 ♖g3! ♔f8 (17...g6)
18 ♘d6! ♖a8

Also horrible is 18...♗xd6 19 ed
f6 20 ♕g6 ♖g8 21 ♗xf6.

19 ♘xf7! ♖g8 1-0.

In view of 20 ♕g6 threatening
♘xh6. Odd but but convincing!

Game 69: Sicilian, 3 b3!?

Westerinen-Dely Szolnok 1975

1 e4 c5 2 ♘f3 e6 3 b3!? d6 4 ♗b2
♘f6 5 ♗d3!?

Insipid is 5 d3 and the text - cf.
moves 9-11 - retains more tension
than 5 ♗b5+ preparing d3.

5...♘c6 6 0-0 ♗e7 7 ♖e1 ♗d7 8 ♘a3

0-0 9 c3! ♘g4 10 ♖c1 ♗f6 11 ♗b1 ♘ge5 12 h3!? ♘xf3+ 13 ♕xf3 a5?!

Florian rightly condemns this, recommending instead 13...a6.
14 ♘b5! ♕b6 15 a4 ♘a7? (69)

16 e5! ♗xe5 (16...de 17 ♕d3) 17 ♖xe5! de 18 ♕d3 ♖fd8 19 ♕xh7+ ♔f8 20 c4 ♘c6

Good as any, e.g. 20...♗xb5?! 21 cb ♖xd2 22 ♗xe5 f6 23 ♗xf6 gf 24 ♕h6+, or 20...f6 21 ♗g6 intending ♕h8+.

21 ♖e1 f6?!

Weakens f6. 21...♘d4 22 ♖xe5; 21...♔e7!? was the best chance.
22 ♖e3 ♘d4 23 ♕h8+! 1-0

Because of 23...♔f7 24 ♗g6+! forcing mate.

Game 70: Sicilian, 3 c3

Torfason-Bengtsson
Graz Student Olympiad 1972

1 e4 c5 2 ♘f3 ♘c6 3 c3 ♘f6!? 4 e5 ♘d5 5 d4 cd 6 cd d6! 7 ♘c3 ♘xc3

Instead 7...de 8 de ♘xc3 doesn't give White much.

8 bc ♗g4?! (70)

Not 8...de 9 d5! with complications favouring White. Sokolov suggests 8...♕a5 or 8...e6.

9 d5!! ♗xf3

Now 9...♘xe5? 10 ♘xe5! ♗xd1 11 ♗b5+ wins at least a piece.
10 gf! ♘xe5 11 ♕a4+ ♘d7 (11... ♕d7?? 12 ♗b5) 12 ♖b1 ♕c7 13 ♗h3 b6 14 ♗e3 0-0-0

Better than 14...♕xc3+? 15 ♔e2! ♕c7 (15...♖d8? 16 ♖hc1, 17 ♗xd7+, 18 ♖c8) 16 ♖hc1 attacking b6.

15 0-0 ♔b7 16 ♗xd7!

Eliminating a possible defender, after which it's just a matter of proving that queen + 2 rooks + bishop in attack beats king + queen + rook in defence.

16...♕xd7 17 ♖b5! ♕c7 18 ♖fb1 ♖b8 19 ♖a5! ♔a8 20 ♖a6! ♖b7 21 ♖1xb6 1-0

Game 71: Sicilian, 3 c3

Featuring an almost 'positional' sacrifice by the Yugoslav. He does something along the same lines in his other win in this collection - game 193.

Sax-Ljubojević
London 1980

1 e4 c5 2 ♘f3 e6 3 c3 d5 4 e5 d4!?

Rather than 4...♘c6 5 d4 - the advance French, which Sax knows well. Now 5 cd cd 6 ♕a4+ ♘c6 7 ♗b5 doesn't win a pawn after 7 ... ♗d7!, so 5 ♗b5+ should probably be played.

5 ♗d3?! ♘c6 6 ♕e2 ♘ge7 7 0-0 ♘g6 8 ♕e4!? ♗e7

Better than 8...dc 9 dc ♘gxe5 10 ♘xe5 ♘xe5 11 ♗b5+ ♘d7 12 ♖d1 with a nasty attack. But White's Q-side is gummed in now.

9 ♘a3 0-0 10 cd cd 11 ♘c2 ♕c7! 12 ♖e1 ♖d8 13 h4

A rather desperate attack, but on 13 b3 Quinteros and Pein give 13...♖d5! 14 ♗c4!? ♘cxe5 15 ♗xd5 ed 16 ♕xd5 ♘xf3+ 17 gf ♕xc2 18 ♖xe7 ♕d1+ 19 ♔g2 ♗h3+! winning the queen.

13...h5 14 g4!? hg 15 h5 *(71)*

The White attack is illusory; now Black turns the tables completely. 15...♘cxe5!! 16 ♘xe5 f5! 17 ♕e2 ♘f4 18 ♕f1 b5! 0-1!

Black's unanswerable build-up is ...♗f6, ...♗b7 and ...♘h3+.

Game 72: Sicilian, 3 ♗b5

Hulak-Simić
Yugoslav Ch, Umag 1976

1 e4 c5 2 ♘f3 ♘c6 3 ♗b5!? ♕b6?! 4 ♘c3 a6?! (development!) 5 ♗xc6 ♕xc6 6 d4 d6 7 0-0 cd (7...♗g4) 8 ♘xd4 ♕c7 9 ♗g5 e6 10 ♖e1 ♘f6

Or 10...♗e7 11 ♗xe7 ♘xe7 12 ♖e3! and ♖d3 with pressure against d6.

11 ♗xf6 gf 12 ♕h5! ♕c5 *(72)*

13 ♘f5! ♗d7

He can't take, i.e. 13...ef?! 14 ef+ ♗e7 15 ♕e2! ♕e5 16 ♕c4 with the threat of ♘d5.

14 ♕h4! ♗e7?

Hulak suggests 14...0-0-0 15 ♕xf6 ♕e5.

15 ♘xe7 ♔xe7 16 e5! ♖hg8 (16...

de 17 ♘e4) 17 ♕xf6+ ♔f8 18 ♘e4
♕c6

Or 18...♕xe5 19 ♕xe5 de 20 ♘f6.
19 ed ♖e8 20 ♕h6+ ♖g7 21 ♖e3
1-0

Game 73: Sicilian, 3 ♗b5

Just 12 at the time, England's
prodigy downs an experienced
Australian Olympiad regular (cf.
game 134).

Short-Fuller
British Ch, Brighton 1977

1 e4 c5 2 ♘f3 ♘c6 3 ♗b5!? ♕b6?!
4 ♗xc6 ♕xc6

Instead Short recommends 4...bc.
5 0-0 g6 6 ♘c3 ♗g7 7 d4 d6 8 dc
dc *(73)*

9 ♗f4! ♗xc3?!
He should decline the pawn.
10 bc ♕xe4 11 ♕c1! ♗f5 12 ♖e1
♕a4
Very unhealthy is 12...♕xc2?! 13

♕a3! b6 14 ♖ad1 with the threat of
♖d2.
13 ♕e3 (threat ♗-e5xf6) 13...♕c6
14 ♘e5 ♕c8 15 ♘c4! ♗e6 (15...♕e6
16 ♘d6+! - Short) 16 ♕e5 ♘f6 17
♘d6+ ed 18 ♕xf6 ♖g8
Or 18...♔d7 19 ♖ad1 d5 20
♖xd5+.
19 ♗xd6 ♕d7 (19...♕d8 20 ♖xe6+)
20 ♖ad1 1-0
The threat of ♗xc5 can't be met.

Game 74: Sicilian, 3 ♗b5

Lutikov-Ermenkov
Albena 1976

1 e4 c5 2 ♘f3 ♘c6 3 ♗b5 g6 4 0-0
♗g7 5 c3!? (also 5 ♖e1 e5 6 b4!?)
5...♘f6 6 d4!? cd 7 cd ♘xe4
He can't 'play safe' with 7...d5?!
8 e5 ♘e4 9 ♘e1! threatening f3.
8 d5 ♘d6 9 ♘a3 ♘e5?! (9...a6) 10
♘xe5 ♗xe5 11 ♖e1 ♘xb5?!
Minev suggests 11...♗f6!? but
then 12 ♗f4! looks strong, i.e. 12...
♕b6 (12...♗xb2? 13 ♗d6; 12...
♘xb5 13 ♘xb5 0-0 14 ♗c7! ♕e8 15
♘d6; 12...♘f5!?) 13 ♗xd6 ♕xd6
14 ♘c4 ♕b8 (14...♕c5 15 b4 ♕d4
16 ♕f3 ♕xa1? 17 ♘d6+!) 15 ♕f3
0-0 16 d6! with pressure.
12 ♖xe5! f6 *(74)*
Others: a) 12...♘xa3 13 ♗g5!
♘b5 14 ♗xe7 ♕xe7 15 ♖xe7+
♔xe7 16 ♕e2+; b) 12...♘d6 13
♗g5 ♘f5 14 ♗xe7! ♘xe7 15 d6; c)
12...d6 13 ♖e1 ♘xa3 14 ♗g5! (14
♕d4!?) 14...0-0 15 ♗xe7.

13 ♘xb5! fe 14 d6 0-0 15 ♗g5!
♕b6

The White attack is crushing, e.g.
15...♖f7 16 de ♖xe7 17 ♕d5+ ♔f8
18 ♘d6!
16 de ♕xb5 17 ef♕+ ♔xf8 18
♕d6+ ♔g8 19 ♗h6 1-0

Game 75: Sicilian, 3...d5?!

C.Hansen-J.Pedersen
Danish Ch Challengers,
Odense 1980

1 e4 e6 2 d4 c5 3 ♘f3 d5?!
Experimental! 3...cd is best. This
position differs from a Tarrasch
French in that White can castle
quickly then attack.
4 ed! ed 5 ♗b5+ ♘c6 (5...♗d7!?) 6
0-0 ♗d6 7 c4!
Guarenteeing a pawn on d5, this
looks like a good answer.
7...a6 8 cd!? (8 ♗a4!?) 8...ab 9 dc6
bc 10 dc ♗xc5 11 ♕c2 ♕b6 12
♘bd2! ♗e6?!
Not 12...♘e7? 13 ♘e4, but best
may be 12...♘f6 although 13 ♘b3

♗e7 14 ♗e3 followed by ♘bd4
poses problems.
13 ♘e4 ♗e7 14 ♗e3 ♕c7 15 ♘d4
♗c4 (15...♗d5 16 ♘xb5) 16 ♖fe1
♗b4?! *(75)*
But what else? b3 was threatened
and 16...♘f6 17 ♘xf6+ didn't help
matters.

17 ♘f6+! gf
The critical try was 17...♔f8 18
♗f4! ♕b7 19 ♕xh7!! If 17...♘xf6
18 ♗f4+ ♕e7 19 ♖xe7+ ♗xe7 21
♘xc6 soon wins.
18 ♗f4+ ♕e7 19 ♖xe7+ ♘xe7 20
♘xc6! ♘xc6 21 ♕e4+ ♔f8 22 ♗h6+
♔g8 23 ♕g4 mate.

Game 76: Sicilian, Kan

Olafsson-Quinteros
Las Palmas 1974

1 e4 c5 2 ♘f3 e6 3 d4 cd 4 ♘xd4 a6
5 ♘c3 ♕c7 6 ♗e2 ♘f6 7 0-0 b5?! *(7
...d6; 7...♘c6)* 8 ♗f3 ♘c6
Another try is 8...♗b7. White has
9 e5!? ♘g8 10 ♗f4 (Minić) or 9 ♖e1
d6 10 a4! b4 11 ♘a2 ♘bd7?! 12

♘xb4 ♘c5 13 ♘d5! ed 14 ed+ ♔d8
15 b4! ♘cd7 16 ♘c6+ ♔c8 17 ♗h2
♗xc6 18 dc ♘e5 19 b5 ♖b8?! 20
♗xe5 de 21 ♗g4+ ♘xg4 22 ♕xg4+
♔d8 23 ♖ad1+ 1-0 Govedarica-
Sofrevsky, Yugoslavia 1976.

9 e5!? b4?! (9...♘g8) 10 ef bc 11
♘xc6 dc 12 ♗f4! ♕d7?! 13 ♕e2
♕b7

The threat was 14 ♖ad1 ♕b7 15
♕c4 ♗d7 16 ♖xd7! ♔xd7 17 ♖d1+
and ♗xc6.

14 bc! ♗d7 15 ♖ab1 ♕a7 16 ♖fd1
gf 17 ♕c4 ♗c5 (76)

On 17...♕c5 18 ♕xc5 ♗xc5 19
♖b7 ♖d8 20 ♖(either)xd7 and 21
♗xc6; 17...♖c8 18 ♗e3 ♕a8 19
♖b6, xa6-a7 is all winning.

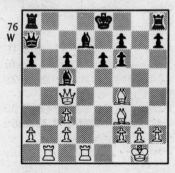

76
W

18 ♖xd7! ♔xd7 19 ♗xc6+! ♔xc6
20 ♕a4+ 1-0

Mate follows by 20...♔d5 21
♖d1+ ♗d4 22 ♖xd4+ ♔c5 23 ♗d6+
♔b6 24 ♖b4.

Game 77: Sicilian, Kan

These early ...b5 moves in the
Kan simply aren't on, as Larry
Christiansen proves yet again.

Christiansen-Gilden
USA National League 1976

1 e4 c5 2 ♘c3 e6 3 ♘f3 a6 4 d4 cd
5 ♘xd4 b5?! 6 ♗d3 ♗b7 7 0-0 ♕c7
8 ♕e2 d6 9 a4! ba?! (9...b4) 10
♖xa4 ♘f6 11 ♗g5 ♗e7 12 f4 0-0?

Loses. Byrne and Mednis give
12...♘bd7 13 ♖c4! ♕b6 14 ♘a4
♕a7 15 ♔h1 d5 16 ♘c6 ♗xc6 17
♖xc6 with advantage to White.

13 e5 ♘d5 14 ♘xd5 ♗xd5 (77)

77
W

15 ♗f6!!

Threat is 16 ♗xh7+! ♔xh7 17
♕h5+ ♔g8 18 ♕g5, and if 15...gf
16 ♕h5 f5 loses to 17 ♘xf5!

15...g6 16 f5! ♗xf6

No good is 16...ef 17 ♘xf5! gf 18
♖g4+!, and on 16...de!? 17 ♗xe5
♗d6 18 ♗xd6 ♕xd6 19 f6 ♕d8!?
(best; Byrne and Mednis give 19...
e5 20 ♕e3! ♘d7 21 ♘f5! winning.)
20 ♕f2 ♘d7 21 ♕h4!? gives a
powerful attack.

17 ef e5 18 ♕g4! ed

Here 18...♘d7 19 ♕g5 ♕d8 20 fg
fg 21 ♗xg6! wins for White.

19 ♖xd4 ♗b7?!

He should try 19...♘d7 20 fg (20
♕g5 ♘xf6) 20...fg 21 ♖xd5 ♘xf6

♕e6+ ♔g7. Now it's easy.
20 fg fg 21 ♗xg6 ♔h8 22 ♕h5!
♖xf6 (else 23 f7) 23 ♖xf6 1-0

Game 78: Sicilian, Taimanov

Velimirović-Vasyukov
Yugoslavia-USSR 1973

1 e4 c5 2 ♘f3 ♘c6 3 d4 cd 4 ♘xd4
e6 5 ♘c3 a6 6 ♗e2 ♕c7

An intriguing idea by the origin-
ator of the system is 6...♘ge7!? 7
♗e3 ♘xd4 8 ♕xd4 b5 (8...♘c6?! 9
♕b6) 9 f4 ♘c6 10 ♕d2 ♗e7 11
0-0-0? ♕a5! 12 e5 (12 ♔b1 b4 13
♘d5 ed 14 ed b3!) 12...b4 13 ♘e4
♕xa2 14 ♘d6+ ♗xd6 15 ♕xd6
♕a1+ 16 ♔d2 ♕xb2 17 ♗c5?! (17
♔e1) 17...♕c3+ 18 ♔c1 b3! 19
♗d3 ♖b8 20 ♖he1 ♖b5! 21 ♗a3
♘b4 22 ♖e2 b2+ 0-1, Martin-
Taimanov, Montilla 1977.
7 0-0 b5?! 8 ♘xc6 ♕xc6 9 ♗f3 ♗b7
10 ♗f4 d6 11 ♖e1 e5 (78)
This fails, so 11...♗e7 or 11...♖d8
should be considered.

12 a4!! b4

Or 12...ef 13 e5 gives White a
tremendous attack.
13 ♘d5 ef 14 c3! b3 (14...bc 15
♖c1) 15 e5 0-0-0 16 ♕xb3 ♔b8 17
♘b4 ♕d7
Not 17...♕b6 18 ♘c6+! ♔c7 19
♕xb6+ ♔xb6 20 ♘xd8.
18 ♗xb7 ♔xb7 19 ♘d5+ ♔a8
Resignation, but 19...♔a7 20
♕b6+ ♔a8 21 ♘c7+, or 19...♔c6 20
♕b6+ ♔xd5 21 ed threatening
♖ad1+ were also fatal.
20 ♘b6+ ♔a7 21 ♘xd7 ♖xd7 22
♖ad1 1-0

Game 79: Sicilian, Taimanov

Romanishin-Hort
Göteborg 1971

1 e4 c5 2 ♘f3 e6 3 d4 cd 4 ♘xd4
♘c6 5 ♘c3 ♕c7 6 g3 d6 7 ♗g2
♗d7? (7...a6) 8 ♘db5 ♕b8 9 ♗f4
♘e5
Very passive is 9...e5 but this is
tricky; White's reply threatens 11
♘xd6+ ♗xd6 12 0-0-0.
10 ♕d4 g5!? 11 ♗xg5 a6 12 ♘a3 b5
13 f4? (79)

Weakening his K-side and allowing complications. 13 ♘e2 would have preserved an advantage.

13...h6! 14 ♗h4

Or 14 fe de! and 15...hg. Black has also given himself the option of ...♖h7 in the event of an attack along the f-file.

14...b4!? 15 fe

Or 15 ♘c4 ♘xc4! 16 ♕xh8 bc 17 ♕xg8 ♕b6! 18 ♕g4 cb with a strong attack.

15...de 16 ♕d3 ba 17 ♖d1 ♕a7! 18 ♖f1? (18 ba) **18...ab 19 ♗h3**

Desperate but dangerous; the threat is 20 ♗xe6! fe (20...♗xe6? 21 ♕d8+) 21 ♕f3 ♗e7 22 ♕f7+ ♔d8 23 ♕g7.

19...♗b4 20 ♔e2 ♕c7!

Wins; 20...♖c8?! 21 ♘b1 ♗b5 22 c4! ♗xc4? 23 ♕xc4 ♖xc4 24 ♖d8 mate. And now 21 ♘d5 fails after 21...ed 22 ♕xd5 ♗b5+.

21 ♕f3 ♗b5+ 22 ♖d3 (22 ♘xb5 ♕xc2+) **22...b1♕! 23 ♖xb1 ♕xc3 0-1**

Game 80: Sicilian, Taimanov

Kuzmin-Sveshnikov
USSR Ch, Top League,
Moscow 1973

1 e4 c5 2 ♘f3 e6 3 d4 cd 4 ♘xd4 ♘c6 5 ♘c3 ♕c7 6 ♗e2 a6 7 0-0 ♘f6 8 ♗e3 ♗b4 9 ♘xc6

On 9 ♘a4!? Black can try 9...♗e7. Instead Gufeld-Dzhindzhihashvili, Gori 1971, continued 9...0-0 10 ♘xc6 dc 11 ♗b6 ♕e5?! (11...♕f4)

12 ♗d3 ♘d7 13 f4 ♕b8 14 ♔h1 ♘xb6 15 ♘xb6 ♖a7 16 e5 ♕c7? (16 ...♗c5) 17 ♘xc8 ♖xc8 18 ♕g4 ♗f8 19 f5! ef 20 ♖xf5 ♕d8 21 ♖xf7! ♔xf7 22 ♗c4+ ♔e8 23 ♕e6+ ♗e7 24 ♖f1 (threat ♖f8+!) 1-0.

9...bc 10 ♘a4 0-0 11 c4!?

Spurning 11 ♘b6 ♖b8 12 ♘xc8 etc., and maintaining his development with attacking threats. Now if 11...♘xe4? 12 c5! ♕e5 13 ♗d4 ♕f4 14 ♗xg7; Geller suggests 11... ♗e7.

11...♗d6?! 12 f4! ♘xe4 13 ♗d3 ♘f6 14 c5 ♗e7 15 ♗d4 ♘d5? *(80)*

16 ♘b6! ♘xb6 (16...♖b8 17 ♘xd5 cd 18 ♗xh7+!) **17 ♗xh7+! ♔xh7 18 ♕h5+ ♔g8 19 ♗xg7! ♔xg7 20 ♕g4+ ♔h7** (20...♔f6 21 ♕g5 mate) **21 ♖f3 ♗xc5+ 22 ♔h1 1-0**

Game 81: Sicilian, Pelikan

Hamilton-Davis
Australia 1975

1 e4 c5 2 ♘f3 ♘c6 3 d4 cd 4 ♘xd4 ♘f6 5 ♘c3 e5!? 6 ♘db5 d6 7 ♗g5

a6 8 ♗xf6!?

Here 8 ♘a3 ♗e6 9 ♘c4 ♖c8! 10 ♗xf6 ♛xf6! 11 ♘xd6+ ♗xd6 12 ♛xd6 ♘d4 13 0-0-0 ♛h6+ 14 ♖d2 ♖d8 15 ♛c5 ♛xd2+! 0-1 is Dugas-Acers, simultaneous display, San Francisco 1977.

8...gf 9 ♘a3 f5

And now 9...b5!? (normal) 10 ♘d5 f5 11 ef ♗xf5 12 ♛f3?! ♘d4 13 ♘c7+ ♛xc7 14 ♛xa8+ ♗c8!? 15 ♗d3?! d5! 16 0-0? (16 c3; 16 ♛xd5? ♗b7) 16...♗xa3 17 ba 0-0 18 f4 ♗b7 19 ♗xh7+ ♔g7 20 ♛xf8+ ♔xf8 21 fe ♘e2+ 0-1 is Bellon-G.Garcia, Orense 1976.

10 ♛h5 d5?! (10...b5!) 11 0-0-0!? ♗xa3 12 ba ♘d4 13 ♘xd5 ♗e6 14 ♗c4 ♖c8 *(81)*

The same reply follows 14...♛a5.

15 ♖xd4!! ed 16 ef! ♗xd5

On 16...♖xc4 Hamilton gives 17 fe ♖c7 18 ♛e5!, and on 16...0-0 17 f6! ♔h8 18 ♗d3.

17 ♖e1+ ♔d7 18 ♗xd5 ♖f8?

Better 18...♛f6 19 ♛xf7+ and White should win.

19 ♗e6+! fe 20 fe+ ♔d6 21 e7 ♖xc2+?! 22 ♔xc2 ♖xf2+ 23 ♔d3! ♛c8 24 ♛e5+ 1-0

Game 82: Sicilian, Richter-Rauzer

Tatai-Radulov
Venice 1971

1 e4 c5 2 ♘f3 ♘c6 3 d4 cd 4 ♘xd4 ♘f6 5 ♘c3 d6 6 ♗g5 ♗d7!? 7 ♛d2 ♖c8 8 f4 ♘xd4 9 ♛xd4 ♛a5 10 e5!?

The Italian produces a novelty which avoids the unclear Black option of 10 0-0-0 ♖xc3!? Now Ciric gives, among others, 10...♘e4 11 ♛xe4 ♖xc3 12 bc ♛xc3+ 13 ♔f2 ♛xa1 14 ed f6! 15 ♗b5 ♛b2! 16 ♗xd7+ ♔xd7 17 de ♗xe7 with equality. The text reply appears to loosen Black's position too much.

10...h6?! 11 ♗h4 g5 12 ef e5 (12...gh? 13 fe) 13 fe de 14 ♛d3! gh 15 0-0-0 ♗c6 (15...♘e6? 16 ♛b5+; 15...♖d8!?) 16 ♛f5 ♖d8 *(82)*

17 ♗b5! ♖xd1+

Not 17...♗xb5? 18 ♛xe5+, and others also lose; 17...♛c7 18 ♖xd8+ ♔xd8 19 ♖d1+ ♗d6 20 ♗xc6 and 21 ♘e4, or 17...♗d6 18 ♖xd6! ♖xd6 19 ♛xe5+ ♖e6 20 ♗xc6+ winning the queen.

18 ♖xd1 ♕c7 19 ♘d5 ♕b8 20
♗xc6 bc 21 ♘b4! 1-0

On 21...♗xb4 22 ♕d7+ ♔f8 23
♕d8 mates; 21...♕c7 22 ♘a6!
decides, and 21...♗d6 22 ♘xc6 ♕c7
23 ♖xd6 ♕xd6 24 ♕c8+ is remorse-
less.

Game 83: Sicilian Richter-Rauzer

**Tal-Larsen
Montreal 1979**

1 e4 c5 2 ♘f3 ♘c6 3 d4 cd 4 ♘xd4
♘f6 5 ♘c3 d6 6 ♗g5 e6 7 ♕d2

Here 7 ♗c4?! (mixing systems)
would transpose to Sursok-Larsen,
Siegen Ol 1970: 7...♕b6!? 8 ♗xf6
gf 9 ♘db5?! ♘e5! 10 ♗b3 ♖g8!? 11
0-0 a6 12 ♘d4? ♕xd4! 0-1.
7...♗e7 8 0-0-0 a6 9 f4 ♕c7!?
(New? - 9...♗d7) 10 ♗e2 ♘xd4

No good is 10...b5? 11 ♘xc6
♕xc6 12 e5.
11 ♕xd4 b5?

Apparently the losing move!
12 e5 de 13 fe ♘d5 14 ♗xe7 ♘xc3
(14...♘xe7? 15 ♘xb5!) 15 ♗f3
♘xd1 *(83)*

Alternatives: a) 15...♔xe7 16 bc!
♖b8 (16...♗b7 17 ♕d6+) 17 ♕b4+
♔e8 18 ♖d6 with a winning attack;
b) 15...♕xe7 16 ♗c6+! ♔f8 17
♕d8+ ♕xd8 18 ♖xd8+ ♔e7 19
♖xh8; c) 15...♘e2+! 16 ♗xe2 ♔xe7
17 ♗f3 ♗b7 18 ♗xb7 ♕xb7 19
♕d6 ♖c8 20 ♖d2 ♕c6 21 ♖hd1
♕xd6 22 ♖xd6 with a favourable
rook ending - Black's best chance.

83
W

16 ♗d6! ♕c4

Or 16...♕a7 17 ♗c5! ♕b8 18
♗xa8 ♕xa8 19 ♕d6 ♕b7 20 ♖xd1
♕d7 21 ♕b6.
17 ♕b6! ♘f2 18 ♗c6+! (18 ♕xf2!
♕f4+ 19 ♔b1 ♗b7 20 ♗c6+) 18...
♗d7 19 ♗xd7+ ♔xd7 20 ♕b7+
♔d8 21 ♕xa8+ ♕c8 22 ♕a7 1-0

Game 84: Sicilian, Sozin

**Skrobek-Jankovec
Zilina 1976**

1 e4 c5 2 ♘c3 ♘c6 3 ♘f3 e6 4 d4
cd 5 ♘xd4 d6 6 ♗e3 ♘f6 7 ♗c4
♗e7 8 ♕e2 0-0 9 0-0-0 ♕c7 10 ♗b3
♘a5

Dubious, according to Mečkarov.
11 g4 a6 12 g5 ♘xb3+ 13 ab ♘d7
14 h4!?

With a threat against which Black
seems to have no sensible defence,
e.g. 14...♘c5 15 b4!?; 14...♘e5 15
f4.
14...b5 15 g6! ♘e5

Or 15...hg 16 h5 g5 17 ♖hg1 with
an attack looming against g7.

16 gh+ ♔h8 17 f4 ♘d7 18 ♖dg1 b4?! *(84)*

Necessary though ineffectual was 18...♗f6.

84
W

19 ♖xg7! ♘f6

Trying to defend g8 and h5. If 19...♔xg7 20 ♕g4+ and 21 ♖g1 mates, or 19...bc 20 ♖hg1 ♘f6 21 ♖g8+ ♖xg8 22 hg♕+ ♘xg8 23 ♕h5+.

20 ♖hg1 ♗b7 21 ♘d5! ed

Or 21...♗xd5 22 ed e5 (22...♕d7 23 de fe 24 ♘f5! ef 25 ♗d4) when Black is two pawns down with a continuing attack against his king. He's helpless now.

22 ♘f5! de 23 ♗d4 d5 24 ♖g8+ 1-0

Game 85: Sicilian, Sozin

Bordonada-Sanz
Nice Olympiad 1974

1 e4 c5 2 ♘f3 ♘c6 3 d4 cd 4 ♘xd4 ♘f6 5 ♘c3 d6 6 ♗c4 e6 7 ♗e3 ♗e7 8 ♕e2 a6 9 0-0-0 ♕c7 10 ♖hg1 0-0
Possible was 10...b5!?, i.e. 11 ♘xc6 ♕xc6 12 ♘xb5?! ♗d7! and White's e-pawn drops.

11 g4 ♘xd4 12 ♗xd4 b5 13 ♗b3 ♘d7 14 g5 ♘c5 15 ♕h5 b4?
Balashov's 15...♗b7 would rule out 16 ♗xg7? ♔xg7 17 ♕h6+ ♔h8 in view of the defensive possibility ...♖g8 and 16 ♗f6!? could be met by 16...♖fc8. Perhaps ♖g3/g4 would do some damage, though.

16 ♗f6! (threat: 17 ♕h6!) **16...♖d8 17 ♖g3 bc 18 ♖h3 h6** *(85)*

Bordonada gives 18...♔f8 19 ♗xg7+! ♔e8 20 ♖f3 ♗f8 21 ♗xf8 ♔xf8 22 g6! and wins (22...hg 23 ♕h8+ ♔e7 24 ♖xf7+ etc.), or 18...♗xf6 19 gf gf 20 ♕h6 ♘xe4 21 ♖g1+ ♘g5 22 ♕xf6.

85
W

19 ♕xh6!

Very pretty; 19...gh 20 ♖xh6 ♗xf6 21 gf with ♖g1+ and ♖h8 mate to follow. Black has only swindles to play for.

19...♘d3+ 20 cd!

The only way, i.e. 20 ♔b1? gh 21 ♖xh6 ♗xf6 22 gf ♘e5!, or 20 ♖dxd3? gh 21 ♖xh6 ♗xf6 22 gf d5! and Black wins (23 ♖dh3 ♕f4+!xh6).

20...cb+ 21 ♔xb2 1-0

Game 86: Sicilian, Sozin

Ermenkov-Triana
Cienfuegos 1975

1 e4 c5 2 ♘f3 d6 3 ♘c3 ♘c6 4 d4
cd 5 ♘xd4 ♘f6 6 ♗c4 e6 7 ♗e3 a6
8 ♗b3 ♗e7 9 ♕e2 ♕c7 10 0-0-0 0-0
11 g4 ♘d7 12 g5 ♘c5 13 ♕h5 b5
14 ♖hg1 ♖e8?

Balashov recommends 14...♘xd4
15 ♗xd4 (transposing to Bordonada-
Sanz, game 85) 15...♗b7, unclear.
15 ♘xc6 ♘xb3+ 16 ab ♕xc6 17
♗d4! b4 (86)

Defensive measures seem to fail, i.e.
a) 17...♗f8 18 ♖d3! when 18...g6
19 ♕xh7+! or 18...e5 19 ♘d5 win;
b) 17...e5 18 ♘d5! ed 19 ♘f6+
♗xf6 20 gf g6 21 ♕h6;
c) 17...g6 18 ♕h6 ♗f8 19 ♕h4
when 19...e5 20 ♘d5, 19...b4 20
♖d3 (threat ♕xh7+), or 19...♗e7
(trying for ...h5) 20 ♗f6 all lose.

86
W

18 ♗xg7! bc

On 18...♔xg7 Balashov gives 19
♕h6+ ♔h8 20 g6 fg 21 ♖xg6 ♗f8
22 ♖g8+! ♔xg8 23 ♖g1+ leading to
mate. Also 19...♔g8 20 g6! fg 21

♖xg6+! soon wins.
19 g6! fg 20 ♖xg6! hg 21 ♕xg6
♗g5+

Also unavailing is the desperate
21...♕xe4.
22 ♕xg5 ♖e7 23 ♖g1 1-0

Game 87: Sicilian, 4 Knights

Adorjan-Quinteros
Amsterdam 1977

1 e4 c5 2 ♘f3 e6 3 d4 cd 4 ♘xd4
♘f6 5 ♘c3 ♘c6!? (5...d6) 6 ♘xc6!?
bc

On 6...dc 7 ♕xd8+ White is
obviously the more comfortable.
7 e5 ♘d5 8 ♘e4 f5!? 9 ef ♘xf6 10
♘d6+ ♗xd6 11 ♕xd6 ♗a6!? 12
c4?! (12 ♗xa6 ♕a5+) 12...♕b6!?
13 ♗d3? (87)

Black threatened 13...♘e4 or 13...
♕xf2+, and 13 c5 ♕b4+ 14 ♕d2
♕xd2+ 15 ♗xd2 ♗xf1 gives him an
impregnable 'knighthold' on d5,
while 13 ♕g3 0-0 is an initiative.

87
B

13...♗xc4!! 14 ♗xc4 ♘e4 15 ♕a3
(15 ♕f4 ♕b4+) 15...♕xf2+ 16 ♔d1

♕d4+ 17 ♗d3 ♘f2+ 18 ♔e2 ♘xh1
19 ♗e3 ♕d5!

He needed to foresee this, otherwise White's bishops are very
dangerous, e.g. 19...♕g4+ 20 ♔f1
♖f8+ 21 ♔g1 is good for White.
**20 ♔f1 ♕e5! 21 g3 ♖b8! (21...
♕xe3?? 22 ♗g6+) 22 ♖e1**

On 22 ♕c3 0-0+! 23 ♔g2 (23
♗f4 ♕xc3 24 bc ♘xg3+ 25 hg g5)
23...♕d5+ 24 ♔g1 ♖f3 is very strong.
22...♖xb2 23 ♗c5 ♖f8+! 0-1

Game 88: Sicilian
Keres Attack

Timman-Röhrl
Madrid (Clare Benedict) 1971

**1 e4 c5 2 ♘f3 e6 3 d4 cd 4 ♘xd4
♘f6 5 ♘c3 d6 6 g4!?**

"... when a win is absolutely
necessary I return to this sharp
variation introduced by ... Keres" -
Karpov.
**6...a6 7 g5 ♘fd7 8 ♗g2!? ♕c7 (?!;
8...♘c6!? 9 f4 ♕c7 - Marić) 9 ♕h5!?
♘c5 10 ♗e3 ♘c6 11 0-0-0 ♗d7 12
f4 g6 13 ♕e2 ♗g7?** *(88)*

14 e5!!

Preserving the initiative for an
attack, whereas 14 ♘db5 ab 15
♘xb5 fails; 15...♕b6 16 ♘xd6+
♔e7 17 e5 ♖xa2.
**14...de 15 ♘db5! ab 16 ♘xb5 ♕b6
17 ♘d6+ ♔e7**

Here Marić's 17...♔f8 18 ♘e4
looks like a misprint in view of 18...
♘d4! Instead (17...♔f8) 18 ♘c4,
19 ♗xc5+ and 20 ♖xd7 regains the
piece.
18 ♕f2! ♖a5

Against 19 ♘c8+! followed by
♗c5+, and 18...♘d4 19 fe was also
rather forlorn.
**19 ♘c4 ♕b5 20 ♘xa5 ♖xa5 21
♗xc5+ ♔e8 22 fe ♘c4 23 b3 ♗xe5
24 a4 1-0**

Game 89: Sicilian,
Scheveningen

Akvist-Kuzmin
Reggio Emilia 1976/7

**1 e4 c5 2 ♘f3 e6 3 d4 cd 4 ♘xd4
♘c6 5 ♗e2 ♘f6 6 ♘c3 d6 7 0-0 ♗e7
8 ♗e3 0-0 9 f4 ♕c7 (9...♗d7) 10
♕e1 ♗d7 11 ♕g3 ♘xd4 12 ♗xd4
♗c6 13 ♗d3 b6!?**

After 13...♖ad8 White can aim
for transposition with 14 ♖ae1!?;
instead 14 ♔h1 ♘h5!? 15 ♕g4 e5,
or 14 ♖ad1 b6 15 e5 de 16 ♗xe5
♕b7 17 f5 ♗c5+ 18 ♔h1 ♘h5 19
♕h3 f6 - unclear according to
Joksić, but Black looks better to
the author.
**14 ♖ae1 ♖ad8 15 ♔h1 ♕b7 16
♖f3! ♖fe8 17 ♕h3 e5?!**

White threatened 18 e5, and 17...g6 18 ♕h6 ♗f8 19 ♕h4 gave him the better of it. The text is an attempt at a freeing combination which doesn't work.

18 fe de 19 ♗xe5 ♘xe4?! (but what?) **20 ♘xe4 ♗xe4** *(89)*

21 ♕g4!

This wins, but not 21 ♗xe4 ♕xe4!, or 21 ♖xe4 ♕xe4! 22 ♖e3! ♕h4!

21...♗g6 22 ♖xf7!! 1-0

After 22...♔xf7 23 ♗c4+ ♖d5 (23 ...♔f8 24 ♕e6) 24 ♕f3+ ♔e6 25 ♗g3+ ♔d7 26 ♗xd5 ♕a6 27 ♗e6+ mates.

Game 90: Sicilian, Scheveningen

Machulsky-Zaichik
Juniors, Tallinn 1976

1 e4 c5 2 ♘f3 ♘c6 3 d4 cd 4 ♘xd4 ♘f6 5 ♘c3 d6 6 ♗e3 e6 7 ♗e2 ♗e7 8 f4 ♗d7?! (8...0-0) 9 g4! ♘xd4 10 ♕xd4 0-0

Of course he can't allow 10...♗c6

11 g5 ♘d7 12 ♕xg7, so this knight becomes misplaced.

11 g5 ♘e8 12 0-0-0 ♗c6 13 ♔b1

A little slow. Savon suggests 13 h4; also quite pointed (at the king!) is 13 ♖hg1.

13...♕b8 (13...f5?!) **14 f5!? b5?!**

He might well have tried 14...ef, as the text permits an immediate breakthrough.

15 f6! gf 16 ♖hg1 ♔h8 17 ♖df1 ♕d8 18 ♘d5! e5 *(90)*

Or 18...ed 19 ed ♗d7 20 ♗d3, with the main threat 21 gf ♘xf6 22 ♖xf6! ♗xf6 23 ♕e4.

19 gf! ♘xf6 (19...ed 20 fe) **20 ♘xe7! ♕xe7**

No better was 20...ed 21 ♗xd4 ♕xe7 22 ♖xf6! ♕e5 23 ♗xe5 de 24 ♖xc6. White's reply, threatening both ♕xc6 and ♗g5, wins a piece now.

21 ♕c3! 1-0

Game 91: Sicilian, Scheveningen

In Jim Peters the American system

of free enterprise has produced that rarest of animals - the sponsored chessplayer.

Peters-Youngworth
USA 1976

1 e4 c5 2 ♘f3 e6 3 d4 cd 4 ♘xd4 ♘f6!? 5 ♘c3 d6 6 ♗e2 ♗e7 7 0-0 0-0 8 f4 ♘c6 9 ♗e3 a6 10 a4

I believe that White's play from moves 10-15 is stylistically indebted to Karpov.

10...♕c7 11 ♔h1 ♘a5 12 ♕d3 d5!?

Tukmakov-Panno, Buenos Aires 1970, concluded 12...♗d7 13 g4 ♔h8 14 g5 ♘g8 15 ♖f3 ♘c6 16 ♖g1 ♘xd4 17 ♗xd4 f5? 18 ♖h3 e5 19 ♘d5 ♕d8 20 fe fe 21 e6!! 1-0.

13 e5 ♘d7 14 ♗f2!? ♗b4?!

Peters suggests 14...♘c5 15 ♕h3 ♘c6! intending ...f6, which would release a lot of pressure.

15 ♘a2 ♗e7 16 ♕h3 ♘c4 17 ♗d3 g6 (17...h6? 18 ♘xe6!) 18 ♕h6! ♘xb2? *(91)*

Necessary was 18...♘c5.

91
W

19 ♗xg6!! hg 20 ♘xe6! fe 21 ♕xg6+ ♔h8 22 ♗d4!

More efficient than 22 ♗b6? ♘xb6 23 ♖f3 ♗h4!

22...♕d8 23 ♖f3 ♖f5 (23...♗h4 24 ♗xb2 ♖f5 25 ♖h3) 24 ♖g3! 1-0

Game 92: Sicilian Scheveningen

Romanishin-G.Garcia
Novi Sad 1975

1 e4 c5 2 ♘f3 e6 3 d4 cd 4 ♘xd4 ♘f6 5 ♘c3 d6 6 ♗e3 a6 7 f4 ♕c7 8 ♕f3 b5 9 ♗d3 (better is 9 g4) 9...♗b7 10 g4 ♘c6 (10 ... h6!?) 11 g5 ♘d7 12 ♕h3?!

Now Black is better. Preferable is 12 0-0-0 or even 12 f5!? leading to unclear complications.

12...♘xd4! 13 ♗xd4 b4 14 ♘e2 e5 15 ♗e3 d5? *(92)*

But not this way! 15...♘c5 with pressure against e4 was correct. In just 3 more moves the tables are drastically turned.

92
W

16 0-0-0! de 17 ♗c4! ♖d8 18 ♗xf7+! ♔xf7 19 g6+! ♔e7

Not 19...♔xg6? 20 ♕e6+ or 19...

♔e8? 20 ♕e6+. Critical is 19...hg!?
20 ♕xh8 ♖c8 21 ♖d2!? (21 ♖xd7+
♕xd7 22 fe) 21...b3! (threat ...
♗b4!) 22 ♔h3 ba! 23 ♖xd7+! ♗e7!
24 ♖xc7 a1♕+ 25 ♔d2 ♖d8+ (25...
♕a5+ 26 ♖c3! ♖d8+ 27 ♔e1!) 26
♖d7 ♕a5+ (26...♕xh1 27 ♖xd8
♗xd8 28 ♕d7+) 27 b4!! (27 c3
♗c8!) 27...♕xb4+ 28 c3 ♕b2+ 29
♔e1 and wins (main line Gufeld
and Ciocaltea), e.g. 29...♗c8 30
♖xe7+ ♔xe7 31 ♕h4+ etc. - a
truely startling variation.

20 fe h6

Another analytic confection
follows 20...♕xe5 21 ♗f4 ♕e6 (21
...♕f6 22 ♖d6) 22 ♗d6+ ♕xd6 23
♖xd6 ♔xd6 24 ♖d1+ ♔c7 25 ♘f4
♘c5 26 ♖xd8 ♔xd8 27 ♕xh7! -
tasty.

21 ♖d6! ♕c4 (21...♘c5 22 ♗xc5)
22 ♖hd1 ♗c8 23 b3! 1-0

Game 93: Sicilian 3 ♗b5+

Larsen has described 3 d4 in the
Sicilian as a kind of giant tactical
trick (it gives Black a central pawn
majority). Ulf Andersson is just the
player to agree with him!

**Andersson-Portisch
Skopje Olympiad 1972**

**1 e4 c5 2 ♘f3 d6 3 ♗b5+!? ♘c6 4
0-0!?**

The alternative is 4 d4 cd 5 ♕xd4
(cf. games 97-8).

**4...♗d7 5 ♖e1 ♘f6 6 c3 a6 7 ♗f1!
e5!? 8 h3! h6?!** (unnecessary) **9 d4**

♕c7 **10 a4! g6?!**

Preferable is 10...♗e7; the fian-
chet⁺o weakens his control over d6.
11 ♘a3 ♗g7 12 dc dc 13 ♘c4 ♖b8?!

Andersson gives 13....0-0 14 ♕d6
♕xd6 15 ♘xd6 with advantage to
White, but the text looks crazy to
me.

14 b4! cb 15 cb ♗e6

By now 15...0-0 16 b5 loses a
pawn.

16 ♘d6+ ♔e7 17 ♗a3!

The immediate 17 b5 allows
Black to block the diagonal with 17
...♘b4! 18 ♗a3 a5. Now after 17...
♕xd6 18 b5 ♘b4 19 ♕xd6+ ♔xd6
20 ♗xb4+ ♔c7 21 ♖ac1+ White's a
lot better.

17...♘e8 *(93)*

**18 ♘xb7! ♕xb7 19 b5+ ♔f6 20 bc
♕c7 21 ♘xe5! 1-0**

Game 94: Sicilian 3 ♗b5+

**Torre-O'Kelly
Malaga 1973**

1 e4 c5 2 ♘f3 d6 3 ♗b5+ ♘d7!? 4

d4 ♘gf6 5 ♘c3!

Another line runs 5 e5 ♕a5+ 6 ♘c3 ♘e4 7 ♗d2 ♘xc3 8 ♗xd7+ ♗xd7 9 ♗xc3 ♕a6 10 d5 with a rather obscure position.

5...cd 6 ♕xd4 e5?! 7 ♕d3 h6 (else ♗g5) 8 ♗d2! ♗e7 9 ♘c4 0-0 10 ♗xd7!

Not 10 ♘xd6? ♘c5, but if now 10 ...♗xd7 11 ♘xd6 is on.

10...♕xd7 11 ♘e3 ♕c6 12 g4!

Presaging an attack; 12...♘xg4 13 ♘xg4 ♗xg4 14 ♖g1 h5 (14...♗e6 15 ♗xh6) would allow 15 h3! ♗e6 16 ♗h6 ♗f6 17 ♗xg7! ♗xg7 18 ♕g3.

12...♗e6 13 ♖g1 ♘d7 14 ♘f5 ♗xf5 15 gf ♔h7 16 ♕h3! ♖g8

Or 16...♘f6?! 17 ♖xg7+ ♔xg7 18 ♗xh6+ ♔g8 19 0-0-0.

17 ♘d5 ♗f6 18 c3 ♖af8 19 ♕h5 ♖h8 20 ♗e3 ♕a4 21 ♔d2! ♖hg8 *(94)*

No better was 21...♕xe4 22 ♘xf6+ ♘xf6 23 ♖xg7+ ♔xg7 24 ♖g1+ etc. Black must cave in now.

22 ♖g6! 1-0

The only defence to 23 ♖xh6+ is 22...fg whereupon 23 fg+ ♔h8 24 ♗xh6 clinches.

Game 95: Sicilian 3 ♗b5+

Browne-Quinteros
Wijk aan Zee 1974

1 e4 c5 2 ♘f3 d6 3 ♗b5+ ♗d7 4 ♗xd7+ ♕xd7 5 c4!?

Logical after swapping the white bishops, since, as this game shows, Black's pawngrabbing reply isn't on. Also good is 5 0-0.

5...♕g4? 6 0-0 ♕xe4 7 d4 cd 8 ♖e1 ♕c6 9 ♘xd4 ♕xc4?

He should try 9...♕d7; now Black's d-pawn is a target.

10 ♘a3 ♕c8 11 ♗f4 ♕d7 12 ♘ab5 e5 *(95)*

13 ♗xe5! de 14 ♖xe5+ ♗e7

One can well believe Minev's cursory 14...♘e7 15 ♘f5! or 14...♔d8 15 ♕f3! winning.

15 ♖d5! ♕c8

The only square; 15...♕xd5 16 ♘c7+. White's next threatens ♘d6+.

16 ♘f5 ♔f8 17 ♘xe7 ♔xe7

17...♘xe7 is met by 18 ♖d8+.

18 ♖e5+ 1-0

Game 96: Sicilian 4 ♕xd4

Vasyukov-K.Grigorian
Vilnius 1975

1 e4 c5 2 ♘f3 d6 3 d4 cd 4 ♕xd4!?
Unusual but not without bite.
The psychologically accurate reply
is 4...♗d7!? preparing ...♘c6. Black
tries another way which, surprisingly
creates a weakness.
4...a6?! 5 ♗e3! ♘f6 6 ♘c3 ♗g4
Preferable was 6...♘c6 although
White is a little better after 7 ♕b6!
♕xb6 8 ♗xb6 e6 9 0-0-0 ♗e7 10
♗e2 0-0 (Gufeld).
**7 e5! ♘c6 8 ♕a4 b5!? 9 ♗xb5! ab
10 ♕xb5 ♕c8**
Black's 8th was a deliberate pawn
sacrifice to gain pressure down the
open Q-side files, but it seems to be
insufficient.
**11 ef ♖b8 12 ♕a4 ♖b4 13 ♕a3
e6!? 14 0-0-0! gf 15 ♖he1 ♗e7 16
h3 ♗h5 (96)**

17 ♘d4! d5 (17...♗xd1 18 ♘xc6
wins) **18 ♘f5! ef**
There's no escape in 18...♗xd1 19
♘xe7, or 18...♗f8 19 ♘xd5! ed 20

♗b6+. The rest is convulsive.
**19 ♗c5 ♖e4 20 f3! d4 21 ♘xe4 fe
22 ♗xe7 ♗g6 23 ♗xf6 e3 24 ♖xd4!**
1-0

Game 97: Sicilian, 4 ♕xd4

In which the theme of this
variation (black square attack)
appears in very stark form.

Ciric-Popović
Trstenik 1979

1 e4 c5 2 ♘f3 d6 3 d4 cd 4 ♕xd4
♘c6 5 ♗b5 ♗d7 6 ♗xc6 ♗xc6 7
♘c3 ♘f6 (7...h6!?) 8 ♗g5 e6 9 0-0-0
♗e7 10 ♖he1 0-0 11 ♔b1
Useless is 11 ♗xf6 ♗xf6! 12
♕xd6 ♗xc3 - or 12...♕a5!? 13 e5?!
♖fd8 - and White's extra pawn is
worthless. Now Krnić recommends
11...♕a5.
**11...♕c7 12 ♕d2! ♖fd8 13 ♘d4
h6? (97)**
Leading with his jaw! Much more
sensible is 13...a6 planning ...b5
with Q-side counterplay.

14 ♗xh6! gh 15 ♕xh6 ♘e8

Or 15...♘h7 16 ♖d3 ♗f8 17 ♖g3+ ♔h8 18 ♕h5 when Ciric̆ gives 18... ♗e8 19 ♕g4 or 18...♕e7 19 ♖h3 f6 20 ♘xe6 and considers White's pressure sufficient to win.

16 ♖d3! ♗f8 17 ♖g3+ ♗g7 18 ♖1e3 d5

A better try than 18...♔f8 19 ♖xg7 ♘xg7 20 ♖g3 f5? 21 ♘xe6+; White's reply to the text proves the accuracy of 16 ♖d3! rather than 16 ♖e3?

19 e5 ♖d7 20 f4!

Not 20 ♖xg7+? ♘xg7 21 ♖g3 ♕xe5! 22 ♘f3 ♕xg3 with good saving chances. Now it's easy enough.

20...♕b6 21 ♖xg7+! ♘xg7 22 ♖g3 f5 23 ef 1-0

Game 98: Sicilian, 4 ♕xd4

Tal-Byrne
Biel Interzonal 1976

1 e4 c5 2 ♘f3 d6 3 d4 cd 4 ♕xd4 ♘c6 5 ♗b5 ♗d7 6 ♗xc6 ♗xc6 7 ♘c3 ♘f6 8 ♗g5 e6 9 0-0-0 ♗e7 10 ♖he1 0-0 11 ♕d2

Deviating from game 97. Now Krnic̆ recommends 11...♕c7(!).

11...♕a5 12 ♘d4 ♖ac8 (12...♖fd8!?) 13 ♔b1 ♔h8

To avert 14 ♘d5 ♕xd2 15 ♘xe7+.

14 f4 h6?! 15 h4!? hg?!

I guess I just don't appreciate the joy of suicide. Here or last move ... ♖fd8 was plausible. Byrne doesn't

intend to hold the piece, and in fact his play would be fine if Tal didn't force him to!

16 hg ♘xe4!? *(98)*

17 ♕d3!!

How simple. White doesn't allow a Q-swap, but focuses against h7, e.g. 17...♘f2? 18 ♖h1+, or 17... ♘xc3+ 18 bc g6 19 ♖h1+ and 20 ♕h3 mating, or 17...f5 18 ♕h3+ ♔g8 19 ♘xe4 ♗xe4 20 g6.

17...♗xg5!? 18 ♘xe4 ♗xe4

Or 18...♗xf4 19 ♖h1+ ♗h6 (19... ♔g8? 20 ♘f6+) 20 ♘f6! g6 21 ♖xh6+ ♔g7 22 ♖h7+! ♔xf6 23 ♖f1+ ♔e7 24 ♕xg6 walking in.

19 ♖xe4 ♗h6 20 g4 f5 21 ♖xe6 ♗xf4 22 ♘xf5 1-0

Game 99: Sicilian, Najdorf

Westerinen-Ghizdavu
Bucharest 1974

1 e4 c5 2 ♘f3 d6 3 d4 cd 4 ♘xd4 ♘f6 5 ♘c3 a6 6 a4!? b6?

With ...b5 ruled out, Black

would do better to adopt Kurajica's suggestion 6...g6! introducing a Dragon system where White is more reluctant to castle long in pursuit of the St. George attack (♗e3, ♕d2, h4 etc.).

7 ♗g5 e6 8 f4 ♕c7 9 ♗xf6 gf 10 ♗e2 ♘c6 11 f5!

Pressurising e6, hindering ...♗b7, threatening ♗h5, and worrying Black's king.

11...♘xd4 12 ♕xd4 ♗e7?

Naturally 12...e5 would be positionally disastrous, but this is soon refuted. Black is hoping for 13 (or 14) 0-0? ♕c5! when the exchange of queens would cancel all White's advantage. Better was 12...♕c5 13 ♕xf6 ♕e5, with slight compensation for the pawn.

13 fe! fe 14 ♖f1! ♗g7 (99)

99
W

15 e5!

This wins, e.g. 15...fe 16 ♕h4+ ♔e8 17 ♗h5+ ♔d7 18 ♖f7+ or 15...♖f8 16 ♕h4! threatening ♕xh7 - but not here 16 ♕e4? f5! 17 ♕xa8 ♗b7.

15...de 16 ♕g4 ♖g8 17 ♖xf6! ♔xf6 18 ♕h4+ ♔f7 19 ♗h5+ ♔f8 20 ♕f2+ 1-0

Game 100: Sicilian, Najdorf 6 ♗e3

The 4th game of the interzonal play-off which earned Adorjan his place in the 1980 Candidate's cycle.

Adorjan-Ribli
Budapest 1979

1 e4 c5 2 ♘f3 d6 3 d4 cd 4 ♘xd4 ♘f6 5 ♘c3 a6 6 ♗e3 e5!?

Staking a claim in the centre and hoping to cover the weakened d5 square with pieces, à la Boleslavsky. 7 ♘b3 ♗e6 8 ♕d2 ♘bd7 9 f3 ♖c8 (9...b5!?) 10 g4!? ♗e7 11 0-0-0 ♘b6 (11...b5!?) 12 h4! (New - Adorjan) 12...0-0 13 h5 ♘c4 14 ♗xc4 ♖xc4 15 g5 ♘d7 16 ♖dg1 ♕c7 17 g6! ♖c8 (100)

No good is 17...fg 18 hg h6 19 ♗xh6, and 17...♘f6 or 17...♗f6 meet the same reply as the game.

100
W

18 ♗h6! ♗f6 19 gh+ ♔xh7 20 ♗xg7! ♗xg7 21 h6!!

Avoiding the blunder 21 ♖xg7+ ♔xg7 22 ♕g5+ ♔f8 23 h6 ♕d8! when Black would win.

21...♗f6 22 ♕g2! 1-0

The point is 23 ♕g7+! ♗xg7 24 hg+ ♔g8 25 ♖h8 mate.

Game 101: Sicilian, Najdorf
6 ♗e3

Polyanchev-Foigel
USSR 1979

1 e4 c5 2 ♘f3 d6 3 d4 cd 4 ♘xd4 ♘f6 5 ♘c3 a6 6 ♗e3 e6 7 f4 b5 8 ♕f3 ♗b7 9 ♗d3 ♘bd7 10 g4 h6! (fight for e5) 11 0-0-0 ♖c8 12 g5 (12 ♘ce2) 12...hg 13 hg ♘e5 14 ♕g2 ♘fg4!?

Seeking a tactical confrontation.
15 ♗f4 b4 16 ♘b1?

Vasyukov gives 16 ♘ce2 ♗e7 17 h3 ♘xd3+ 18 ♖xd3 ♘e5 when Black stands a little better in view of the central position.
16...♗e7! 17 h4

Or 17 h3 ♗xg5 18 ♗xg5 ♕xg5+ when either 19 ♖d2 ♕h6 or 19 ♘d2? ♘xd3+ win.
17...♕a5 18 ♗e2 ♕xa2! 19 b3 *(101)*

On 19 ♗xg4 ♘c4! 20 c3 bc 21 ♘xc3 ♕a1+ Black wins.

101
B

19...♘f2!! 20 ♕xf2 ♗xe4 21 ♗c4 ♖xc4! 22 bc?!

Preferable was 22 ♗xe5! de 23 bc ed 24 ♖h2 (24 ♖he1 ♖xh4! threatening ...♗xg5+) 24...0-0 25 ♕xd4, but the Black bishops are very strong (25...♗f5 threatening ...b3!).
22...♘xc4 0-1

Very effective; 23 ♖dg1 ♗xh1 24 ♖xh1 ♕b2+ 25 ♔d1 ♕xb1+ 26 ♗c1 ♗xg5! and massacre.

Game 102: Sicilian, Najdorf
6 ♗e2

An alert game by White; it's not usually a good idea to play b4 in the Sicilian (backward c-pawn), but here it's a case of "look! b4 you leap!"

Kavalek-Quinteros
Nice Olympiad 1974

1 e4 c5 2 ♘f3 d6 3 d4 cd 4 ♘xd4 ♘f6 5 ♘c3 a6 6 ♗e2 ♘bd7 (6...e5!? - game 103) 7 ♗e3 ♘c5 8 f3 e6 9 a4 b6

White threatened a bind with a5. Interesting is 9...e5!? 10 ♘b3 ♘xb3 11 ab ♗e6 12 ♗c4 ♕c7 13 ♕d3 ♖c8 when Black doesn't look too bad; 10 ♘f5 ♗xf5 11 ef d5 (11... g6!?) looks quite good.
10 0-0 ♗b7 11 ♕d2 ♖c8 12 ♖fd1 ♗e7 13 b4! ♘cd7 15 b5! a5?! *(102)*

Better was 14...ab, if only to gain time while White chooses between all four good-looking recaptures.

102
W

15 ♘c6! ♗xc6?!

Preferable was 15...♕c7 when, for example, 16 ♗f4 e5 17 ♗g5 ♗xc6 18 bc ♕xc6 19 ♘b5! 0-0 (19 ...♕xc2? 20 ♖ac1!) 20 ♘xd6 ♗xd6 21 ♕xd6 ♕xd6 22 ♖xd6 ♖xc2 23 ♗b5 still favours White.

16 bc ♖xc6 17 ♗b5 ♖c8 18 e5! de 19 ♘e4 ♘d5 (19...♖c7 20 ♗xb6) 20 c4 ♗b4 1-0

There's not much after 21 ♕f2 ♘xe3 22 ♖xd7.

Game 103: Sicilian, Najdorf 6 ♗e2

Rashkovsky-Gutman
USSR 1974

1 ♘c3 c5 2 ♘f3 d6 3 e4 a6 4 d4 cd 5 ♘xd4 ♘f6 6 ♗e2 e5 7 ♘b3 ♗e6 8 f4!

To dislodge Black's bishop by f5 or, if Black captures on f4, reassert his space advantage in the centre.

8...♕c7 9 g4!? ef 10 ♗xf4 ♘c6 (10 ...h6!? Geller) 11 g5 ♘d7 12 ♕d2 ♘ce5 13 0-0-0 ♗e7 14 ♘d4! g6

Otherwise ♘f5 comes. Now White avoids 15 ♘xe6 as he wishes to occupy the d5 square.

15 h4 0-0-0 (15...0-0 16 h5) 16 ♘d5 ♗xd5 17 ed ♔b8 18 ♖h3! ♖c8 19 ♖c3 ♕d8 *(103)*

Or 19...♕b6 (19...♕a5?? 20 ♖xc8+) 20 ♖b3 ♕a7 21 ♘c6+ ♘xc6 22 dc ♖xc6 23 ♗f3 ♖b6 24 ♖e3 and Black's horribly placed; 24... ♘e5? 25 ♖xe5!

103
W

20 ♘c6+! bc 21 dc ♘b6

On 21...♘xc6 22 ♗xd6+ White regains the piece a pawn up, if he doesn't have better; 21...♖xc6 22 ♖xc6 ♘xc6 23 ♗xd6+ Kc8?? 24 ♗xa6 mate.

22 ♗xe5! de 23 ♕e3! 1-0

Black sees 23...♕c7 (23...♘d5 24 ♖xd5 ♕xd5 25 ♕b6+) 24 ♖b3 ♗d8 (24...♕a7 25 ♖d7) 25 ♖xd8 ♕xd8 26 ♖xb6+ ♔c7 27 ♖b7+ ♔xc6 28 ♗f3+ ♔d6 29 ♕a3+ ♔e6 (29...♖c5 30 ♕xa6+) 30 ♕b3+ and mate very soon.

Game 104: Sicilian, Najdorf
6 ♗c4

Fischer-Rubinetti
Palma de Mallorca Interzonal 1970

1 e4 c5 2 ♘f3 d6 3 d4 cd 4 ♘xd4
♘f6 5 ♘c3 e6 6 ♗c4 a6 7 ♗b3 b5 8
0-0 ♗b7 (8...b4 9 ♘a4 - cf. game
106) 9 ♖e1 ♘bd7

Otherwise 9...♗e7 10 ♗xe6! fe 11
♘xe6 and 12 ♘xg7+ gives White 3
pawns and a very strong attack for
the piece, so Black plays to eliminate
the white bishop first.
10 ♗g5! h6 11 ♗h4

Ivkov suggests 11 ♗xf6 and 12 a4
b4 13 ♘a2 with a positional
advantage to White, whereas
Fischer's move retains more violent
possibilities but, according to Ivkov,
Black can try for a blockade with
11...g5 12 ♗g3 ♘e5. His next
elicits a sacrifice.
11...♘c5?! (104)

104
W

12 ♗d5! ed 13 ed+ ♔d7 14 b4 ♘a4
15 ♘xa4 ba 16 c4 ♔c8 17 ♕xa4
♕d7 18 ♕b3 g5 19 ♗g3 ♘h5

Or 19...♗g7 20 c5 dc 21 bc ♕xd5

22 c6 with an ending in which
White is more mobile.
20 c5! dc 21 bc ♕xd5?!

A little better was 21...♗xd5
when 22 c6 regains the piece but
requires accuracy to prove the win.
**22 ♖e8+! ♔d7 23 ♕a4+ ♗c6 24
♘xc6! 1-0**

Because of 24...♕xc6 25 ♕xc6+
and 26 ♖xa8, or 24...♖xe8 25
♘b4+, or 24...♔xe8 25 ♖e1+ ♗e7
26 ♘xe7+ ♕d7 27 ♘d5+ ♔d8 28
♕a5+ (or ♗c7+) wins.

Game 105: Sicilian, Najdorf
6 ♗c4

Saverymuttu-Juhnke
British-German Universities,
Hamburg 1971

1 e4 c5 2 ♘f3 d6 3 d4 cd 4 ♘xd4
♘f6 5 ♘c3 a6 6 ♗c4 e6 7 ♗b3 b5 8
f4!? ♗b7 9 0-0 ♘bd7 10 ♖e1 ♘c5

Here 10...♗e7 (recommended by
Maric̀) invites 11 ♗xe6 fe 12 ♘xe6
with an unclear but dangerous
attack.
11 ♗d5!? ♕c7

This time, with the Q-bishop at
home, White's attack after 11...ed
12 ed+ ♔d7 13 b4 ♘a4 14 ♗xa4 ba
15 c4 is more obscure, and should
be put to the test, but Black has
prepared a faulty tactic.
**12 b4! ed?! 13 ed+ ♘e6!? 14
♗b2! ♘xd5 15 ♘xe6 fe 16 ♘xd5
♕c6** (105)

Instead 16...♗xd5 17 ♕xd5 is

quite horrible.

17 ♖xe6+! ♔f7 (17...♔d7 18 ♕g4!)
18 ♖f6+! ♔g8

Equally hopeless is 18...gf 19 ♕h5+ ♔e6 (19...♔g8 20 ♘xf6+; 19 ...♔g7 20 ♕g5+) 20 ♖e1+ ♔d7 21 ♕f7+ ♔c8 22 ♖e8+ ♕xe8 23 ♕c7 mate.

19 ♖xf8+! ♕xf8 20 ♗xg7+! ♔e8

Or 20...♔xg7 21 ♕g4+ ♔f7 22 ♕f5+ ♔e8 23 ♖e1+ ♔d8 24 ♕f6+ wins.

21 ♕h5+ ♔d8 22 ♗f6+ 1-0

Game 106: Sicilian, Najdorf
6 ♗c4

Ermenkov-Ostojić
Kecskemet 1977

1 e4 c5 2 ♘f3 d6 3 d4 cd 4 ♘xd4 ♘f6 5 ♘c3 a6 6 ♗c4 e6 7 ♗b3 b5 8 0-0 ♗e7

A sensible avoidance of sacrifices on e6; White's reply hopes to induce 9...♗b7?! 10 ♗xe6, mean-

while developing the queen for K-side action.

9 ♕f3!? ♕b6 10 ♗e3 ♕b7 11 ♕g3!? g6 12 ♗h6! b4

Black has to go for a pawn to compensate for the hampered development. 12...♘xe4 13 ♘xe4 ♕xe4 14 ♖ad1 was the other way, although then too the pressure in the centre seems to give White the advantage.

13 ♘a4 ♘xe4 14 ♕e3 d5

Ermenkov gives 14...♘f6 15 ♗g7 ♖g8 16 ♗xf6 ♗xf6 17 ♘xe6!

15 c4! bc 16 ♘xc3 ♘c5

Swapping would give White a new pawn to play c4 again.

17 ♖fe1 ♘xb3 18 ab! ♘d7 *(106)*

This leads to a pretty finish but 18...♘c6 19 ♘xd5! ed 20 ♘xc6 or 18...♗d7 19 ♖ac1 ♘c6 20 ♘xd5 was equally intolerable. One is left wondering where Black went wrong?

19 ♘xe6! fe 20 ♕xe6 ♘b6 21 ♕f6! ♖g8 22 ♗g5 ♖a7 23 ♘b5! 1-0

Elegant and decisive. 23...ab 24 ♖xa7 or 23...♖f8 24 ♘d6+ ♔d8 25 ♕xf8+.

Game 107: Sicilian, Najdorf
6 &c4

Satyanarana-Neelakantan
Indian Ch, Vijayawada 1979

1 e4 c5 2 ♘f3 d6 3 d4 cd 4 ♘xd4
♘f6 5 ♘c3 e6 6 &c4 &e7 7 &e3 a6
8 &b3 b5

Here 8...♘c6(!) transposes to
Sozin lines.

9 ♕f3! ♕c7 10 0-0-0 0-0(?!) 11 g4!
&b7 12 g5 ♘fd7 13 g6!

Very strong! Now on 13...hg 14
♘xe6! fe 15 &xe6+ and 16 ♕h3+
wins.

13...♘c5 14 gh+ ♔h8

Or 14...♔xh7 15 ♕h5+ ♔g8 16
♖hg1 &f6 17 ♖g3 with an enormous
attack.

15 ♖hg1 ♘bd7 *(107)*

Essential was 15...&f6.

107
W

16 ♖xg7! ♔xg7

On 16...&f6 17 ♖g2 b4 18 ♖dg1!
bc 19 ♖g8+! mates.

17 ♖g1+ ♔h8 18 ♕g4 &f6 19 ♘h6!
♘xe4 (19...♔xh7 20 &xf8) 20
&g7+ 1-0.

Game 108: Sicilian, Najdorf
Poisoned Pawn

Vitolins-Arakas
'Vapra'-'Iiud', Valka 1978

1 e4 c5 2 ♘f3 d6 3 d4 cd 4 ♘xd4
♘f6 5 ♘c3 a6 6 &g5 ♘bd7 7 f4

Instead 7 &c4 (-b3) rules out
Black's plan; a horrific example is
Tatai-Hamann, Amsterdam II 1970:
7 &c4 ♕a5!? 8 ♕d2 e6 9 0-0-0 b5
10 &d5?! ed? (10...b4! Marović) 11
ed ♘c5 12 ♖he1+ ♔d7 13 ♘c6 ♕b6
14 b4! ♘a4 15 ♕d3! ♘xc3 16 ♕xc3
♘g4 17 &d8?? ♕xf2 18 ♖f1?? ♕e3+
0-1; but White missed 17 Qxg7!!
and 18 ♕xg7!! winning instantly.
7...♕b6 8 ♕d2 ♕xb2 9 ♖b1 ♕a3
10 &xf6 gf (10...♘xf6 11 ♘d5) 11
♘d5 ♖b8 12 ♖b3 ♕a4? *(108)*

Instead 12...♕xa2 adds a possible
back rank check to the melée.
White now 'develops' in style.

108
W

13 &xa6! ab?!

Not 13...♕xa6? 14 ♘c7+. Also
13...e6 14 ♘xf6+!? favours White.
14 ♕c3! ♕xb3

The only try, though of course it's easy now, e.g. 14...♗b7 15 ♖xb7! ♖d8 16 ♘c7 mate!

15 cb ♗b7 16 ♘c7+ ♔d8 17 ♕a5 ♔c8 18 0-0? (18 ♘e8!) 18...♘xe4 19 ♖c1 ♘c5 20 b4 e5 21 ♘xa6 ♖b7 22 bc 1-0

Game 109: Sicilian, Najdorf

Hecht is one of the very few GMs ever to give up full-time chess.

Hecht-Schaufelberger
Bath (Clare Benedict) 1973

1 e4 c5 2 ♘f3 d6 3 d4 cd 4 ♘xd4 ♘f6 5 ♘c3 a6 6 ♗g5 e6 7 ♕f3!? ♗d7 (7...h6 – Bukić) 8 0-0-0 ♘c6 9 ♗e2 ♕a5 10 ♕g3! b5?

This allows a combination.

11 ♘xc6 ♗xc6 *(109)*

12 ♖xd6! ♖c8

On 12...♗xd6 13 ♕xd6 ♖c8 14 e5 (Bukić) 14...♘g8!? makes the win hard to prove, but 14 ♗h5!! seems to win, i.e. 14...♕c7 15

♕xe6+ ♔f8 16 ♗xf7! and now a) 16...♕d7 17 ♗xf6 ♕xe6 18 ♗xe6 ♖e8 19 ♗xg7+ with 4 pawns for the exchange; b) 14...♘xe4 15 ♘xe4 ♗xe4 16 ♗e7+! ♕xe7 17 ♕xc8+ ♔xf7 18 ♕xh8 ♕xf2 19 ♔b1 ♕xc2+ 20 ♔a1 ♕xg2 21 ♖c1/d1 with the exchange and an attack; c) 16...♗d7 17 ♕b3 involves material plus and a continuing attack, and 14...♗d7 loses after 15 e5! ♘g8 16 ♗xf7+. White could also transpose to game possibilities with 14 ♗xf6.

13 ♗xf6 gf 14 ♗h5 ♗h6+

Or 14...♗xd6 15 ♕xd6 ♗d7 16 ♗xf7+.

15 ♔b1 b4 16 ♖xe6+ ♔f8 17 ♕d6+ ♔g7 18 ♘d5 ♗xd5 19 ed ♖hd8 20 ♕e7 ♔h8 21 ♕xf7 ♖f8 22 ♕b7 ♖c7 23 ♖xa6! 1-0

Game 110: Sicilian Polugayevsky Najdorf

E.Pedersen-Gallmeyer
Denmark 1971

1 e4 c5 2 ♘f3 d6 3 d4 cd 4 ♘xd4 ♘f6 5 ♘c3 a6 6 ♗g5 e6 7 f4 b5!? 8 e5 de 9 fe ♕c7! 10 ef ♕e5+ 11 ♗e2 ♕xg5 12 0-0 ♕e5? (12...♖a7) 13 ♗f3 ♖a7 14 ♘c6! ♕c5+

On 14...♘xc6 Marić gives 15 ♗xc6+ ♗d7 16 ♗xd7+ ♖xd7 17 ♕f3 ♗c5+ 18 ♔h1 0-0 19 ♘e4 with a K-side attack.

15 ♔h1 ♖d7 *(110a)*

Now 15...♘xc6 is met by 16 ♘e4 ♕e5 (16...♕d4 17 ♘d6+! ♕xd6 18 fg! wins) 17 fg ♗xg7 (17...♕xg7 18

♘f6+ and 19 ♗xc6) 18 ♘d6+ ♔e7 19 ♗xc6 and if 19...♛xd6? 20 ♖xf7+.

110a
W

16 ♘xb8! ♖xd1 17 ♖axd1 gf 18 ♘e4 ♛c7

Not 18...♛e5? 19 ♘c6 ♛c7 20 ♘xf6 mate.

19 ♘xf6+ ♔e7 20 ♗h5! ♗g7 *(110b)*

Or 20...♛xb8 21 ♘g8+! ♖xg8 (21 ...♔e8 22 ♗xf7 mate) 22 ♖xf7+ ♔e8 23 ♖g7 mate.

110b
W

21 ♘c6+! ♛xc6

On 21...♔f8 22 ♘d7+! mates, i.e. 22...♗xd7 (22...♔g8 23 ♘e7 mate!, or 22...♛xd7 23 ♖xd7 ♗xd7 then

as...) 23 ♖xf7+ ♔e8 24 ♖f6 mate, or 23...♔g8 24 ♘e7 mate.

22 ♘g8+! ♔e8

Or 22...♔f8 23 ♖xf7+ ♔xg8 24 ♖d8+, or 22...♖xg8 23 ♖xf7+ ♔e8 24 ♖fd7+ ♔f8 25 ♖f1+ mating.

23 ♗xf7+ ♔f8 24 ♖d8+ 1-0

Game 111: Sicilian, Polugayevsky Najdorf

The winner of this game became German correspondence champion as a result of the event.

Maeder-Czaya
West German Corres Ch 1978

1 e4 c5 2 ♘f3 d6 3 d4 cd 4 ♘xd4 ♘f6 5 ♘c3 a6 6 ♗g5 e6 7 f4 b5!? 8 e5 de 9 fe ♛c7! 10 ef ♛e5+ 11 ♗e2 ♛xg5 12 ♛d3!?

Not 12 fg?! ♗xg7 followed by ... 0-0 and Black's K-bishop is an immense piece - the point of Black's play in this variation.

12...♛xf6 13 ♖f1 ♛e5 14 ♖d1!

Or 14 0-0-0 ♖a7 15 ♘f3 ♛f4+! with a vital tempo. White now threatens 15 ♘xe6 so Black prepares ...♖d7 as a reply.

14...♖a7 15 ♘f3 ♛c7 16 ♘g5! f5

Maeder gives 16...♛b6 17 ♗h5 g6 18 ♘ce4, or 16...♗e7 17 ♖xf7 ♛xh2 with either 18 ♖xe7+ ♔xe7 19 ♛e3! or 18 ♗h5 ♛xh5 19 ♖xe7+ winning.

17 ♛d4! ♖g8 *(111)*

18 ⌘xf5!! ♗e7

Or 18...ef 19 ♗h5+ g6 20 ♘d5 and 21 ♘f6+.

19 ⌘f7 ♛c5 20 ⌘xe7+ ♛xe7 21 ♘ce4 1-0

On 21...⌘d7 22 ♗h5+ g6 (22...♚f8? 23 ♘xh7 mate) 23 ♘f6+ ♚f8 (23...♚d8? 24 ♛b6 mate!) 24 ♘6xh7+ ♚e8 25 ♗xg6+! ⌘xg6 26 ♛h8+ it's all over.

Game 112: Sicilian, Najdorf

Spassky-Rashkovsky
USSR Ch, Moscow 1973

1 e4 c5 2 ♘f3 d6 3 d4 cd 4 ♘xd4 ♘f6 5 ♘c3 a6 6 ♗g5 e6 7 f4 ♛c7 8 ♗d3!? ♘bd7 9 ♛e2 b5 10 0-0-0 ♗b7 11 ⌘he1

Very straightforward. White intends e5, so perhaps Black should respond with 11...0-0-0 or 11...e5 himself.

11...♗e7?! 12 e5 de 13 fe ♘d5 14 ♗xe7 ♘xc3 *(112)*

On 14...♘xe7 15 ♛g4 is hard to meet, e.g. 15...0-0 (15...♚f8 16

♛xe6!?; 16 ⌘f1) 16 ♘xe6 fe 17 ♛xe6+ ⌘f7 18 ♗xh7+ ♚xh7 19 ♛xf7.

15 ♛g4! ♘xd1 16 ♘xe6! ♛c6

In response to 16...fe Geller gives the flashy 17 ♗d6 ♛b6 18 ♛g5! ♛d8 19 ♛g6+!! - maybe 19 ♗g6+ would only be worth one exclamation mark?

17 ♘xg7+! ♚xe7 18 ♛g5+ f6

Or 18...♚f8 19 ♘f5 ♛xg2 20 ♛e7+ ♚g8 21 e6! with indefensible threats.

19 ef+ ♚d8 20 f7+ ♚c7 21 ♛f4+ 1-0

After 21...♚b6 (21...♚c8? 22 ⌘e8+; 21...♛d6 22 ♘e6+ ♚c6 23 ♗e4+) 22 ⌘e6 White will come out with queen and three pawns versus two rooks and a continuing attack.

Game 113: Sicilian, Najdorf

Kamashvaran-Aaron
India 1972

1 e4 c5 2 ♘f3 d6 3 d4 cd 4 ♘xd4 ♘f6 5 ♘c3 a6 6 ♗g5 e6 7 f4 ♘bd7 8

♗c4!? ♕c7

Sokolov gives 8...♕a5, 8...♕b6!?, and 8...b5?! 9 ♗xe6! This latter is unclear, although 8...♗e7 9 ♗xe6! is clear.

9 ♕e2 ♘b6 10 ♗b3 ♗e7 11 0-0-0 h6?! 12 ♗xf6 ♗xf6 *(113)*

113
W

13 ♘db5!?

This attack is very hard to assess. **13...ab 14 ♘xb5 ♕c5 15 ♘xd6+ ♔f8 16 f5! ♕e5 17 c3 ♗e7?!**

To evict the knight, which fails. Critical are 17...♗d7!? or 17...g6/g5!?, respectively developing or giving the king some room; 17...♘d5?! mixes it unwisely.

18 ♘xf7! ♔xf7 19 ♕h5+ ♔f8?!

On 19...♔g8!? Sokolov gives 20 ♖hf1! although I can only see a draw by ♕e8-g6 after 20...♗f6! Instead 20 ♕e8+ ♗f8 21 ♖d8 looks more like a winning attempt, e.g. 21...♕f6 22 fe ♕e7? 23 ♕xf8+! or 22...♔h7 23 e5! threatening ♗c2+; 23...♕f4+ 24 ♔b1 ♗xe6 25 ♕xe6! wins.

20 ♖hf1 ♗g5+ (20...♗f6 21 ♖d8+!) **21 ♔b1 ♗e7 22 fe ♗xe6 23 ♖f7+! ♔e8 24 ♖f5+ 1-0**

Game 114: Sicilian, Najdorf

Calvo-Kavalek
Las Palmas 1973

1 e4 c5 2 ♘f3 d6 3 d4 cd 4 ♘xd4 ♘f6 5 ♘c3 a6 6 ♗g5 e6 7 f4 ♕c7 (?! - Velimirović) 8 ♕e2!? ♘bd7 9 0-0-0 ♗e7 10 g4 h6?

Commencing a bad plan. 10...e5? 11 ♘f3 also favours White, but 10...b5!? is more obscure.

11 ♗h4 g5?! 12 fg ♘h7 *(114)*

114
W

13 ♘f5! ef 14 ♘d5 ♕d8

After 14...♕a5 15 ef ♘e5 16 ♘xe7 ♔xe7 17 ♗e1! and White won 10 moves later in O.Rodriguez-Quinteros, Sao Paulo 1972.

15 ef ♘e5 16 ♗g3 ♗xg5+ 17 ♔b1 0-0

So Black castles into a pawn storm, but h4 was a big threat anyway, e.g. 17...♔f8 18 h4 ♗e7 19 ♘xe7 ♕xe7 20 ♖xd6! ♕xd6 21 ♗xe5 and if 21...♕e7 22 ♗g7+ gives material plus.

18 h4 ♗f6 19 g5! hg 20 hg ♗xg5

Or 20...♘xg5 21 ♘xf6+ ♕xf6 22 ♖xd6! and Black collapses.

21 ♗xe5 de 22 ♕g4

The threat is ♕h3. If 22...♕d7 23 ♘f6+ wins, or 22...f6 23 ♖xh7! ♔xh7 24 ♕h5+ ♔g8 25 ♕g6+ ♔h8 26 ♗c4 is decisive.

22...♔g7 23 f6+! ♔g8 (23...♕xf6 24 ♖xh7+) 24 ♕e4! 1-0

Game 115: Sicilian, Najdorf

Grefe-Browne
USA Ch, El Paso 1973

1 e4 c5 2 ♘f3 d6 3 d4 cd 4 ♘xd4 ♘f6 5 ♘c3 a6 6 ♗g5 e6 7 f4 h6!? 8 ♗h4 ♗e7

This vigorous contesting of the h4-d8 diagonal involves the drawback that ...0-0 will now invite a rapid g4-g5 by White.

9 ♕f3 ♘bd7 10 0-0-0 ♕c7 11 ♗e2 ♖b8 12 ♕g3 ♖g8?!

A 'failed' Browne TN. The idea is to follow up with ...g5, opposing the rook to White's queen, and gaining the e5 square. But White contests this vigorously by proving, once again, that the Najdorf king is a beleagured piece.

13 ♖hf1! g5?! 14 fg ♘e5 15 ♘f3! b5

If Black tries to win a piece by 15...hg 16 ♗xg5 ♘h7 he walks into 17 ♗xe7! ♖xg3 18 ♗xd6 with clear advantage to White.

16 ♘xe5 b4 *(115)*

On 16...de Marić gives 17 gf!! ♖xg3 18 fe ♖g5 19 ♗h5! ♕xe7 20

♖xf7 ♕xf7 21 ♗xf7+ ♔xf7 22 ♗xg5 hg 23 ♖d8 and wins. All quite true!

115
W

17 ♘xf7! bc 18 gf! ♖xg3 19 fe ♖g5 20 ♗xg5 hg 21 ♘xd6+ 1-0

Game 116: Sicilian, Najdorf

Lombardy-Quinteros
Manila 1973

1 e4 c5 2 ♘f3 d6 3 d4 cd 4 ♘xd4 ♘f6 5 ♘c3 a6 6 ♗g5 e6 7 f4 ♗e7 8 ♕f3 h6 9 ♗h4 ♕c7 10 0-0-0 ♘bd7 11 ♗e2 ♖b8 12 ♕g3 ♖g8?!

Incidentally, this move is doubly incorrect as the pawn is already defended. On 12...b5!? 13 ♕xg7?? ♖g8 14 ♕xh6 ♗f8 White's queen is trapped.

13 ♖hf1! b5?! *(116)*

A 'failed' Quinteros TN! Had Lombardy analysed Browne's game (see game 115) before this?

116
W

14 ⓩxe6!! fe 15 ♕g6+ ♚d8

White continues in like manner after 15...♚f8: 16 e5! de 17 f5! with lines opening against the king.

16 e5! de 17 f5! ef

Minić gives 17...♛c6 18 ♗xf6 ♗xf6 19 ♗f3 ♕b6 20 fe ♕xe6 21 ♗d5! ♗g5+ (21...♚e8 22 ♗f7 ♕f8 23 ♗xg8 ♕xg8 24 ♖xf6) 22 ♕xg5 hg 23 ♗xe6 ♖e8 24 ♗g4 with a tremendous position for White.

18 ♗xf6 ♗xf6 19 ⓩd5 ♕c6 20 ♖xf5 ♖f8

The threat was 21 ⓩxf6 and 20...♗g5+ 21 ♖xg5 ♕xg6 22 ♖xg6 didn't help - the threat is still 23 ⓩf6.

21 ♗g4! ♖b6 22 ♖xf6! gf

Also 22...♖xf6 23 ♕xg7 ♖e6 24 ♗h5! didn't help.

23 ♕g7 ♖b7 (23...♖e8 24 ⓩxb6 etc.) 24 ♕e7 mate.

Game 117: Sicilian, Najdorf

Parma-Balashov
Moscow 1971

1 e4 c5 2 ⓩf3 d6 3 d4 cd 4 ⓩxd4 ⓩf6 5 ⓩc3 a6 6 ♗g5 e6 7 f4 ♕c7 8 ♕f3 b5

Parma gives this a ?, presumably in view of his forcing continuation - though that's unclear. The move paid off in Psakhis-Tukmakov, USSR 1979, however: 9 0-0-0?! b4! 10 e5 ♗b7 11 ♕h3 de 12 ⓩcb5 ab 13 ♗xb5+ ♗c6! 14 fe ♗xb5 15 ef ♗d7! 16 ⓩf5 gf 17 ♗xf6 ♖g8 18 ♕xh7 b3!? 19 ⓩd6+ ♗xd6 20 ♖xd6 ♖f8 0-1 (21 ♖d2 ba!).

9 ♗xf6!? gf 10 e5 ♕b7

On 10...♗b7 11 ⓩe4 involves a self-pin but 11 ♕h5 threatens ⓩxe6 and if 11...♕d7 12 0-0-0 embarrassing the black queen looks powerful.

11 ⓩe4 fe 12 fe de (117)

117
W

13 ♗d3!?

The alternative was 13 ⓩxe6 fe (13...♗xe6?? 14 ⓩf6+) 14 ♗d3, unclear, according to Parma, as would now be 13...ed 14 ⓩf6+ ♚e7 15 ♗e4 ♕c7 16 0-0! ♖a7 17 ⓩd5+ ed 18 ♕f6+ ♚e8 19 ♗xd5. Black's way is riskier.

13...f5?! 14 ⓩxe6! fe 15 ♗xe4 ♕b6

On 15...♕f7 the simple 16 ♕xf7+ ♚xf7 17 ⓩxf8 ♖a7 18 ⓩxh7 is winning, so Black offers a last complication.

16 ♘xf8 ♖xf8 17 ♕h5+ ♖f7 18 ♕xe5+ ♗e6 19 0-0-0!

And not 19 ♗xa8 ♕f2+ 20 ♔d1 ♖d7+ 21 ♔c1 ♕d2+ and 21...♕d1+. White still has 2 threats now and if 19...♕e3+ 20 ♔b1 ♖e7 21 ♕h8+ ♔f7 22 ♖hf1+ wins.

19...♖a7 20 ♖d6 ♕e3+ 21 ♔b1 ♖ae7 22 ♖xe6 1-0

Game 118: Sicilian, Najdorf

Rantanen-Denman
Skopje Olympiad 1972

1 e4 c5 2 ♘f3 d6 3 d4 cd 4 ♘xd4 ♘f6 5 ♘c3 a6 6 ♗g5 e6 7 f4 ♗e7 8 ♕f3 ♕c7 9 0-0-0 ♘bd7 10 ♗e2!? (10 ♗d3 - see game 119) 10...b5 11 ♗xf6 ♘xf6!?

On 11...gf 12 ♕h5 ♘c5 13 ♗f3 ♗b7 14 f5 with white-square pressure, or 11...♗xf6 12 e5 ♗b7 13 ♕h3 de 14 ♘xe6!? looks a good sac. Now the Finn becomes a shark.

12 e5! ♗b7 *(118a)*

118a
W

13 ef! ♗xf3 14 ♘xf3 ♖c8 (14... ♗xf6!?) 15 fe ♕b6?

No good is 15...♕xe7 16 ♘f5!, but on 15...b4!? Rantanen gives only 16 ♘d5?! ed 17 ♖he1 ♕c4 which favours Black. Here 16 ♘e4 d5!? or 16 ♘ce2 ♕xe7, are all better for Black than the game.

16 ♖he1 h5 (16...♔xe7?? 17 ♘d5+) 17 f5! e5 18 f6! g6 *(118b)*

Horrible, but on 18...ed there follows 19 ♘d5, 20 fg and 21 ♘f6 mate; on 18...gf 19 ♘d5 ♕b8 20 ♘f5 ♔d7 21 ♘xf6+! ♔e6 22 ♖xd6+ ♔xf5 23 ♘e4!; and on 18...♖xc3 19 fg ♖g8 20 ♘f5.

118b
W

19 ♖xe5! de 20 ♗c6+! 1-0

Game 119: Sicilian, Najdorf

Zaid-Ayrapetov
USSR 1975

1 e4 c5 2 ♘f3 d6 3 d4 cd 4 ♘xd4 ♘f6 5 ♘c3 a6 6 ♗g5 e6 7 f4 ♗e7 8 ♕f3 ♕c7 9 0-0-0 ♘bd7 10 ♗d3 h6

On 10...b5 typically obscure is 11 ♖he1 ♗b7 12 ♘d5!? ed 13 ♘f5

♗f8(?!) 14 e5!? de 15 fe ♘xe5 16
♘xg7+! ♗xg7 17 ♗xf6 ♗xf6 18
♕xf6 ♖g8 19 ♖xe5+ ♔f8 20 ♖de1
♕c6 21 ♖e6 1-0 (21...♕c8 22
♖e7 ♖g7 23 ♖xf7+ ♖xf7 24 ♕h8
mate), Enevoldsen-Hamann, Denmark 1972.

11 ♗xf6!?

There was a choice. 11 ♗h4 g5!?
(Gufeld); 11 h4!? (Velimirović); 11
♕h3!? ♘c5 (11...♘b6 Browne or
11...♘f8-g6 Trifunović) 12 ♖he1
♖g8? 13 e5! de 14 fe hg 15 ef ♗xf6
16 ♘d5 ♕d8 17 ♗h7! ♖h8 18 ♘f5
g4 19 ♕g3 ♔f8 20 ♘xf6 1-0 (20...
♕xf6 21 ♕d6+ ♔e8 22 ♘xg7+),
Planinc-Najdorf, Wijk aan Zee 1973.
**11...♘xf6 12 ♖he1 b5 13 e5 ♗b7
14 ♕h3 de 15 fe ♘d7** *(119)*

119
W

**16 ♘xe6! fe 17 ♗g6+ ♔d8 18 ♕xe6
♗c8**

White threatened 19 ♖xd7+♕xd7
20 ♖d1; 18...♗c6 19 ♘d5 ♗xd5 20
♖xd5 would threaten ♖ed1, ♗f5
winning.
19 ♘d5 ♗g5+

Or 19...♕c5 20 ♘xe7 ♕xe7 21
♕b6 mate!
**20 ♔b1 ♕c5 21 ♘b6! ♖a7 22 ♗f5
♕e7 23 ♕c6 ♖c7 24 ♕a8! 1-0**

Game 120: Sicilian, Najdorf

Vitolinsh-Gutman
USSR 1973

1 e4 c5 2 ♘f3 d6 3 d4 cd 4 ♘xd4
♘f6 5 ♘c3 a6 6 ♗g5 e6 7 f4 ♘bd7 8
♕f3 ♕c7 9 0-0-0 b5 10 ♗xb5!
Indubitably a good move, though
unclear, which both sides have
contested vigorously for years (cf.
games 121-3).
10...ab 11 ♘dxb5 ♕b8

Instead 11...♕b6 12 e5 ♖a5! 13
ef gf favoured Black in Balashov-
Polugayevsky, Manila 1976. Minev
gives 11...♕b7!? 12 ♘xd6+ ♗xd6
13 ♖xd6 ♖b8 14 b3 ♕a7 15 ♖hd1
0-0 as unclear.
**12 ♖he1 h6 13 ♗h4 ♗b7 14 ♕d3
♘c5 15 ♕c4!? ♘fd7** (Superior is 15
...♗e7) **16 b4! ♘a6** *(120)*

120
W

**17 ♘d5! g5 18 fg ed 19 ed+ ♘e5 20
♖xe5+! de 21 d6 hg 22 d7+ ♔d8**

On 22...♔e7 Gipslis gives 23
♗xg5+ f6 24 ♗xf6+! ♔xf6 25 ♖f1+,
i.e. 25...♔e7 26 ♕f7+ ♔d8 27 ♕e8
mate or 25...♔g5 26 h4+! ♖xh4 27
♕g8+.
23 ♕xf7 1-0

Game 121: Sicilian, Najdorf

Sibarević-Bukić
Banja Luka 1976

1 e4 c5 2 ♘f3 d6 3 d4 cd 4 ♘xd4 ♘f6 5 ♘c3 a6 6 ♗g5 e6 7 f4 ♘bd7 8 ♕f3 ♕c7 9 0-0-0 b5 10 ♗xb5! ab 11 e5!

Apparently strengthening White's play. Sibarević gives the possibility 11...♗b7 12 ♘dxb5 ♕b6 13 ♕e2 de 14 fe ♘d5 15 ♘xd5 ♗xd5 16 ♖xd5! ed 17 ♘d6+ ♗xd6 18 ed+ ♔f8 19 ♕e7+ ♔g8 20 ♕xd7 with advantage to White.

11...♕b8? 12 ef gf 13 ♖he1! h5

And not 13...fg 14 ♘c6 ♕-moves 15 ♖xe6+! fe 16 ♕h5 mate.

14 ♕h3! e5 15 ♘d5! fg *(121)*

Counter-attack by 15...♖xa2 16 ♔b1 ♕a7 fails to 17 ♘xf6+.

16 ♘c6 ♕b7 17 ♖xe5+! ♗e7

On 17...♘xe5 18 ♘f6 mate! or 17 ...de 18 ♘f6+! ♘xf6 19 ♖d8 mate.

18 ♖xe7+ ♔f8 19 ♕f5 ♘e5 20 ♕f6 ♖h7 1-0

In view of 21 ♖e8+! ♔xe8 22 ♕d8 mate.

Game 122: Sicilian, Najdorf

Poleshchuk-Foigel
Corres 1977

1 e4 c5 2 ♘f3 d6 3 d4 cd 4 ♘xd4 ♘f6 5 ♘c3 a6 6 ♗g5 e6 7 f4 ♘bd7 8 ♕f3 ♕c7 9 0-0-0 b5 10 ♗xb5! ab 11 e5! ♕b7!? 12 ♘dxb5

Black looks better after 12 ef ♕xf3 13 gf (13 fg? ♕e3+; 13 ♘xf3) 13...gf 14 ♗h4 b4, but if now 12... ♕xf3 13 gf White threatens both ef and ♘c7+ with advantage.

12...de 13 fe ♖xa2!? 14 ♔b1!

Better than 14 ♘xa2 ♕xb5 15 ♕a8 ♘b6, or 15 ef? ♕xg5+. Also 14 ♕xb7 ♖a1+ 15 ♔d2 ♖xd1+ 16 ♖xd1 ♗xb7 17 ef gf is O.K. for Black in view of his bishops.

14...♖a5 15 ef ♕xf3 *(122)*

This loses. Kondratiev and Stolyar give 15...♖xb5 16 ♘xb5 ♕xb5 17 ♖xd7! ♕xd7 18 fg ♗g7 19 ♖d1 ♗d4 (19...♕c7 20 ♕c6+!) 20 ♗f6 ♗b7 21 ♕b3 and White wins; disaster also strikes after 15...gf 16 ♗xf6 ♕xf3? 17 ♘c7 mate.

16 ♘c7+! ♔d8 17 fg+ ♔xc7 18 gh♕

♕a8! 19 ♗d8+! 1-0

After the forced 19...♔xd8 20 ♕xf8+ ♔c7 21 ♕d6+ ♔d8 (or 21 ...♔b7 22 ♕b4+) Black's attack fizzles out, e.g. 22 ♔c1 ♖a1+ 23 ♘b1 ♕xg2 24 ♖hg1.

Game 123: Sicilian, Najdorf

Semkov-Georgiev
Varna 1977

1 e4 c5 2 ♘f3 d6 3 d4 cd 4 ♘xd4 ♘f6 5 ♘c3 a6 6 ♗g5 e6 7 f4 ♕c7 8 ♕f3 ♘bd7 9 0-0-0 b5 10 ♗xb5!

This time Black will win, although not because of this move; alternatives are possible, of course, e.g. 10 ♗xf6!? ♘xf6?! 11 e5 ♗b7 12 ♕h3 de 13 ♘cxb5! ab 14 ♗xb5+♔e7 15 fe ♕xe5 (15...♘d5) 16 ♖he1 ♕f4+ 17 ♔b1 ♗d5 18 ♘c6+ ♗xc6 19 ♗xc6 ♖b8 (19...♖a7 20 ♕c3 ♘d7 21 ♖d4 ♕b8 22 ♖ed1) 20 ♕a3+! ♕b4 21 ♕a7+ 1-0, Rogulj-Georgiev, Varna 1977.

10...ab 11 e5 ♖a5!?

! Minev, ?! Kondratiev and Stoljar who suggest 12 ef gf 13 ♕h5(!) with advantage to White. Minev regards 12 ♘dxb5 ♖xb5 13 ♘xb5 ♕b8 as unclear.

12 ef gf 13 ♖he1 b4

Not 13...fg 14 ♘d5 ♕b7 15 ♖xe6+! fe 16 ♕h5+ ♔d8 17 ♘xe6 mate. Black intends to answer 14 ♘d5 by 14...♖xd5 15 ♕xd5 ♗e7! with advantage.

14 ♘c6?! ♖g8 15 ♘e4

Or 15 ♘d5 ♖xd5 16 ♕xd5 ♘c5!

17 ♗xf6 ♗b7, and on 15 ♘xa5 bc the roof falls in.

15...♖xa2 16 ♔b1 *(123)*

16...♗b7! 17 ♘xf6+?

Better is 17 ♔xa2 although Black's on top; 17...♗xc6 18 ♗h4 f5!, or 18 ♗xf6 ♗xe4 19 ♕xe4 ♘xf6.

17...♘xf6 18 ♗xf6 ♖g6!

Avoiding any obscurities with 18 ...♗xc6 19 ♕b3! intending 20 ♖xe6+.

19 ♗h4 ♗xc6 20 ♕b3 ♖a5 21 f5 ♕a7! 0-1

Game 124: Sicilian, Dragon

Fischer-Camara
Siegen Olympiad 1970

1 e4 c5 2 ♘f3 d6 3 d4 ♘f6 4 ♘c3 cd 5 ♘xd4 g6 6 ♗e3 ♗g7 7 f3 ♘c6 8 ♕d2 ♗d7!?

Intending to delay ...0-0 and give White less to attack.

9 ♗c4 ♖c8 10 ♗b3 ♕a5 11 0-0-0 ♘e5 12 h4! ♘c4?!

This leads to problems. The

aggressive 12...b5!? or the defensive 12...h5, look plausible.

13 ♗xc4 ♖xc4 14 ♘b3! ♕c7 15 ♗d4 ♗c6

Now, according to Trifunović, 15 ...0-0?! allows 16 ♗xf6 ♗xf6 17 ♘d5 ♕c8 18 ♘xf6+ ef 19 h5 with a winning attack.

16 e5! de 17 ♗xe5 ♕c8 18 ♕e2 ♗d7? *(124)*

But 18...b5 19 ♘a5 offers no joy.

124
W

19 ♖xd7! ♔xd7 (forced) **20 ♘b5! ♕c6**

The threat was 21 ♖d1+ ♔e8 22 ♗xf6 ♗xf6 23 ♘d6+. The text loses quickly but 20...♖c6, though more tenacious, was also hopeless (21 ♘xa7).

21 ♖d1+ ♔e8 22 ♘c7+ ♕xc7 23 ♗xc7 ♖xc7 24 ♕b5+ 1-0

Game 125: Sicilian, Dragon

Auchenberg-Podzielny
West Germany 1972

1 e4 c5 2 ♘f3 d6 3 d4 cd 4 ♘xd4

♘f6 5 ♘c3 g6 6 ♗e3 ♗g7 7 f3 0-0 8 ♗c4 ♘c6 9 ♕d2 ♗d7 10 0-0-0 ♕a5 11 ♗b3 ♖fc8

The best rook.

12 h4 ♘e5 13 h5!? ♘xh5 14 ♗h6 ♘d3+!? 15 ♔b1!

Better than 15 cd ♗xd4, or 15 ♕xd3 ♗xh6+. Nilsson now suggests 15...♘xb2 16 ♔xb2 ♗xh6 17 ♕xh6 ♖xc3 instead of Black's next, which lands him in unexpected difficulty. **15...♗xd4? 16 ♘d5! ♕d8?!** *(125)*

Or 16...♕xd2 17 ♘xe7+ ♔h8 18 ♖xd2 ♖e8 19 ♖xd3 with a small but clear positional advantage.

125
W

17 ♖xh5!!

A bombshell. Now 17...gh 18 ♕g5+ ♔h8 19 ♖xd3 ♗e5 20 f4 wins a piece.

17...♗h8 18 cd e6!? 19 ♗g5! f6 20 ♖xh7! fg

Neither 20...♔xh7 21 ♖h1+ ♔g8 22 ♖xh8+! ♔xh8 23 ♗xf6+, nor 20...ed 21 ♗xd5+! ♔xh7 22 ♖h1+ ♔g7 23 ♗h6+ ♔h7 24 ♗f8+ would save him.

21 ♖e7! ed 22 ♕xg5 ♔f8 23 ♕xd5! ♗e8 24 ♖f7+ 1-0

Game 126: Sicilian, Dragon

Donchev-Perenyi
Bulgaria 1977

1 e4 c5 2 ♘f3 d6 3 d4 cd 4 ♘xd4
♘f6 5 ♘c3 g6 6 ♗e3 ♗g7 7 f3 ♘c6
8 ♕d2 0-0 9 ♗c4

In this game White avoids castling
to hasten his own attack. The
immediate 9 0-0-0, however, gives
Black an interesting and critical
possibility: 9...d5!? 10 ed ♘xd5 11
♘xc6 bc 12 ♗d4 e5! 13 ♗c5 ♗e6!
14 ♘xd5 cd 15 ♗b5?! d4! 16 ♗xf8
♕xf8 17 ♔b1 ♖b8 18 ♗a4 d3! 19
cd e4 20 d4 ef 21 gf? (21 ♗b3) 21
...♕a3! 22 ♗b3 ♖xb3! 0-1, Polgar-
Dely, Kecskemet 1972.
9...♗d7 10 h4 ♘e5 11 ♗b3 ♖c8 12
h5 ♘xh5 13 g4 ♘f6 14 ♗h6 ♗xh6
15 ♕xh6 ♖xc3!?

Thematic and reasonable attempt
to pry White's interest away from
the K-side. He already has a pawn
for the exchange.
16 bc ♕a5 17 ♕e3?! ♖c8 18
♔d2? *(126)*

It was time to castle!

126
B

18...♖xc3! 19 ♗xf7+

Desperation, in view of 19 ♕xc3
♘xf3+! 20 ♘xf3 (20 ♔d3 ♘e5+) 20
...♘xe4+, winning the queen.
19...♕f8 20 ♘e6+ ♗xe6 21 ♕xc3
♘xf3+! 0-1

Game 127: Sicilian,
Accelerated Dragon

Portisch-Deže
Vršac 1971

1 c4 c5 2 d4 g6 3 ♘f3 cd 4 ♘xd4
♘c6 5 e4

This transposition is the most
common route to these Maroczy vs.
Dragon set-ups.
5...♘f6 6 ♘c3 d6 7 ♘c2!? ♗g7 8
♗e2 ♘d7 (8...0-0) 9 ♗e3 ♗xc3+?!

Always a risky swap; black
square bishop are important pieces!
Here, also, White retains a lion's
share of the centre.
10 bc ♕a5 11 ♕d2 ♘c5 12 f3 ♕a4
13 0-0 ♗e6 14 ♘b4! ♖c8 15 ♘d5
♘d7?

Sokolov's 15...♘e5!? looks right,
and if 16 ♕d4 ♗d7! (plan ...♘e6);
16 ♗d4!?
16 ♕b2 b6?! *(127)*

127
W

17 c5!! bc

Forced; the other captures allow 18 ♗b5 ♕a5 19 c4!, threatening ♕xh8 and ♗d2! trapping the queen.

18 ♗b5 ♕a5 19 ♗xc6 ♖xc6 20 ♕b7! 1-0

A rooks drops, i.e. 20...♕a6 21 ♕xa6 and ♘c7+, 20...♖a6 21 ♕c8+, or 20...♗xd5 21 ed ♖c7 22 ♕a8+. Elegant.

15 ♖xc4!! ♖xc4 (15...♘b6 16 ♖xc8+ ♘xc8 17 ♗b5+) **16 ♕xd5 ♖a4 17 ♗b5+ ♔f8** (17...♔d8 18 ♕xd6+) **18 ♖c1! 1-0**

Game 128: Sicilian, Accelerated Dragon

One of Geller's excellent novelties and it is to Michael Stean's credit that he puts it to the test.

Geller-Stean
Teesside 1975

1 ♘f3 c5 2 c4 g6 3 d4 cd 4 ♘xd4 ♘c6 5 e4 ♘f6 6 ♘c3 d6 7 ♗e2 ♘xd4 8 ♕xd4 ♗g7 9 ♗g5!

Accurate, before ♕d2. Feeble would be 9 ♕e3 0-0 10 b3? ♘xe4!

9...♗e6 10 ♖c1 ♕a5 11 ♕d2 ♖c8 12 f3!?

The innovation; 12 b3 b5! 13 ♘xb5 ♕xd2+ 14 ♗xd2 ♘xe4 lets Black equalise. Black should now reply 12...0-0 accepting a slight spacial inferiority.

12...♗xc4? 13 ♘d5! ♕xa2 (forced) **14 0-0! ♘xd5** *(128)*

On 14...b5 Geller had prepared 15 ♖a1 ♕b3 16 ♖a3!

Game 129: Sicilian, Accelerated Dragon

Bukić-Romanishin
Moscow 1977

1 d4 g6 2 c4 c5 3 ♘f3 cd 4 ♘xd4 ♘c6 5 e4 ♘f6 6 ♘c3 d6 7 ♗e2 ♘xd4 8 ♕xd4 ♗g7 9 ♗g5! ♗e6 10 0-0 (10 ♖c1!? cf. game 128) **10... 0-0 11 ♕d2 ♖c8 12 b3 b5?!**

Thematic, but inaccurate in view of White's reply. Better is 12...♕a5. **13 e5!**

Not 13 ♘xb5? ♘xe4, nor 13 cb? ♖xc3. After the text, however, 13 ...de 14 ♕xd8 ♖fxd8 15 ♘xb5 favours White because of his Q-side pawn majority for the imminent endgame.

13...b4!? 14 ef ef 15 ♗e3 bc 16 ♕xc3 f5 17 ♗d4 ♗xd4 18 ♕xd4 ♕a5! 19 ♖fd1!

Better than 19 ♕xd6 allowing
...♖f-d8-d2xa2 drastically under-
mining White's advantage.
**19...♖fd8 20 ♗f3 ♖c5 21 ♕f6
♖d7?** *(129)*

Bukić gives 21...♕c7 22 h4 h5 23
♖d3, and White is clearly much
better. This simply hastens the end.

**22 b4! ♕xb4 23 ♖db1 ♕xc4 24
♗e2! 1-0**

The point; 24...♕c2 25 ♗d3!
♕c3 26 ♖b8+ ♖c8 27 ♕xc3.

Game 130: Sicilian, Accelerated Dragon

Uhlmann-Ljubojević
Niksic 1978

**1 c4 c5 2 ♘f3 g6 3 d4 ♗g7 4 e4 cd
5 ♘xd4 ♘c6 6 ♗e3 d6 7 ♘c3 a6 (7
...♘f6) 8 ♗e2 e6?**

This doesn't develop - it blocks in
his own Q-bishop and weakens the
d-pawn. Natural and best is 8...♘f6.
9 ♕d2 ♘e5 10 ♖d1! ♕c7? *(130)*

Uhlmann suggests 10...f5 preparing to defend d6 with ...♘f7.

11 ♘db5! ab 12 ♘xb5 ♕c6

Here on 12...♕d7 13 ♘xd6+ ♔f8
14 f4 doesn't regain the piece but
Uhlmann gives simply 13 0-0 'with
a winning position' - judgement,
rather than analysis?
13 ♘xd6+ ♔e7

Alternatively 13...♔f8 is met by
14 f4 ♘d7 15 ♘xc8.
14 ♕b4! ♔f6 15 f4 g5

Or 15...♘d7 16 e5+ - Uhlmann;
16 ♘e8 mate is stronger!
16 fe+ ♔g6 17 ♘xf7! 1-0

Game 131: Trompowsky Attack

Vaganian was the right sort of
tactician to score heavily with this
opening while it was being re-
searched in the mid-70s.

Vaganian-Botterill
Hastings 1974/5

1 d4 ♘f6 2 ♗g5 g6!? 3 ♗xf6 ef 4 e3 ♗g7 5 ♘e2 b6?!

Vaganian suggests 5...f5!? with the intention of ...c5, but the latter advance always results in a weak black d-pawn. One scheme is ...d5, ...f5, ...c6, ...♘-d7-f6-e4, when it's hard for either side to make progress.

6 ♘f4 d5 7 h4! h5 8 c4!? dc

Of course 8...c6 9 cd cd 10 ♕b3 is terrible for Black, but now his g6 and f7 points are sensitive.

9 ♗xc4 ♗b7 10 ♘c3 ♗h6? *(131)*

This threat is too slow; not 10... 0-0? 11 ♘xg6, but Vaganian suggests 10...♘c6.

131
W

11 ♗xf7+! ♔xf7 12 ♕b3+ ♔e8 13 ♘xg6 ♕d7

Or 13...♖h7 14 ♕g8+, and if 13... ♔d7 White can go for 14 ♕f7+ ♔c8 15 ♘e7+ ♔d7 16 ♘c6+ ♔xc6 17 ♖c1 which promises a quick mate.

14 ♘xh8 ♕g7 15 ♕e6+ ♔f8 16 ♘d5 ♘d7 17 ♘e7! 1-0

Efficient; 17...♕xg2 18 ♘eg6+! ♔g7 19 ♕f7 mate.

Game 132: Trompowsky Attack

Vaganian-Kupreichik
USSR Ch, Top League,
Leningrad 1974

1 d4 ♘f6 2 ♗g5 c5!? 3 d5 ♕b6 (3... ♘e4!?) 4 ♘c3!

Better than 4 ♕c1 ♘e4! 5 ♗h4 g5 6 ♗g3 ♗g7 7 c3 ♕h6! (plan ...♘xg3) and Black is better.

4...♕xb2 5 ♗d2! ♕b6 6 e4 d6 7 f4 g6? (7...e6 Vaganian) 8 e5 de 9 fe ♘fd7 10 ♘f3 ♗g7 11 ♖b1 ♕d8 12 e6 fe 13 ♘g5! ♘f6 14 ♗b5+ ♔f8 15 de a6 *(132)*

If he can't play this he's about lost; 15...♕d4 was the alternative.

132
W

16 ♗e3!! ♕a5

No good is 16...♕xd1+ 17 ♖xd1 ab (17...♗h6 18 ♖d8+ ♔g7 19 ♖xh8 ♗xg5 20 ♖xc8, or 19...♔xh8 20 ♘f7+) 18 ♖d8+ ♘e8 19 0-0+ ♗f6 20 ♖xc8 ♔g7 21 ♘f7! and White wins.

17 0-0! h6

Or 17...ab 18 ♖xb5 ♕c7 19 ♘d5 ♕e5 20 ♗xc5! (Vaganian).

18 ♕d3! ♔g8

Here 18...hg 19 ♕xg6 ♔g8 20 ♕f7+ ♔h7 21 ♗d3+ decides. The rest is annihilation.

19 ♕xg6 ♗xe6 20 ♘xe6 ♖h7 21 ♖xf6! ♘d7 22 ♗xd7 1-0

Game 133: Trompowsky Attack

Gurgenidze-Kapengut
USSR 1975

1 d4 ♘f6 2 ♗g5 c5!? 3 ♗xf6! gf 4 d5 ♕b6 5 ♕c1 f5!? (5...♘h6 6 e3) 6 e3 ♗g7 7 c3 e6 8 ♘h3! h5?!

Weakening; better was 8...d6. Accepting the pawn by 8...ed exposes both d5 and f5 to White's pieces.

9 ♗e2 e5!? 10 f4! e4 11 ♘a3 ♕g6?! 12 ♘b5 ♘a6 13 d6!

Locking up Black's Q-side. 13... ♕xg2 is met by 14 ♖g1 ♕xh3 15 ♖xg7 and White can soon bring his other rook into action.

13...♗f8 14 ♕d2! ♕xg2 *(133)*

133
W

15 ♕d5!!

It's the double rook sacrifice. After 15...♕xh1+ ♔d2 ♕xa1 17 ♕e5+ ♔d8 18 ♕xh8 ♕xb2+ 19 ♔e1 ♔e8 20 ♕e5+ ♔d8 21 ♘g5! is decisive, and of course 15...♖g8 16 ♖g1 is no good.

15...f6 16 ♕xf5! ♕xh1+ (else 17 ♖g1) 17 ♔d2 ♕xa1 18 ♕g6+ ♔d8 19 ♕xf6+ ♔e8 20 ♕e5+ ♔f7

Or 20...♔d8 21 ♕xh8 ♕xb2+ 22 ♔e1! etc.

21 ♗c4+! 1-0

Mates by 21...♔g6 22 f5+! ♔h7 23 ♘g5+ ♔h6 24 ♕f6.

Game 134: Torre Attack

Fuller-Dankert
Esbjerg II 1979

1 d4 d5 2 ♘f3 ♘f6 3 ♗g5!? e6 4 ♘bd2 ♗e7 (4...c5!?) 5 e3 0-0

An alternative scheme is 5... ♘bd7!? 6 ♗d3 c5 7 c3 b6 intending ...♗b7, ...♕c7 and ...0-0-0 - Fuller.

6 ♗d3 b6 7 ♘e5 ♗b7 8 ♕f3 ♘bd7? (8...♘fd7!) 9 ♕h3 g6

On 9...♘e4? White intended 10 ♘xe4! de 11 ♗a6! winning, i.e. 11... ♗xa6 12 ♘c6 ♕e8 (12...♕c8? 13 ♘xe7+) 13 ♗xe7, 11...♗xg5 12 ♗xb7 winning the exchange, or 11 ...♘xe5 12 ♗xb7 ♖b8 13 ♗xe4 winning a pawn.

10 ♕h4! ♘b8 (10...♖e8 11 ♗b5!) 11 f4 c5 12 c3 ♘c6 13 ♘df3 (13 ♗a6 h6) 13...♖c8 14 0-0 ♖c7 15 ♗h6! ♘h5 16 ♘g5 ♘xe5

Of course 16...♘g7 17 ♗xg7 ♗xg5 18 fg ♔xg7 19 ♕h6+ and 20 ♘g4!

was all bad news.

17 fe ♗c8 *(134)*

A trick; 18 ♗xf8? ♗xg5. The attack must work now, however.

18 g4! ♘g7 19 ♖f6! ♘e8

Or 19...♗xf6 20 ef ♕xf6 21 ♖f1 ♕d8 22 ♗xg7.

20 ♗xf8 ♗xf6 21 ef ♕xf6 (20... ♘xf6 21 ♘xh7!) 22 ♖f1 ♕h8 23 ♘xf7! 1-0

The finish is 23...♖xf7 24 ♖xf7 ♔xf7 25 ♕e7+ ♔g8 26 ♗h6 ♘g7 27 ♗b5-e8-f7 mate.

Game 135: Colle System

Rajković-Matulović
Stip 1976

1 d4 d5 2 ♘f3 ♘f6

My researches also uncovered the game Jacqueline Levy (whilst cooking dinner) - Chess Challenger 10 (with 11 mins/move), which diverged with 2...♗f5 3 c4 dc 4 ♕a4+ ♗d7 5 ♕xc4 ♘f6 6 ♘g5 e6 7 g3 ♗c6 8 ♗h3! ♗xh1 9 ♘xf7 ♔xf7 10 ♕xe6+ ♔g6 11 ♗f5+ ♔h5 12

♕e3 ♗b4+ 13 ♔f1 h6 14 ♕f4 g5 15 g4+ ♔h4 16 ♕g3 mate.

3 e3 ♗g4 4 ♘bd2 ♘bd7 5 h3 ♗h5 6 c3 c6 7 ♕b3?!

White's opening is innocuous; Black's bishop on the h5-d1 diagonal or the g6-b1 diagonal assures him easy equality. Better was 7 ♗d3 intending 0-0, ♖e1 and e4.

7...♕c7 8 ♗d3 e6 9 c4?! ♗e7 10 0-0 0-0 11 ♖e1 ♖ac8 12 cd?!

Matulović suggests 12 ♘f1 dc 13 ♗xc4 c5 with a slight plus for Black. 12 e4 looks consistent, but Black can reply 12...de 13 ♘xe4 ♗xf3 14 gf e5 with a fine game.

12...cd 13 ♘f1 ♘e4! 14 ♘3d2 f5 15 ♘xe4?

A fatal opening of the f-file. He should try 15 f3 ♗h4 16 ♖e2 ♘d6 when Black has an ideal Dutch Defence position.

15...fe 16 ♗e2 ♗h4! 17 g3 *(135)*

17...♖xf2!! 0-1

The idea is 18 ♔xf2 ♖f8+ 19 ♔g2 ♖xf1! and now:

a) 20 ♔xf1 ♕xg3,

b) 20 ♖xf1 ♕xg3+ 21 ♔h1 ♗xe2, or

c) 20 gh ♖f2+!! 21 ♔xf2 ♕h2+

22 ♔f1 ♗f3! 23 ♗xf3 ef, all mating.

Game 136: QGD, Semi-Tarrasch Defence

Vaisman-Grabczewski
Wrocław 1974

1 ♘f3 ♘f6 2 c4 e6 3 ♘c3 d5 4 d4 c5 5 cd ♘xd5

On 5...ed 6 g3 steers the game along normal Tarrasch lines; the text allows a big centre, although 6 e3 is also good (cf. game 137).
6 e4!? ♘xc3 7 bc cd 8 cd ♘c6 9 ♗c4 b5!? 10 ♗e2

Of course not 10 ♗xb5? ♕a5+. Now 10...♗b4+ 11 ♗d2 ♕a5 still gives White a slight edge due to his central superiority, with either 12 d5!? (Partos) or 12 a3 ♗xd2+ 13 ♕xd2 ♕xd2+ 14 ♔xd2.
10...a6 11 0-0 ♗b7 12 a4 b4 13 d5 ed?

Black's position is very sensitive as a result of his delayed development. Necessary is 13...♘a5.
14 ed ♘a5 *(136)*

15 ♗b5+! ab 16 ♖e1+ ♔d7 (16... ♗e7 17 d6) 17 ♘e5+ ♔c7 18 ♕c2+! ♘c4

Here 18...♔b8 19 ♗f4 threatening ♘xf7+ is unanswerable, and 18... ♔b6 19 ♗e3+ ♔a6 20 ab+ ♔xb5 21 ♕d3+. The text allows the prettiest win.
19 ♘xc4 bc 20 ♕xc4+ ♔b8 21 ♖e8!! ♕xe8 22 ♗f4+ ♔a7 23 ♕d4+ ♔a6 24 ♗c7 1-0

Game 137: QGD, Semi-Tarrasch Defence

Kasparov-Begun
Sokolsky Memorial, Minsk 1978

1 d4 d5 2 c4 e6 3 ♘c3 ♘f6 4 ♘f3 c5 5 cd ♘xd5 6 e3 ♘c6 7 ♗d3 ♗e7 8 0-0 0-0 9 ♘xd5 ♕xd5

Black's K-side is sensitive, i.e. 9... ed 10 ♕c2 forking 2 pawns - Ubilava (but 10...♘b4!?) or simply 10 dc ♗xc5 (10...♘b4 11 ♗b1 ♗xc5 12 a3) 11 ♗xh7+, or 11 ♕c2. White continues to play on the b1-h7 diagonal.
10 e4!? ♕d8 11 dc ♗xc5 12 e5! ♗e7 (else ♕c2) 13 ♕e2 ♘b4 14 ♗b1 ♗d7 15 a3 ♘d5 16 ♕e4 g6 17 ♗h6 ♖e8 18 h4! ♕b6 19 h5! f5?

It looks bad to play 19...♕xb2 20 ♖a2 but the text gives White more access to Black's king. Maybe 19... ♗f8 would hold out longer.
20 ef6 ♘xf6 21 ♕e1! ♘xh5 22 ♘e5 ♗b5 *(137)*

Or 22...♗c6 (to prevent ♕e4) 23 ♘xg6 hg 24 ♕xe6+; White's attacking play is all justified now.

137
W

23 ♗xg6! ♘f6

No better was 23...hg 24 ♕e4 ♘g7 25 ♕xg6 ♗f8 26 ♘g4.

24 ♗xh7+! 1-0

The choice was 24...♔h8 25 ♘f7+! ♔xh7 26 ♕b1+ ♔g8 27 ♕g6 mate, or 24...♔xh7 25 ♕b1+!, or 24...♘xh7 25 ♕e4 ♘f8 26 ♕g4+. Fierce!

Game 138: QGD, Chigorin Defence

Bouwmeester-Boey
Perfors Memorial Corres 1979

1 d4 d5 2 c4 ♘c6 3 ♘c3! dc 4 ♘f3 ♘f6 5 e4 (5 d5 ♘a5 6 ♕a4+ c6) 5 ...♗g4 6 ♗e3 e6 7 ♗xc4 ♗b4 8 ♕c2 ♕e7!?

Maybe new. White has a strong centre but Black has developed all his pieces; an earlier game went 8... 0-0 9 0-0-0 ♗xc3 10 bc ♕e7 11 h3 ♗h5 12 ♗d3 ♕a3+ 13 ♕b2 ♕xb2+ The text improves this line for Black, however; White could try 9 ♗b5 instead.

9 0-0-0?! ♗xc3 10 bc ♕a3+ 11 ♔d2

Not 11 ♔b1? ♘xe4 12 ♕xe4 ♗f5.
11...e5! 12 d5 ♘a5 13 ♗e2 0-0 14 ♘xe5? *(138)*

Heemsoth suggests 14 ♖b1 c6 15 dc ♖fd8+ 16 ♔e1 ♘xc6 17 ♖xb7, although White's development remains a problem.

138
B

14...♘xe4+! 0-1

A 'correspondence resignation'. On 15 ♕xe4 ♕xa2+ 16 ♔c2 ♘b3+ 17 ♔d3 ♗f5+ picks up the queen. Trickier is 15 ♔e1 ♗xe2 16 ♖c1 (16 ♔xe2 ♘xc3+, or 16 ♕xe2 ♕xc3+ 17 ♗d2 ♘xd2 18 ♖xd2 ♖ae8 19 f4 f6) 16...♗a6 17 ♕xe4 ♖ae8 18 ♕d4 f6 to take the ♖c1 if White's knight moves.

Game 139: QGD, Chigorin Defence

Ian Rogers, the young Australian IM candidate, is an aggressive player whom this defence suits well.

Booth-Rogers
Australia 1976

1 d4 ♘c6 2 c4 (2 d5!) 2...d5 3 ♘f3

♗g4 4 ♘c3 e5!

A TN according to Davis; 4...e6 is normal, but 4...dc 5 d5 ♗xf3 6 ef ♘e5 7 ♗f4 favours White.

5 cd ♗xf3 6 dc (6 ef ♘xd4 is equal.)

6...♗xc6 7 d5 (7 de ♕h4!?) 7...♗d7 8 g3?!

This provides a target later. The solid 8 e4 was more apposite.

8...f5! 9 ♗g2 ♘f6 10 0-0 ♗c5 11 ♕b3 ♖b8 12 e4 0-0 13 ♗e3!?

The check with 13 d6 merely opens the position for Black, so he tries to swap bishops instead. There is a strong attack on the way, however.

13...♗d6! 14 ♗xa7 ♖a8 15 ♗e3 (15 ♕xb7!?) 15...f4 16 gf?! ef 17 ♗d4 *(139)*

139
B

17...f3! 18 ♗xf3 ♗xh2+!

The idea is a quick mate after 19 ♔xh2 ♘g4+ 20 ♗xg4 ♕h4+ 21 ♔g2 ♕xg4+ and ...♖f3-h3. He should try 19 ♔g2 ♘g4 20 ♖h1 with defensive chances.

19 ♔h1! ♘g4 20 ♘e2 ♕h4 21 ♔g2 ♘e3+! 22 fe (22 ♕xe3 ♕h3+, ... ♗g3+, ...♕h2 mate) 22...♗h3+! 23 ♔xh2 ♗xf1+ 24 ♔g1 ♖xf3 0-1

Game 140: Queen's Gambit Accepted

Portisch-Radulov
Nice Olympiad 1974

1 d4 d5 2 c4 dc 3 ♘f3 ♘f6 4 e3 c5 5 ♗xc4 e6 6 0-0 ♘c6 7 ♕e2 a6 8 a4 ♕c7 9 ♘c3 ♗d6 (9...♗e7) 10 ♖d1! 0-0 11 h3 b6?!

'Theory' is 11...e5 12 de ♘xe5 about equal.

12 d5! ed 13 ♗xd5! ♗b7 (13... ♘xd5 14 ♘xd5 ♕b8 15 ♘xb6) 14 e4 ♖ae8 15 ♗g5! ♘d4

Preferring active counterplay to the grovelling 15...♗e7 or 15...♘d7.

16 ♘xd4 ♘xd5 17 ♘xd5 ♗xd5 18 ♘f5 ♖xe4 19 ♕h5 ♖fe8!? *(140)*

Radulov defends his 'bishop centre' through a back rank possibility, since both 19...♖e5 and 19...g6 lose after 20 ♗f6!, and 19... ♗h2+ 20 ♔h1 ♗a8 21 ♘xg7! was unpleasant.

140
W

20 ♘xg7! ♖8e5

Or 20...♔xg7 21 ♕h6+ ♔g8 22 ♗f6 ♗f8 23 ♕g5+.

21 f4! ♖xf4 (forced) 22 ♘e8! ♕c6

(22...♖xe8) 23 ♘xd6?!

Instead 23 ♕h6 was simple; now Black could try 23...h6!, e.g. 24 ♕xh6 ♖e2! 25 ♗xf4 ♖xg2+ 26 ♔f1 ♗c4+ 27 ♘xc4 ♕f3+ turning the tables. Varnusz claims that there was still a win by 24 ♘c8, i.e. 24...♖xg5 25 ♕xg5+ hg 26 ♘e7+ etc., but simply 24...♕xc8 looks good enough; 25 ♖xh6 ♖e6! seems to hold. But Black misses his chance. **23...f6? 24 ♖e1! 1-0**

In view of 24...♖xg5 25 ♖e8+ ♔g7 26 ♖e7+! ♔f8 27 ♖f7+! mating.

Game 141: Queen's Gambit Accepted

Pytel-Castro
Dortmund 1977

1 d4 d5 2 c4 dc 3 e4!? e5 (3...c5!) 4 ♘f3 ed (4...♗b4+) 5 ♗xc4 ♘c6 6 0-0 ♗g4?

Very careless! Of course 7 ♗xf7+ ♔xf7 8 ♘g5+ ♕xg5! 9 ♕b3+ ♗e6 is no good for White, but the weakness at b7 is more significant than Black thinks.

7 ♕b3 ♕d7 *(141)*

8 ♗xf7+!

And not 8 ♕xb7 ♖b8 9 ♗xf7+?, hoping for 9...♔xf7? 10 ♕xc6, but getting 9...♖d8! 10 ♕a6 ♗xf3 (threat ♕g4) 11 gf ♖b6 12 ♕c4 ♘e5. Five bonus points for seeing and rejecting this one!

8...♕xf7 9 ♕xb7 ♖c8 (9...♔d7!? 10 ♕xc6+!) 10 ♕xc6+ ♗d7 11 ♕a6 ♘f6

Planning a manoeuvre to blockade the pawn at e6, though it doesn't work. Black's position is very bad.

12 e5! ♘e4 13 ♖e1 ♘c5 14 e6! ♘xe6

No use either are 14...♗xe6 15 ♕xc8+, or 14...♘xa6 15 ef+ ♔xf7 (15...♔d8 16 ♗g5+) 16 ♘e5+ and 17 ♘g6+.

15 ♘g5 1-0

Game 142: QGD, Orthodox Defence

Attard-Csom
Nice Olympiad 1974

1 d4 ♘f6 2 c4 e6 3 ♘f3 d5 4 ♘c3 ♗e7 5 ♗g5 0-0 6 e3 ♘bd7 7 cd ed 8 ♗d3 ♖e8 9 0-0 c6 10 ♖c1

Inaccurate. 10 ♕c2 ♘f8 gives a standard position for commencement of the minority attack with 11 ♖ab1 planning b4-b5xc6 or 11 ♗xf6!? ♗xf6 12 b4; the text can be met by 10...♘e4 with immediate equality if Black wishes.

10...♘f8 11 ♗xf6 ♗xf6 12 b4 a6 13 a4 ♗e7!?

The bishop is a 'killer' on the b8-h2 diagonal. Against 14 b5 Csom gives 14...♗d6 15 bc bc 16 ♘e2 ♗d7 17 ♘g3 g6 intending ...h5-h4 with a slight advantage to Black. Maybe.

14 ♕b3 ♗d6 15 e4?

Vigorous - but there's a tactical flaw.

15...♗g4! 16 e5

Otherwise he drops a pawn; 16 ♘d2 ♗f4 and 17...de, 18...♕xd4 or 16 ♘e5 ♗xe5 17 de de and 18...♖xe5.

16...♗xf3 17 gf *(142)*

Or 17 ed ♕g5 18 g3 ♕h6 winning a pawn at least.

142
B

17...♖xe5!!

Doom! If 18 de ♕g5+ 19 ♔h1 ♕xe5 20 f4 ♕xf4 21 ♔g2 ♕xh2+ 22 ♔f3 ♗e6! 23 ♘e2 ♕h3+ 24 ♘g3 ♘d4+ wins the queen. But declining doesn't help either.

18 f4 ♖h5 19 f3 ♕h4 20 ♖c2 ♘e6 0-1

Game 143: QGD, Dutch Variation

Doubleday-South
Ottawa Ch 1977

1 d4 ♘f6 2 c4 e6 3 ♘c3 d5 4 ♗g5
c5!?

Tricky. Exchange variation players can avoid this by 4 cd(!) ed 5 ♗g5.

5 cd cd 6 ♕a4+ ♕d7!? 7 ♕xd4

Not 7 de ♕xa4 8 ef+ ♔xf7 9 ♘xa4 b5.

7...♘c6! 8 ♕a4 ♘xd5 9 0-0-0!? ♗e7

Not 9...♘xc3 10 bc ♕c7 11 ♖d8+! Now, theory gives 10 ♗d2 leading to equality; White's try simply leaves the bishop vulnerable and his development laggard.

10 ♗f4? ♘cb4! 11 ♕xd7+ (11 ♕b3 ♕c6) 11...♗xd7 12 ♘xd5 ed! 13 a3 (13 ♔b1 ♗f5+ 14 ♔a1 ♘c2+ 15 ♔b1 ♘e3+) 13...♖c8+ 14 ♔b1 ♗f5+ 15 ♔a1 ♘c2+ 16 ♔a2 0-0 17 e3? *(143)*

Superior was 17 ♘f3 but Black is obviously much better.

143
B

17...♘xa3! 18 ba ♖c2+ 19 ♔b3

Here 19 ♔b1 ♗e2+! 20 ♔c1 ♗xa3 mate, or 19 ♔a1 ♗f6+ 20 ♖d4 ♖c1+ was all easy.

19...♗f6 20 ♖xd5

On 19 ♖b1 ♖c3+ (19...♖xf2 20 ♗g3! ♖d2 21 ♘f3!) 20 ♔a2 ♗xb1 21 ♔xb1 ♖fc8 threatening ...♖b3+

decides, as does 19 ♖d4 ♗xd4 20
ed ♖xf2.
20...♖b2+ 21 ♔c4 ♖c8+ 22 ♖c5
b5+! 23 ♔d5 ♖d2+ 0-1

Game 144: QGD, Slav Defence

**Petrosian-Kupreichik
44th USSR Ch, Leningrad 1976**

1 d4 d5 2 c4 c6 3 cd (3 ♘f3) 3...cd
4 ♘c3 ♘f6 5 ♘f3 ♘c6 6 ♗f4 e6

Apparently 6...♗f5 7 e3 e6 8
♗b5!? ♘d7! 9 0-0 ♗e7 leads to
equality.
7 e3 ♗d6 8 ♗g3 ♘e4?! (8...0-0) 9
♘xe4 de 10 ♘d2 ♗xg3?!

Now White's development is fluid,
his pawns compact, and the h-file
gives attacking chances. But 10...
f5 was a bit 'loose'.
11 hg e5 12 de ♕a5 13 ♕b3! ♕xe5
(13...♘xe5 14 ♕b5+) 14 ♗e2 ♕e7
15 ♖c1 0-0?! *(144)*

Ugrinović gives 15...♗e6 16 ♗c4
♗xc4 17 ♕xc4 f5 18 g4 ♘e5 19
♕b5+ ♔f8 20 ♕e2!, and 15...♗f5
16 ♕d5 ♗g6 17 ♗b5 seems to win a
pawn. The text is more drastic.

16 ♘xe4! ♕xe4 17 ♗d3 ♕b4+ (17...
♕e5/e7!?) 18 ♕xb4 ♘xb4 19
♗xh7+ ♔h8 20 ♗b1+! ♔g8 21 ♖c4!
a5

Or 21...♘c6 22 ♗h7+ ♔h8 23
♗d3+! ♔g8 24 ♖ch4 g6 (24...f5 25
♗c4+) 25 ♖h8+ ♔g7 26 ♖1h7+
winning an exchange. This way
White must play a different trick to
prevent ...f5.
22 ♗h7+ ♔h8 23 ♗f5+! 1-0

After 23...♔g8 24 ♖ch4 g6 (24...
f6 25 ♗g6 mates) White plays ♖h8+,
♖1h7+, ♖xf8, ♖7h8 and ♖xc8; 24
...g5!? is met by 25 ♖h8+ ♔g7 26
♖1h7+ ♔f6 27 ♖xf8 ♗xf5 28
♖hxf7+! and 29 ♖xf5.

Game 145: QGD, Slav Defence

**Miles-Preissman
Haifa Olympiad 1976**

1 d4 d5 2 c4 c6 3 ♘f3 ♘f6 4 ♘c3
dc 5 a4

5 e4!? is the speculative Tolush-
Geller Gambit.
5...e6 6 e3 (6 e4!?) 6...♗b4?!

Miles suggests 6...c5, transposing
to a QGA in which Black has lost
a tempo but gained the use of b4
without playing ...a6 (cf. Portisch-
Radulov, game 140).
7 ♗xc4 ♘bd7 8 0-0 0-0 9 ♕b3 ♕e7
10 e4!

A strong pawn offer. If Black
declines with 10...♖d8 11 e5 ♘d5
12 ♘e4 cramps him, and 10...e5 11
de ♗xc3 12 ♕xc3 ♘xe4 13 ♕d4
followed by ♗g5 was unpleasant.

10...♗xc3 11 bc ♘xe4 12 ♗a3 c5
13 ♖fe1 ♘ef6 14 a5!?

And not 14 ♗xe6? fe 15 ♖xe6
♕f7 16 ♘g5 c4! 17 ♕xc4 ♘b6,
Miles, who suggests 14 ♘g5 ♕h8 15
d5 with advantage. But this 'Larsen
move' turn out well; imperative
was 14...h6.

14...♖b8? *(145)*

15 ♗xe6! fe

It goes like clockwork now.
Declining the piece was a miserable
alternative.

16 ♖xe6 ♕f7 17 ♘g5 c4!? 18 ♕xc4
♘b6 19 ♕e2! ♕g6 20 ♗xf8 ♕xg5
21 ♗d6! 1-0

Game 146: QGD, Semi-Slav

This is the kind of game that
brings to mind Steinitz's maxim:
never move pawns in front of the
king unless you can't avoid it.

Toth-Coppini
Banco di Roma 1979

1 d4 d5 2 c4 c6 3 ♘c3 ♘f6 4 e3 e6

5 ♘f3 ♘bd7 6 ♗d3 ♗d6!? 7 e4 de 8
♘xe4 ♘xe4 9 ♗xe4 h6!?

Hindering ♗g5 or ♘g5. Larsen
has played 9...0-0 10 0-0 (10
♗xh7+? ♔xh7 11 ♘g5+ ♔g8 12
♕h5 ♘f6) 10...c5!? here.

10 0-0 0-0 11 ♗c2 (11 b3!?) 11...
e5 12 ♖e1 ed 13 ♕xd4 ♘f6?!

Pachman prefers 13...♗c5. Black
is still undeveloped and this allows
White to cramp him a bit more.

14 ♖d1 ♗e7 15 ♕e5 ♗d7? *(146)*

Instead 15...♕e8 was necessary.
Black's small inaccuracies have
accumulated!

16 ♗xh6! gh 17 ♕g3+ ♔h8 18 ♘e5!

This quiet move is the clincher.
Now 18...♖g8?? 19 ♘xf7 mate, or
18...♕c7? 19 ♘g6/f7+ are killers.
18...♕c8 can be met as in the game.
18...♗c5 19 ♕f4 ♔g7 20 ♖d3 ♖h8
21 ♖xd7! ♕xd7 (21...♘xd7 22
♕xf7 mate) 22 ♘xd7 1-0

Game 147: QGD, Semi Slav, Meran

Geller-Whiteley
Moscow (Teams) 1977

1 d4 d5 2 c4 c6 3 ♘f3 ♘f6 4 ♘c3 e6 5 e3 ♘bd7 6 ♗d3 dc 7 ♗xc4 b5 8 ♗b3!? b4

Kan gives 8...a6? (preparing c5) 9 e4 b4 10 e5 bc 11 ef cb 12 fg ♗xg7 13 ♗xb2 ♕a5+ 14 ♘d2! with an edge for White.

9 ♘e2 (9 ♘a4? ♗a6!) **9...c5 10 0-0 ♗b7 11 ♘f4 cd?**

Better is 11...♗d6 - this opens the e-file. Sacs on e6 don't work yet but Black's knights are led a merry dance from here on - vintage Geller. **12 ed! ♘b6**

If 12...♗d6 13 ♘g5 keeps White on the boil.

13 ♘g5 ♗d5 14 ♘xd5 ♘fxd5 15 ♗a4+ ♘d7

The bishop's a killer but 15... ♘xa4 16 ♕xa4+ ♔e7 is horrific.

16 ♕h5 ♔e7

Ugly - but 16...g6 17 ♕h3 ♗g7 18 ♘xe6 fe 19 ♕xe6+ ♘e7 20 d5! was also terminal.

17 ♖e1 g6 18 ♕f3 ♘b6 *(147)*

One threat was ♗-c6xd5.

147
W

19 d5! ♘xd5 20 ♘xf7! (20 ♗c6) **20 ...♕xf7 21 ♕xd5 0-0-0 22 ♕a8+ 1-0**

Game 148: Semi-Slav, Meran

Salesses-Corsetti
Argentinian Corres Ch 1979

1 d4 d5 2 c4 c6 3 ♘f3 ♘f6 4 ♘c3 e6 5 e3 ♘bd7 6 ♗d3 dc 7 ♗xc4 b5 8 ♗b3!? b4 9 ♘e2 ♗e7 (9...c5 - game 147) **10 0-0 0-0 11 ♘f4 ♗a6 12 ♖e1 ♕b6 13 e4 ♖fd8** *(148)*

So far Kan-Yudovich, Moscow 1947. White's next is an improvement.

148
W

14 ♘xe6! ♖e8?!

Feeble; he must try 14...fe 15 ♗xe6+ when a) 15...♔h8 16 ♘g5 h6 (or 16...♖f8 17 e5) 17 ♘f7+ gives an attack or exchange win, and b) 15...♔f8 16 e5 ♘d5 17 ♘g5 ♗xg5 18 ♗xg5 with a powerful attack.

15 ♘fg5!? ♘f8?!

Heemsoth suggests 15...h6 16 ♘xf7 ♔xf7 17 ♘c7+ etc.; now Black contrives a self-mate.

16 ♘xf7! ♔xf7 17 ♘g5+ (18 ♘d8+! ♔g6 19 ♗f7 mate) **17...♔g6 18 ♗f7+ ♔h6 19 ♘e6+ g5 20 ♗xg5 mate**

Game 149: Nimzo-Indian Defence

Browne-Ljubojevic
Tilburg 1978

1 d4 ♘f6 2 c4 e6 3 ♘c3 ♗b4 4 e3
0-0 5 ♗d3 c5 6 ♘f3 d5 7 0-0 cd 8
ed dc 9 ♗xc4 b6 10 ♗g5 ♗b7 11
♖e1 ♘bd7 12 ♖c1 ♖c8 13 ♕b3!?

New and strong. The safe reply is
13...♗e7 14 ♘e5; Ljubojevič
suggests 13...♗a5!? 14 ♘e5 ♘xe5
15 de ♕d4 16 ef ♕g4 with complications. Instead he falls into a
positional trap.

13...♕e7?! 14 ♗d5!! ♗a6

Not 14...♗xd5? 15 ♘xd5 etc, and
14...♗xc3 15 ♗xb7 ♖b8 16 ♖xc3
♖xb7 17 d5 also favours White.

15 ♕a4! ♗xc3 16 bc ♘b8 17 ♗b3
b5?

Intending ...♕b7 followed by ...
♘c6, but getting himself all tangled
up. Miles and Speelman suggest 17
...♗d3 intending ...♗g6.

18 ♕a5 ♕b7?!

18...♕c7 must be better.

19 ♗xf6 gf *(149)*

20 d5! ed 21 ♕b4 ♕d7 22 ♕h4
♔g7 23 ♘d4 1-0

There was nothing to do about
24 ♗c2.

Game 150: Nimzo-Indian Defence

Rytov-Timman
Tallinn 1973

1 d4 ♘f6 2 c4 e6 3 ♘c3 ♗b4 4 e3
b6!? 5 ♘e2 (5 ♗d3 ♗b7 - cf. game
156) 5...♗a6 6 a3 ♗xc3 7 ♘xc3 d5
8 b3

Here 8 cd?! ♗xf1 messes up
White's castling and leaves him with
a feeble bishop. Nei mentions 8 b4
♗xc4 9 ♗xc4 dc 10 ♕e2 a5!, and
Black stands well.

8...0-0 9 ♗e2 ♘c6 10 b4? (10 a4,
10 0-0) 10...♗xc4 11 ♗xc4 dc 12
♕e2 *(150)*

Black's follow-up looks unlikely,
but it fingers the weakness in
White's structure.

12...b5! 13 ♘xb5 ♕d5! 14 ♘xc7

♛xg2 15 ♔f1

Better than 15 ♖f1 ♖ac8 16 ♘a6 which is met by 16...e5.

15...♛f3 16 ♘xa8! ♘xd4! 17 ed

It seems that 17 ♖a2 loses too, i.e. 17...♘b3 18 ♗b2 ♖d8 19 ♗d4 ♘xd4 20 ed ♖xd4, or 18 ♗d2 ♘e4 19 ♘c7 c3.

17...♛c3+ 18 ♔e2 ♛xa1! 19 ♛g2 ♛a2+ 20 ♔e1 ♛b1

The return to the white squares marks the end. If 21 ♔e2 ♛c2+ 22 ♔f3 ♛e4+ 23 ♔g3 ♛g4 mate.

21 ♔d2 ♘e4+ 22 ♔e3 ♛d3+ 23 ♔f4 g5+ 24 ♔e5 ♖d8! 0-1

Game 151: Nimzo-Indian Defence

Kruger-Iskov
Dortmund II 1978

1 d4 ♘f6 2 c4 e6 3 ♘c3 ♗b4 4 e3 b6 5 ♘e2 ♗a6 6 ♘g3 0-0 7 e4!? ♘c6 8 ♗d3 e5

'Theory'. The pawn is taboo; 8...♘xd4?? 9 ♛a4 picks up a piece. But now 9 0-0? ♘xd4! 10 ♛a4 ♗xc3 11 bc ♘e6 12 ♗a3 (12 ♛xa6 ♘c5) 12...♗b7 was an effective exchange sac in Lombard-Korchnoi, Switzerland 1978.

9 d5 ♗xc3 10 bc ♘a5?

Keene gives 10...♘e7.

11 ♛e2 d6 12 ♗g5 h6 13 ♗d2 ♘d7 14 ♘f5 ♛f6?!

An attack with jam on it! The threat was 15 ♗xh6 gh 16 ♛g4+

♛g5 17 ♘xh6+, and if Black stops it g4-g5 is enormous.

15 h4 ♘c5?! *(151)*

Imperative is 15...♖e8 but ♖-h3-g3 is very strong.

151
W

16 ♗g5! hg

Or 16...♘xd3+ 17 ♛xd3! hg 18 hg ♛xg5 19 ♛h3 f6 20 ♘e7+ ♔f7 21 ♛e6+ ♔e8 22 ♘c6 mate, but not 17 ♔f1 ♗xc4!? with chances.

17 hg ♛xg5 18 ♛h5!

The point - 18...♛xh5 19 ♘e7+ mates, or 18...f6 19 ♘e7 mate. Black chooses to enjoy a little joke before resigning.

18...♘xd3+ 19 ♔f1 ♛xg2+ 20 ♔xg2 ♘f4+ 21 ♔f3 1-0

Game 152: Nimzo-Indian Defence

Ray Keene is a fine positional player, but is quite capable of high-powered tactics when he feels like it! (cf. game 182). His opponent in this game is a young Australian.

Keene-Kerr
Sydney 1979

1 d4 ♘f6 2 c4 e6 3 ♘c3 ♗b4 4 e3
b6 5 ♘e2 ♗a6 6 ♘g3 0-0 7 e4 ♘c6 8
♗d3 e5 9 a3!? ♗xc3+ 10 bc d6

On 10...ed 11 cd ♘xd4 White
intended 12 ♗b2 ♘c6 13 ♘f5 with
an attack: the immediate threat is
14 ♘xg7! ♔xg7 15 ♕g4+ ♔h8 16
♕g5. Black could return the pawn
by 12...c5 13 ♗xd4 cd 14 ♗e2 with
a bind (probably best).

11 ♗g5 h6

Necessary in order to prevent
♘h5.

**12 ♗e3 ♘a5 13 ♕e2 ♕d7 14 ♘f5
♕a4?** *(152)*

Offside! This leads to a delicate
winning manoeuvre.

152
W

15 ♗xh6! gh 16 ♕e3 ♘e8

If 16...♘g4 17 ♕g3 h5 18 h3.

17 ♕xh6 ♕d7

The threat was 18 ♘e7 mate, and
17...f6 allows 18 ♕g6+ ♔h8 19
♘e7, 20 ♕h6 mate.

18 ♕g5+! ♔h7 19 ♕h4+! ♔g8 (19
♔g6 20 ♕h6 mate) **20 ♕g3+! ♔h8
21 ♕h3+! ♔g8 22 ♘h6+ 1-0**

Game 153: Nimzo-Indian
Defence

Quinteros-Ribli
Montilla 1974

1 d4 ♘f6 2 c4 e6 3 ♘c3 ♗b4 4 ♕c2
c5 5 dc 0-0 6 ♗f4 ♘a6 7 a3?!

White sacrifices any initiative he
may have gleaned from the opening.
Correct was 7 ♗d6! ♖e8 first, e.g.
8 a3 ♕a5 9 ♖b1 ♗xc3 10 bc ♘xc5
11 ♖b5 ♕a4 12 ♕xa4 ♘xa4 13 f3
b6 14 e4 with a good game.

7...♗xc3+ 8 ♕xc3 ♘e4!? 9 ♕d4

9 ♕c2 is met by 9...♕a5+!? when
Black has an initiative.

9...♘axc5!? 10 ♖d1

Ribli had planned the double-
edged 10 b4 ♘b3 11 ♕xe4 ♘xa1 12
♗e5 (12 ♕b1 ♕f6) 12...a5! 13
♗xa1 ab.

10...d5! 11 b4

Or 11 f3? ♘b3 and 12...♕a5+
wins for Black, and 11 cd ed 12
♕xd5 ♗e6 is worth a pawn, e.g. 13
♕xd8 ♖fxd8 14 f3 ♗b3! 15 ♖xd8+
♖xd8 16 fe ♖d1+ 17 ♔e3 ♖xf1 18
♔xe4?! ♗d5+ and ...♗xg2.

11...♘a4 12 f3 ♘ec3! 13 ♖d3 f6!

Turning the game into a rout,
since 14 ♖xc3 e5 costs the exchange.

**14 ♗d2 e5 15 ♕h4 d4 16 e3 ♗f5 17
♗xc3**

Minić gives 17 ed? ♗xd3 18 ♗xd3
e4. Now 17...♗xd3?! 18 ♗xd3 is
trenuous counterplay, but Black
has something better in mind.

17...♘xc3 18 ♖d2 *(153)*

18...de! 19 ♖xd8 ♖axd8 20 ♘e2 ♖d2 21 g4 (21 ♔f1 ♘xe2) 21...♗d3 22 ♔f1 ♘xe2 23 ♘xe2 ♖xe2 24 ♔g1 ♖d8 0-1

Game 154: Nimzo-Indian Defence

V.E.Kozlov-V.Kozlov
All-Union USSR Sporting Soc Ch Yaroslav 1979

1 d4 ♘f6 2 c4 e6 3 ♘c3 ♗b4 4 ♕c2 c5 5 dc ♘a6 6 a3 ♗xc3+

The alternative is 6...♕a5!? with the idea of exchanging queens, e.g. 7 ♗d2 ♘xc5 8 ♖d1 ♗xc3 9 ♗xc3 ♕a4 10 ♕xa4 ♘xa4 but White retains an advantage with 11 ♗d4.

7 ♕xc3 ♘xc5 8 b4?!

Barden and Harding recommend 8 f3! keeping those horses out.

8...♘ce4 9 ♕d4 d5 10 e3 (10 c5!?) 10...0-0 11 ♗b2? *(154)*

An oversight. The K-side needs developing.

11...e5! 12 ♕d1

Of course 12 ♕xe5 ♘xf2 is kaput, and 12 ♕d3 ♗f5 was embarrassing.

12...♘g4 13 ♘h3 (13 f3 ♕h4+) 13...♘xe3! 14 fe ♗xh3 15 ♕f3

Very unhealthy for White is 15 gh ♕h4+ 16 ♔e2 ♕f2 17 ♔d3 ♕xb2.

15...♕h4+! 16 g3 ♕h6 17 ♗xh3 ♕xh3

Bang go the white squares. Balashov and Kozlov give 18 ♗xe5 ♖ae8 19 ♗d4 dc with a winning position; there's little to be done.

18 cd ♘g5! 19 ♕e2 (19 ♕f1 ♕g4) 19...♖ac8! 20 e4

Or 20 ♗xe5 ♕f5 21 ♗f4 (21 ♕b2 ♕xe5) 21...♕xd5 22 ♖f1 ♘e4 and the king can't hide.

20...f5! 21 ef ♖xf5 22 ♖f1 ♖xf1+ 23 ♕xf1 ♕xh2 0-1

Game 155: Nimzo-Indian Defence

This line (4 ♗g5) is known as Spassky's variation; the game won a brilliancy prize.

Spassky-Kinmark
Göteborg 1971

1 d4 ♘f6 2 c4 e6 3 ♘c3 ♗b4 4 ♗g5
0-0 (4...h6!) 5 e3! (5 e4?! c5) 5...d6
6 ♗d3 ♗xc3+ 7 bc e5 8 ♘e2 h6 (8...
♘bd7) 9 ♗xf6!? ♕xf6 10 ♘g3

Prevents ...♗f5. Sokolov gives
Black's reply a ?! mark, suggesting
instead 10...c5, but in that case
White could continue a la Botvinnik
with 11 dc!? dc 12 ♗e4!

10...c6 11 0-0 d5 12 f4! ed (? -
Cafferty; 12...e4) 13 cd ♕e7

Sokolov gives this a ?! and there
can be no doubt 13...dc 14 ♗xc4
♘d7 was more appropriate here.

14 ♕f3 ♘d7?

Even worse is 14...♗g4? 15 ♕xg4!
♕xe3+ 16 ♔h1 ♕xd3 17 ♘f5 etc.
but the text blocks in his Q-bishop.
14...dc 15 ♗xc4 ♗e6 needed a try.

15 cd cd 16 ♘f5 ♕a3 17 ♕g4! (17
♕g3!) 17...g6 18 ♘xh6+ ♔h7 (155)

He's already lost but the best try
was 18...♔g7!? 19 ♘f5+ ♔g8 (19...
♔h8 20 ♕h4+ ♔g8 21 ♕h6! gf 22
♖f3) 20 ♖ad1 ♘f6 21 ♘h6+ ♔g7 22
♕g5 ♘e4 23 ♕xd5! ♘c3 24 ♕g5
♘xd1 25 ♖xd1 threatening 26 f5,
or if 25...♖h8 26 ♘xf7! wins.

155
W

19 ♘xf7!! ♕xd3

Or 19...♖xf7 20 ♕xg6+ ♔h8 21
♕xf7 ♕xd3 22 ♖f3 ♘b6 23 ♖g3,
mating.

20 f5! ♕a6 21 ♘g5+ ♔g8

21...♔g7 is killed by 22 ♘e6+.

22 ♕h6 ♘f6 23 fg (plan ♖xf6) 23...
♔g7 24 ♘h7! 1-0

There was no defence, e.g. 24...
♗d7 25 ♘xf6 ♖xf6 26 ♕h7+ ♔f8
27 g7+.

Game 156: Queen's Indian Defence

Defosse-Frank
Belgium 1977

1 d4 ♘f6 2 c4 e6 3 ♘f3 b6 4 ♘c3
♗b4!?

This might be better termed the
'NIDQID Hybrid' opening since
it can arise via either move order -
cf. game 133.

5 ♕c2 ♗b7 6 e3 ♘e4 7 ♗d3 f5 8
a3?!

Tempo loss. Better was 8 0-0
with a) 8...♗xc3 (theory); b) 8...
♘xc3 9 bc ♗e7 - tempo loss!; c) 8
...♘xc3 9 bc ♗xf3!? when 10 gf is
reminiscent of Janowski-Lasker,
Paris 1909 (which see!), and 10 cb
♕g5!? is quite tricky.

8...♗xc3+ 9 bc 0-0 10 0-0 ♖f6!? 11
♘d2 ♖h6 12 g3? (156)

Natural and wrong. 12 f3! is
playable since 12...♕h4 13 fe gives
Black insufficient, and on 12...
♘xd2 either 13 ♕xd2 ♕h4 14 g3,
or 13 ♗xd2 ♕h4 14 h3 (plan ♗e1)

are safe enough while Black's Q-rook is at home. Now, a thunderbolt.

156
B

12...♕h4!! 13 ♘f3

Not 13 gh ♖g6+ 14 ♔h1 ♘xf2 mate.

13...♘g5!! 14 gh 0-1

14 ♘xh4 ♘h3 mate. After the text, 14...♘xf3+ and now a) 15 ♔h1 ♖xh4! 16 h3 ♘xd4+ with 3 pawns more; b) 15 ♔g2 ♘e1+ 16 ♔h3 ♗g2+ 17 ♔g3 ♖g6+ 18 ♔f4 ♖g4+ 19 ♔e5 with a choice of knight mates.

Game 157: Queen's Indian Defence

Bobotsov-Kolarov
Varna 1971

1 d4 ♘f6 2 c4 e6 3 ♘f3 b6 4 ♘c3 ♗b7 5 ♗g5!? ♗e7 6 ♕c2 c5 7 ♖d1 (7 e3?! ♗xf3) 7...♘c6 8 e3 0-0 9 ♗e2 cd!?

Intending 10 ed d5! with comfortable equality, so White opts for an unclear but dangerous pawn sac instead.

10 ♘xd4!? ♘xd4 11 ♖xd4 ♗xg2 12 ♖g1 ♗c6 13 ♗d3!

Worse than useless is 13 ♗h6? ♘e8 14 ♖dg4 f5! 15 ♖4g3 (15 ♖xg7 ♘xg7 16 ♗xg7 ♖f7) 15...♗f6, whereas now, according to Bobotsov, Black is forced to play 13...g6 14 ♗h6 ♔h8 15 ♗xf8 ♗xf8 when he has adequate compensation for the exchange, but the reason was hard to see -

13...♖e8? 14 ♖h4 g6 *(157)*

157
W

15 ♗xg6!! hg

Or 15...fg 16 ♗xf6 ♗xf6 17 ♖xh7! forcing mate.

16 ♖h6! ♔g7?!

Or 16...♘e4!? 17 ♗xe7 ♕xe7 18 ♘xe4 ♗xe4 19 ♕xe4 ♕b4+ 20 ♔f1 ♕xb2 21 ♖g3! and the attack must win.

17 ♖xg6+ fg 18 ♗h6+! 1-0

Game 158: Queen's Indian Defence

Spassky-Tal
Montreal 1979

1 d4 ♘f6 2 c4 e6 3 ♘f3 b6 4 e3

♗b7 5 ♗d3 d5 6 b3 (6 cd) 6...♗d6
(6...♗b4+!? 7 ♗d2 ♗d6!) 7 0-0 0-0
8 ♗b2 ♘bd7 9 ♘bd2 ♕e7 10 ♖c1
♖ad8!?

A classy waiting move; if 10...
♘e4 11 ♕c2 f5 Black has weakened
e5 whereas White holds f3 in
reserve, but now on 11 ♕e2 ♘e4
Black needn't follow up with ...f5.
11 ♕c2 c5 12 cd
12 ♖fd1 cd 13 ed is met by 13...
♖c8!
**12...ed 13 dc bc 14 ♕c3 ♖fe8 15
♖fd1** *(158)*

Tal gives 15 ♖fe1 c4!? 16 bc ♗b4
17 ♕c2 dc - with the point, presumably, 18 ♗xc4? ♗xf3 19 gf
♗xd2 20 ♕xd2 ♘e5 21 ♕e2 ♖d2!

158
B

15...d4! 16 ed cd 17 ♕a5?
Very embarrassing was 17 ♕xd4
♘e5! but 17 ♘xd4!? should be
tried. Spassky presumably feared
the 'Greek gift' theme 17...♗xh2+?!
18 ♔xh2 ♘g4+ 19 ♔g1 (or 19 ♔g3
♕e5+!?) 19...♕h4 20 ♘4f3 ♕xf2+ -
but it's unsound. I strongly
recommend the reader to exercise
his fantasy on this incredibly
complex position. Tal himself

intended (17 ♘xd4) 17...♕e5! 18
♘f3 ♕h5 with an attack.
**17...♘e5 18 ♘xe5 (18 ♖e1) 18...
♗xe5 19 ♘c4**
Or 19 ♘f1 ♘d5 20 ♘g3 ♘f4 21
♗f1 h5! (Tal) and White's king will
be pulverised. It's over now.
19...♖d5! 20 ♕d2
Or 20 ♗a3 ♕e6 21 ♕d2 ♗xh2+!
22 ♔xh2 ♖h5+ 23 ♔g1 ♖h1+! 24
♔xh1 ♕h3+.
**20...♗xh2+! 21 ♔xh2 ♖h5+ 22
♔g1 ♘g4 0-1**

Game 159: Queen's Indian Defence

**Korchnoi-Karpov
21st game, Candidates Final
Moscow 1974**

**1 d4 ♘f6 2 ♘f3 e6 3 g3 b6 4 ♗g2
♗b7 5 c4 ♗e7**

Modest. 5...♗b4+ 6 ♗d2 ♗e7 is
supposed to misplace White's Q-
bishop, although W.Müller-Dr.Vajs,
Euro Master (corres) 1979 isn't an
advert: 7 0-0 0-0 8 ♘c3 d5 9 cd
♘xd5?! 10 ♖c1 ♘d7 11 ♘xd5 ♗xd5
12 ♕c2 c5?! 13 e4 ♗b7 14 ♗c3
♖c8 15 ♖fd1 cd 16 ♘xd4 a6 17
♗h3! ♖c7?! 18 ♘xe6! 1-0 (18...fe
19 ♗xe6 ♕h8 20 ♗xg7+!).
**6 ♘c3 0-0 (6...♘e4) 7 ♕c2 c5 8 d5!
ed 9 ♘g5 ♘c6?!**

Allowing a piece to settle on d5.
Also unhelpful was 9...h6?! 10
♘xd5 and 10...hg? 11 ♘xe7+ or 10
...♗xd5 11 ♗xd5 favour White. 9...

g6 is recommended by Matanović.
10 ᐧxd5 g6 11 ♕d2! ᐧxd5?! 12 ♗xd5 ♖b8? *(159)*

This is all based on an oversight. Necessary was 12...♗xg5 13 ♕xg5 ♕xg5 14 ♗xg5, although the bishop pair and Black's backward d-pawn ensure Black much the worse of it.

159
W

13 ᐧxh7! ♖e8
A way of resigning. The trick goes 13...♔xh7 14 ♕h6+ ♔g8 15 ♕xg6+! ♔h8 16 ♕h6+ ♔g8 17 ♗e4! f5 18 ♗d5+ ♖f7 19 ♕g6+.
14 ♕h6 ᐧe5 15 ᐧg5 ♗xg5 16 ♗xg5 ♕xg5 17 ♕xg5 ♗xd5 18 0-0 (18 cd?? ᐧf3+!) **18...♗c4 19 f4 1-0**

Game 160: King's Indian, 4 Pawns Attack

Orienter, supposedly non-playing captain of the Austrian team, decided his bottom board was off colour, and that he's better have a go himself...

Orienter-Toran
Madrid 1971

1 d4 ᐧf6 2 c4 g6 3 ᐧc3 ♗g7 4 e4 d6 5 f4!? 0-0 6 ♗e2 c5 7 d5 e6 8 ᐧf3 ed 9 e5!? (wild) **9...de 10 fe ᐧg4 11 ♗g5 ♕d7?**
He should not avoid equalising by 11...f6! 12 ef ♗xf6; the text costs too much development.
12 ᐧxd5 ᐧxe5? (12...ᐧc6) **13 ᐧxe5 ♗xe5 14 ♗f6!**
Threatening ᐧe7+, and if 14...ᐧc6? 15 ♗xe5 ᐧxe5 16 ᐧf6+ wins.
14...♗d6 15 ♕d2 ♖e8 16 ♗c3! ♗e7 17 ♕h6 f6 18 0-0 ᐧc6 *(160)*
Black's in a horrific way now.

160
W

19 ♖xf6! ᐧd4 20 ♗g4! ♕d8
Or 20...♕xg4 21 ᐧxe7+ and mates on f8.
21 ♖f7! ♔xf7 22 ♕xh7+ ♔f8 23 ♗xd4 1-0

Game 161: King's Indian, Sämisch

Platonov-Shamkovich
39th USSR Ch, Leningrad 1971

1 c4 g6 2 ᐧc3 ♗g7 3 d4 d6 4 e4 ᐧf6 5 f3 ᐧc6

The Sämisch Panno proper is 5...
0-0 6 ♗e3 ♘c6.

6 ♗e3 a6 7 ♘ge2 ♖b8 8 ♘c1 e5 9 d5?

Korchnoi prefers 9 ♘b3 with a small plus to White; the text allows a thematic pawn offer seeking black square play - which is obscure and should probably be put to the test, though who likes defending?

9...♘d4! 10 ♘1e2 c5! 11 dc bc 12 ♘xd4

Black also retains the initiative after 12 ♕d2.

12...ed 13 ♗xd4 ♖xb2 14 ♘b5? *(161)*

Misconcieved! 14 ♕c1, driving the rook back, is Korchnoi's sensible suggestion; this 'exchange win' backfires elegantly.

161
B

14...♘xe4!! 15 ♗xb2

Or 15 ♗xg7 ♕a5+ 16 ♘c3 ♘xc3 and 17 ♕d3 ♘e4+ 18 ♔d1 ♘f2+, or 17 ♕c1 ♘e4+ 18 ♗c3 (18 ♔d1 ♘f2 mate!) 18...♕xc3+ with an extra piece.

15...♕a5+ 16 ♘c3

Not 16 ♔e2 ♗xb2 17 fe ♗g4+.

16...♗xc3+ 17 ♗xc3 ♕xc3+ 18 ♔e2 ♗e6! 0-1

Game 162: King's Indian, Sämisch

**Korchnoi-Balashov
Moscow 1971**

1 d4 ♘f6 2 c4 g6 3 ♘c3 ♗g7 4 e4 d6 5 f3 e5 6 ♘ge2 c6 7 ♗g5 ♕a5 8 ♕d2 ♘bd7 9 d5 cd 10 cd h6?

Feeble tempo-loss; he should castle.

11 ♗e3 a6 12 ♘g3 h5 13 ♗d3 ♘h7 14 0-0 0-0 15 a4 ♘c5? *(162)*

Losing the exchange! Kotov suggests 15...♕d8 16 a5 ♘df6 17 ♘a4 and naturally White's progress on the Q-side ensures him much the better of it.

162
W

16 b4! ♕xb4 17 a5 ♗h6!?

The trap springs shut after 17...♘b3 18 ♕b2 and ♖a4; another way was 17...♘xd3 18 ♕xd3 with the threat of ♖b1 and if 18...b5 19 ab (else ...♕c4) 19...a5 20 ♖a4! ♗a6 21 ♕d2 ♕b3 22 ♖b1.

18 ♗xh6 ♘b3?!

Relatively best, though still losing, was 18...♕d4+ 19 ♔h1 ♕xd3 20 ♕xd3 ♘xd3 21 ♗xf8.

19 ♕b2 ♕d4+ 20 ♖f2! ♘xa1 21 ♗xf8 h4 (21...♔xf8 22 ♗f1) 22 ♘ge2 1-0

On 22...♕xd3 23 ♘c1! and 24 ♗xd6 the knight remains trapped.

Game 163: King's Indian, Sämisch

This game was repeated move for move in Jansen-Vangelov, Albena 1978!

Stefanov-Andreyev
Bulgaria 1975

1 d4 ♘f6 2 c4 g6 3 ♘c3 ♗g7 4 e4 d6 5 f3 0-0 6 ♗g5 (6 ♗e3) 6...c5! 7 d5 ♕a5 8 ♕d2 a6 9 0-0-0?
Suicidal.
9...b5 10 cb ab 11 ♗xb5 ♗a6 12 ♗a4!? ♘xe4?!
Not best, since White could reply 13 fe ♗xc3 14 ♕xc3 ♕xa4 15 ♗h6 winning the exchange, and on 15... f6 16 ♗xf8 ♔xf8 17 ♘f3 ♕xa2 18 ♘g5!
13 ♘xe4? ♕xa4 14 ♔b1? *(163)*

163
B

14...♕xa2+!! 15 ♔xa2 ♗d3+ 16 ♔b3 c4+ 17 ♔b4 ♘a6+ 18 ♔b5 ♖fb8+ 19 ♔c6 ♖c8+ 20 ♔b7
Or 20 ♔d7 ♖c7 mate; 20 ♔b6 ♗d4+; 20 ♔b5 ♘c7+ 21 ♔c6 (21 ♔b4 ♖cb8 mate; 21 ♔b6 ♖ab8+ meeting 22 ♔a5 or 22 ♔a7 with 22...♖b5 and 23...♖a8 mate, and 22 ♔c6 with 22...♘e6 and 23...♖c7 mate.) 21...♘e6+ 22 ♔b7 ♖cb8+ 23 ♔c6 ♘d8+ 24 ♔d7 ♖b7+ 25 ♔e8 ♘e6 mate.
20...♖c7+! 21 ♔xa8 ♗d4 0-1

Game 164: King's Indian, Fianchetto

Delfaro-Browne
USA 1976

1 ♘f3 ♘f6 2 g3 g6 3 ♗g2 ♗g7 4 0-0 0-0 5 c4 d6 6 d4 ♘bd7 7 ♘c3 e5 8 e4 ed
Now it is important for White to play h3 at some point during the next four moves. A similar lapse occurred in Knudsen-Reshevsky, Esbjerg 1979; 8...c6 9 ♖b1?! a5 10 b3?! ♖e8 11 ♖e1 ed 12 ♘xd4 ♘g4! 13 f3 ♕b6! 14 ♘ce2 ♘ge5 15 ♗e3 ♘c5 16 ♕d2 ♕b4! 17 ♘c3 a4 18 a3 ♕xa3!! 19 ♘c2 ♕xb3 20 ♖xb3 ♘xb3 and Black won very prettily.
9 ♘xd4 ♖e8 10 ♖e1 ♘c5 (10...c6) 11 ♖b1?! a5 12 b3?! c6 13 a3?

♘g4! 14 b4?

Awful! 14 ♗e3 was called for; on 14 ♘de2? Browne intended 14...♘xf2! 15 ♔xf2 ♘xc3 16 ♘xc3 ♕f6+ 17 ♕f3 ♘d3+!

14...ab 15 ab ♕f6! 16 ♘de2

Best was 16 ♗e3 but after 16...♘xe3 17 fe White was busted anyway. The rest of the game is a mopping up cavalry charge.

16...♕xf2+ 17 ♔h1 *(164)*

164
B

17...♘d3! 18 ♖f1 ♗xc3! 19 ♖b3

On 19 ♕xd3 ♗xf1+! wins the exchange, and 19 ♘xc3 ♕d4 20 ♕f3 allows a new twist in the old theme; 20...♘(either)f2+ 21 ♔g1 ♘h3+ 22 ♔h1 ♕g1+!

19...♘e1! 20 ♖xf2 0-1

Game 165: King's Indian, Fianchetto

Romanishin-Grünfeld
Riga Interzonal 1979

1 c4 ♘f6 2 g3 g6 3 ♗g2 ♗g7 4 d4 0-0 5 ♘f3 d6 6 0-0 ♘c6!? 7 ♘c3 a6

8 b3!?

The old way of playing the Panno - 8 d5 ♘a5 9 ♘d2 - still looks good but the text is both flexible and fashionable.

8...♖b8 9 ♗b2 b5 10 cb ab 11 ♖c1 ♘a5

Better seems to be Adorjan's novelty from his 1979 match with Ribli - 11...b4 12 ♘b1 ♘a7! Now Romanishin produces an effective novelty of his own.

12 ♕c2! ♗b7 13 ♖fd1 (13 ♘xb5?? ♗e4) **13...♕d7 14 e4 b4 15 e5! bc**

Romanishin and A.Petrosian both suggest 15...♘e8 as an interesting alternative.

16 ♗xc3! ♗h6 *(165)*

Instead 16...♘c6 is met by 17 ef followed by d5 'fixing' Black's weak c pawn.

165
W

17 ef! ♗xc1 18 ♕xc1 ♗xf3

Black's outlook is grim, e.g. 18...♘c6 19 d5 ♘e5 20 ♘xe5 ♘xe5 21 ♗xe5 with a terrible black-square grip and 2 pawns for the exchange. **19 ♗xf3 ♕f5** (19...♘c6? 20 ♗xc6 ♕xc6 21 d5) **20 fe! ♖fe8 21 ♕e3 ♖b6 22 d5 ♘b7 23 g4! 1-0**

After 23...♕d7 24 ♕d4 forces
mate.

Game 166: King's Indian, Classical

White in this game is Tom
Timman - Jan's brother. No mean
player himself, but up against a
'mean' Cvetković.

T.Timman-Cvetković
Graz Students Olympiad 1972

1 c4 ♘f6 2 ♘f3 g6 3 ♘c3 ♗g7 4 e4
d6 5 d4 0-0 6 ♗e2 e5 7 0-0 ♘c6 8
d5 ♘e7 9 ♘e1 ♘e8!? 10 ♘d3 f5 11
f4!?
The energetic reaction to Black's
9th, which gives less central control
than 9...♘d7. Black's reply is a
novelty, according to Sokolov, who
recites 11...ef 12 ♗xf4 fe (12...
♗xc3?! 13 bc fe 14 ♗g5!) 13 ♘xe4
and White is slightly better.
11...c6!? 12 ef?!
More natural was 12 fe.
12...cd!? 13 fe
Complex and obscure play would
arise from 13 fg!? dc!? (13...♘xg6
14 ♘xd5) 14 gh+ ♔h8.
13...♗xf5 14 ♘xd5 de 15 ♘c5?
More apposite seems Sokolov's
15 ♘f2, also aiming at e4 but
reserving c5 as a reply to ♘d6.
Now White stands badly, controlling neither e4 nor d4.
15...♘ed6 16 ♗d3 ♕h4!
This threatens the powerful 17...

♕d4+.
17 ♗xf5 ♗xf5 18 b3?! *(166)*

166
B

18...♗c2!
Simple, but hard to see. If 19
♕xc2? ♖xf1+ 20 ♔xf1 ♖f8+ wins;
21 ♔g1 ♕e1 mate, or 21 ♔e2 ♖f2+.
**19 ♖xf8+ ♖xf8 20 ♕e2 ♕d4+ 21
♘e3 ♕xa1 22 ♕c2 ♗h6! 0-1**

Game 167: King's Indian, Classical

Ghitescu-J.Timman
Wijk aan Zee 1974

1 d4 ♘f6 2 c4 g6 3 ♘c3 ♗g7 4 e4
d6 5 ♘f3 0-0 6 ♗e2 e5 7 0-0 ♘c6 8
d5 ♘e7 9 ♘e1 ♘d7 10 f3 f5 11 g4!?
To block the K-side; now 11...
f4? 12 h4! (to meet ...g5 by h5 or
...h5 by g5) means that White could
play on the Q-side with no attack
to fear as also after 11...h5? 12 g5
or 11...fg 12 fg.
11...♘f6 12 ♘d3 c6!
Keeping fluid play. White should
reply 13 ♘f2; 13 ♔g2 can be met

by 13...b5!
13 ♔h1? *(167)*

13...fg 14 fg ♘xg4! 15 ♖xf8+ ♕xf8 16 c5

Ineffectual was 16 ♗xg4 ♗xg4 17 ♕xg4 ♕f1+ 18 ♔g1 ♕xd3 19 ♗g5 ♕f3+.

16...♘f2+ 17 ♘xf2 ♕xf2 18 cd ♗h3! 19 ♗f3

On 19 ♔g1 Timman intended 19 ...♕xg1+ 20 ♔xg1 ♘c8 21 dc bc 22 ♗e3 ♘xd6 23 ♖d1 ♗f8.

19...♘c8 20 dc bc 21 d7 ♗xd7 22 ♕xd7? ♕f1 mate

A collapse, but 22 ♔e2 ♕xe2 23 ♗xe2 ♗e6 24 ♗e3 ♘b6 25 ♖d1 ♗f8 gives a sound extra pawn ans an easy GM victory.

Game 168: King's Indian, Petrosian

Sakins-Dambitis
Corres, Lithuania 1978

1 d4 ♘f6 2 c4 g6 3 ♘c3 ♗g7 4 e4 d6 5 ♘f3 0-0 6 ♗e2 e5 7 d5 ♘bd7

8 ♗e3

The idea behind Petrosian's variation - typified by 7 d5 - is to induce a weakening of the white squares in Black's K-side by 8 ♗g5 h6 9 ♗h4 g5 10 ♗g3.

8...♘g4!? 9 ♗d2?

Still best was 9 ♗g5 f6 10 ♗h4 etc.

9...f5! 10 h3? *(168)*

Asking for it, but the natural 10 ♘g5 ♘c5! 11 b4 fails to 11...f4! when either 12 ♗xg4 ♘d3+! 13 ♔e2 ♗xg4+ 14 f3 ♕xg5, or 12 ♘xh7 ♕h4! 13 ♗xg4 ♘d3+ 14 ♔e2 ♘xf2! 15 ♕e1 ♗xg4+ 16 ♔f1 f3! favour Black.

10...♘xf2!! 11 ♔xf2 fe 12 ♘xe4 ♕h4+ 13 ♔e3

13 ♘g3 is met by 13...♘c5!

13...♗h6+ 14 ♔d3 ♕xe4+!

The point; 15 ♔xe4 ♘c5 mate! Now it's a rout.

15 ♔c3 ♗g7! 16 ♖f1

Or 16 ♗d3 ♖xf3! 17 ♕xf3 ♕d4+ and 18...e4! winning.

16...♘c5 17 b4 ♖xf3+! 18 gf

No better is 18 ♖xf3 ♕d4+ 19 ♔c2 e4.

18...♕d4+ 0-1
The end is 19 ♔c2 ♗f5+.

Game 169: King's Indian, Smyslov

A spectacular game, not because of sacrifices (there are none) but because of the ease with which a former world champion drifts into a lost position through, apparently, 'playing for the draw'.

**Smyslov-Bronstein
Teesside 1975**

1 d4 ♘f6 2 ♘f3 g6 3 c4 ♗g7 4 ♘c3 0-0 5 ♗g5!?
This ultra-solid plan (of strong-pointing the d4 square) is Smyslov's patent.
5...d6 6 e3 c5!? 7 ♗e2 ♘c6 8 0-0 ♗f5 9 dc?
Abandons all hope of advantage. 9 d5!? was correct.
9...dc 10 ♕xd8?! (10 ♘d2) 10... ♖fxd8 11 ♖ad1 *(169)*

Krnić's 11 ♗xf6 ♗xf6 12 e4 also favours Black (control of d4 - utter defeat for Smyslov's opening strategy).
11...♘e4! 12 ♘xe4 ♗xe4 13 b3 h6 14 ♗f4?!
A little better was 14 ♗h4. Now White is virtually lost as the Black pieces surround his vulnerable Q-side.
14...♘b4! 15 a3 ♘a2! 16 ♖xd8+ ♖xd8 17 ♖d1 ♖xd1+ 18 ♗xd1 ♘c3 19 ♘d2 ♗d3! 0-1
He loses a piece, i.e. 20 ♗g4 f5 21 ♗h3 e5 22 ♗g3 f4! (and ...♘e2+); 20 ♗f3 e5 21 ♗g3 e4! 22 ♗g4 f5 23 ♗h3 ♘e2+ 24 ♔h1 ♘xg3+ and 25 ♗c3.

Game 170: Benoni Defence

**Donner-Planinc
Wijk aan Zee 1973**

1 d4 ♘f6 2 c4 c5 3 d5 e6 4 ♘c3 ed 5 cd d6 6 ♘f3 g6 7 ♘d2!? (7 e4) 7 ...♗g7
A 'sane' ploy against White's plan is Trifunović's 7...♘bd7 8 ♘c4 ♘b6 9 e4 ♘xc4 10 ♗xc4 ♗g7 etc. The inimitable Planinc has other ideas.
8 ♘c4 0-0 9 ♗f4 b6!?
Here goes. 10 ♘xd6? loses a piece after 10...♘h5 11 ♘xc8 ♘xf4. An intriguing alternative is the 'waiting' 10 e3!?
10 ♗xd6 ♖e8 11 ♗g3 ♘e4 12 ♘xe4 ♖xe4 13 e3 b5! 14 ♘d6 ♖b4 15 ♗xb5

15 ♕f3?! is inaccuate.
15...♗f8! 16 ♗c6 *(170)*
Not 16 ♘xc8⁻♖xb5 winning a piece.

170
B

16...♗a6!
Giving White a chance to go wrong; the best reply is 17 ♕d2 allowing ...♘xc6 with complex play.
17 ♗xa8?! ♖xb2 18 ♕a4?
Prevents ...♕a5+ but essential was 18 ♘e4 when it's muddy though maybe 18...♕a5+ 19 ♘d2 ♗d3! stopping ♖b1 and threatening ...c4 is effective.
18...♕f6! 19 ♖c1
Other moves are met by ...♖e2+ or ...♕c3+.
19...♗xd6 20 f4 ♕f5! 21 e4 ♖e2+ 22 ♔d1 ♕h5 0-1

Game 171: Grünfeld Defence

Knaak-Forintos
Skopje Olympiad 1972

1 d4 ♘f6 2 c4 g6 3 ♘c3 d5 4 ♘f3
♗g7 5 ♗g5 ♘e4 6 cd ♘xg5 7 ♘xg5 e6 8 ♕a4+
Keeping an extra pawn, since 8...♗d7 can be met by 9 ♕b3 (9...♕xg5? 10 ♕xb7). More modest alternatives, such as 8 ♘f3 or 8 ♕d2, don't seem to compensate White for the 'minor exchange'.
8...c6! 9 dc ♘xc6 10 ♘f3 ♗d7 11 0-0-0 (11 e3? ♘xd4) **11...0-0** (11... ♘xd4? 12 ♖xd4) **12 e3?! *(171)***
The Hungarian had prepared a TN here; a queen move was necessary.

171
B

12...♘xd4!
Now it's good. Forintos puts forward 13 ♕a3 ♘xf3 14 gf ♖e8 with advantage to Black, but the sacrifice needed testing:
13 ♖xd4(?) ♗xa4 14 ♖xd8 ♖fxd8 15 ♘xa4 ♖ac8+ 16 ♘c3
16 ♔b1?? is a disaster in view of 16...♖d1 mate.
16...♗xc3 17 bc ♖xc3+ 18 ♔b2 ♖dc8
Black's winning because more pawns must fall and the K-bishop is hard to develop. Now if 19 ♘e1 ♖3c6! 20 ♘d3 ♖b6+ 21 ♔a1 ♖c2

and ...♖d2 (Forintos).

19 ♘d4 e5 20 ♘b3 ♖c2+ 21 ♔b1 ♖xf2 22 ♘c1 e4 23 ♗b5 0-1

The pawns all drop, e.g. 23...♖8c2 24 ♗d7 ♖xg2 25 h3 f5 and ...♖h2.

Game 172: Grünfeld Defence

Knaak-Uhlmann
East German Ch 1979

1 d4 ♘f6 2 c4 g6 3 ♘c3 d5 4 cd ♘xd5 5 e4 ♘xc3 6 bc ♗g7 7 ♗c4 0-0 8 ♗e3 b6?!

This is too slow - 8...c5 was correct.

9 h4!? ♗b7 10 ♕f3 ♕d7 11 ♘e2

Not 11 h5 ♕c6!, but now if 11...♕c6?? 12 ♗d5.

11...h5 12 ♗g5 ♘c6 13 ♘f4! e6

Forced, since 13...♘a5 allows 14 ♘xg6, and 13...♔h7/8 14 ♘xh5 gh 15 ♕xh5+ ♔g8 16 ♖h3 etc.

14 ♖d1!? ♘a5 15 ♗d3 c5? *(172)*

He had to divert White's attention with 15...♕c6.

172 W

16 ♘xh5! gh 17 ♗f6!

Threatening 18 ♕g3 winning.

17...♗xf6 18 ♕xf6 ♕d8 19 ♕h6 f6

On 19...f5, keeping ...f4 as a defence against ♖h3, Benko gives 20 ♕g6+! ♔h8 21 ♕xh5+ ♔g8 (21...♔g7 22 ♖h3 f4 23 e5) 22 ef ef (22...♕e7 23 f6! ♖xf6 24 ♖h3) 23 ♕g6+ ♔h8 24 ♕h6+ ♔g8 25 ♗xf5! ♕e7+ 26 ♗e6+ winning.

20 ♕g6+ ♔h8 21 e5 f5

Or 21...♕e7 22 ♕h6+ (22 ♖h3?! f5!) 22...♔g8 23 ♖h3 ♖f7 24 ♖g3+ ♔g7 25 ♕h7+! ♔f8 26 ♕h8+.

22 ♕h6+ ♔g8 23 ♖h3 ♔f7 24 ♖g3 1-0

'Best' is 24...♕c8 25 ♖g7+ ♔e8 26 ♗b5+ ♗/♘c6 27 ♕g6+ ♔d8 28 dc+.

Game 173: Leningrad Dutch

Vadasz-Holzl
Hungary-Austria 1974

1 ♘f3 g6 2 d4 f5 3 h4!?

Aggressive and unsettling, although a classicist would term it premature (cf. game 26).

3...♘f6 4 h5 ♘xh5

Better than 4...♗g7 5 hg hg 6 ♖xh8+ ♗xh8 when 7 ♘e5 gives White the initiative.

5 ♖xh5!? gh 6 e4!? d6?

Not 6...fe?? 7 ♘e5 winning outright. Florian suggests 6...♗g7! 7 ♘h4 0-0 8 ♘xf5 with about equal practical chances.

7 ♘g5! c6 8 ♕xh5+ ♔d7 *(173)*

173
W

9 ♘e6! ♕b6

Now 9...♕e8 (the answer to 9 ♘f7) is met by either 10 ♕xf5 or 10 ♕xe8+ ♔xe8 11 ♘c7+; 9... ♔xe6?? 10 ♕xf5 is mate, and whether 9...♕a5+ 10 ♗d2 ♕b6 is superior is a moot point; White's position looks winning now.

10 ♘d2 ♕a5 11 c3! ♘a6

Or 11...♔xe6 12 b4! wins. The critical try was 11...b5 when 12 ♕xf5 ♔e8 (12...♗h6 13 ♘b3) 13 ♕h5+ ♔d7 14 ♘c4! ♕a4/a6 15 ♘e5+ and 16 ♘c5+ does the trick.

12 ♘c4 ♕b5 13 ♘e5+ dc 14 ♗xb5 cb 15 ♕xf5 ♔e8 16 ♕xe5 ♖g8 17 ♕h5+ ♔d7 18 ♕b5 1-0

Game 174: Catalan

Sosonko-Hübner
Tilburg 1979

1 d4 ♘f6 2 c4 e6 3 g3!? d5 (3... c5!?) 4 ♗g2 dc 5 ♘f3 a6 6 0-0 b5

Sosonko gives this a ?!; 6...♘c6 was possibly a better try.

7 ♘e5 ♘d5 8 ♘c3 c6

Again probably inaccurate; 8... ♗b7 should be tried.

9 ♘xd5 ed

Instead 9...cd 10 e4 ♗b7 11 ♕h5! is very dangerous, i.e. 11...g6 12 ♘xg6! fg 13 ♕e5 ♖g8 14 ♕xe6+, or 11...♕e7 12 ed ♗xd5 13 ♗xd5 ed 14 ♖e1 winning. No better was 9... cd 10 e4 ♗e7 11 ed ed 12 ♘xf7! ♔xf7 13 ♕h5+ ♔f8 (13...g6 14 ♕xd5+; 13...♔e6 14 ♖e1+) 14 ♗xd5 winning.

10 e4 ♗e6 11 a4! b4

Against 11...♗e7 Sosonko had intended 12 ab cb 13 ed ♗xd5 14 ♘xf7! ♔xf7 15 ♕h5+. Clearly Black's position is already very ropey.

12 ed ♗xd5?

Necessary was 12...cd allowing White an attractive choice between 13 ♘xc4 of 13 f4!? continuing his attack.

13 ♕g4! h5 *(174)*

Or 13...♗xg2 14 ♖e1, or 13...♗e6 14 ♕h5 threatening ♘xc6.

174
W

14 ♗xd5! cd

Instead 14...hg 15 ♗xf7+ ♔e7 16

♗g5+ loses a piece, and 14...♕xd5 15 ♕c8+, a rook. There's nothing left.
15 ♕f5! ♖a7 16 ♖e1 ♖e7 17 ♗g5 g6 18 ♗xe7 1-0

Game 175: English

Here Vaganian apparently falls victim of an opening transposition whilst avoiding Planinc's favourite Benoni; the end position is dazzling.

Vaganian-Planinc
Hastings 1974/5

1 d4 ♘f6 2 c4 c5 3 ♘f3 cd 4 ♘xd4 e6 5 ♘c3 ♗b4!? 6 ♘b5
Dubious, according to Vaganian, since Black can equalise now or soon with ...d5. He gives 6 ♗d2 or 6 g3.
6...0-0 7 a3 ♗xc3+ 8 ♘xc3 d5 9 ♗g5 h6!? 10 ♗xf6 (10 ♗h4) 10...♕xf6 11 cd ed 12 ♕xd5?!
This is far too risky; best was 12 e3.
12...♖d8 13 ♕f3?
Black's initiative now becomes serious; 13 ♕b3 was called for.
13...♕b6! 14 ♖d1 ♖xd1+ 15 ♘xd1 ♘c6 16 ♕e3?!
Counterplay isn't on; Vaganian doesn't criticise this, but 16 e3 must be better when play might go 16...♗e6 17 ♗e2 ♖d8 18 0-0 ♖d2 with considerable pressure.
16...♘d4! 17 ♕e8+ ♔h7 18 e3

♘c2+ 19 ♔d2 *(175)*

19...♗f5!! 20 ♕xa8 ♕d6+ 21 ♔c1 ♘a1!
The threat is ...♘b3 mate and leading to a very pretty finish. But White is lost now, e.g. 22 ♗c4 ♕c5 23 b3 ♘xb3+ etc., or 22 b4 ♘b3+ 23 ♔b2 ♕d2+! 24 ♔xb3 ♕c2 mate.
22 ♕xb7 ♕c7+! 0-1

Game 176: English

Stean-Filguth
Sao Paulo 1979

1 c4 ♘f6 2 ♘c3 e6 3 ♘f3 b6 4 e4 ♗b7 5 ♗d3!?
Convolutions of this sort are only permitted in blocked positions - cf. game 71.
5...d6· 6 ♗c2 c5 7 d4 cd 8 ♘xd4 ♗e7 9 0-0 0-0 10 b3! ♘c6 11 ♗b2 ♕d7 (11...a6) 12 ♘xc6 ♗xc6 13 ♕d3 ♖fc8 14 ♖ae1!
White has developed well against this 'universal system' and is poised to attack - the threat is 15 ♘d5! ed

16 ed ♗b7 17 ♗xf6 and 18 ♕xh7+.
14...g6 15 f4 a6?! 16 ♕e2! ♖a7

Against 16...b5 Byrne and Mednis give 17 ♘d5! ed 18 ed ♘xd5 19 cd ♗xd5 20 f5 ♖e8 21 ♕d2 ♕b7 22 fg fg 23 ♕c3, mating.

17 ♖d1 ♕c7 18 f5 gf *(176)*

176
W

19 ♘d5!! ♘xd5

The main line runs 19...ed 20 ed ♗a8 21 ♖xf5 ♘e8 22 ♕g4+ ♔f8 23 ♖xf7+! ♔xf7 24 ♕e6+ ♔f8 25 ♖f1+ ♗f6 26 ♗xf6 ♘xf6 27 ♕xf6+ ♔g8 28 ♗f5! Black has 'pinned' his hopes on the c-file but to no avail.

20 ed ♗xd5 21 ♖xd5! ed 22 ♗xf5 ♕c5+

Or 22...♖b8 23 ♕g4+ ♔f8 24 ♕g7+ ♔e8 25 ♕g8+ ♗f8 26 ♖e1+.

23 ♔h1 d4 24 ♕g4+ 1-0

Ivkov mentions 6...♘c6 7 ♗xc6+! - the value of a tempo (cf. game 127).

7 ♘f3 f6 8 ♘d2 ♕d7!? 9 0-0 ♗e7 10 ♘c4 ♘c6 11 ♕a4

Another interesting try is 11 f4!?

11...♘d8 12 ♕xd7+ ♔xd7?

An odd decision leaving him in a tangle.

13 ♗e3 ♘c6 14 ♖ac1 ♘a6?! (14... b6!?) 15 ♘d5! ♘d4?! 16 ♗xd4 ed 17 ♖fe1!? (17 ♘cb6+!?) 17...♖b8 18 e3 de 19 ♖xe3 ♗d8 20 ♖ce1 ♘b4 *(177)*

He was too far gone for a defence now, i.e. 20...♘c7 21 ♖e7+.

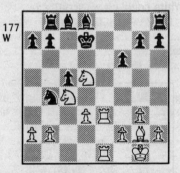

177
W

21 ♗h3+! ♔c6 22 ♖e6+! ♗xe6 23 ♖xe6+ ♔d7

No better was 23...♔xd5 24 ♖d6 mate! nor 23...♔b5 24 ♘c3 mate!

24 ♖xf6+! 1-0

Game 177: English

Ivkov-Dunkelblum
Caorle 1972

1 c4 ♘f6 2 ♘c3 c5 3 g3 d5 4 cd ♘xd5 5 ♗g2 ♘c7 6 d3 e5

Game 178: English

Suba-Roos
Buenos Aires Olympiad 1978

1 c4 ♘f6 2 ♘c3 d5 3 cd ♘xd5 4 g3

g6 5 ♗g2 ♘xc3 6 bc ♗g7 7 h4!?
(7 ♖b1) 7...♘d7 8 ♕b3!?

Suba considers 8 h5 gh 9 ♖xh5
♘f6 unclear, but the isolated h-
pawn doesn't add to Black's
position.

8...c5 9 ♗a3 ♕c7 10 h5 ♖b8!? 11
♘f3 b5 12 hg hg 13 ♖xh8+ ♗xh8
14 ♘g5 e6?!

Black had better chances to resist
after 14...♘e5 15 f4 ♗f6!?

15 ♘xe6! ♕e5!?

On 15...fe 16 ♕xe6+ ♔f8 17 ♗d5
♘e5 18 ♗xc5+! ♔g7 19 ♕d6 the
pawn mass favours White.

16 ♘f4 b4 17 d4!

White could blow everything with
17 ♗b2? which Black meets with
17...bc 18 ♗xc3 ♖xb3 19 ♗xe5
♗xe5.

17...♕d6 18 cb ♕xd4 (178)

178
W

19 ♖c1!!

A piece sac. If 19 ♖d1 ♕c3+ 20
♕xc3 ♗xc3+ 21 ♔f1 cb would be
quite O.K. for Black.

19...cb 20 e3 ♕g7?

Suba gives the exciting 20...♘c5!
21 ♕xb4! ♕xb4! (21...♖xb4 22 ed)
22 ♗xb4 ♖xb4 23 ♖xc5 ♗a6 and

White is a pawn up.

21 ♕xb4! ♕e5

No good was 21...♖xb4 22 ♖xc8+
♔e7 23 ♗xb4+ ♔f6 24 ♗c3+ ♘e5
25 ♖e8!

22 ♘d3! ♕f6 23 ♗h3! 1-0

White threatens 24 ♗xd7+, and
23...♖xb4 24 ♖xc8+ costs a piece,
while 23...♔d8 24 ♕c4 ♕a6 loses
fastest to 25 ♕xf7 ♕xa3 26 ♖xc8+!

Game 179: English

A 'quiet' game in which White
doesn't attack, he just carries out
his positional theme. Yet, how
many players can do that?

**Andersson-Westerinen
Geneva 1977**

1 c4 ♘f6 2 ♘f3 g6 3 g3 ♗g7 4 ♗g2
0-0 5 0-0 d6 6 ♘c3 ♘c6 7 d3!? e5 8
♖b1 a5 9 a3 ♗d7

Another idea is 9...♗f5 intending
...♕d7, and 9...h6 is not without
merit.

**10 b4 ab 11 ab ♕c8 12 ♗g5!
♗h3?!** (179)

179
W

This allows White to force an 'uglification' in the Black position.
13 🖤xf6! 🖤xf6 14 ♘d5 🖤d8
Not 14...🖤g7? because of 15 b5!
15 🖤xh3 ♛xh3 16 🏰a1! 🏰xa1?
He should play the passive 16...🏰b8 since White is now able to penetrate the Q-side.
17 ♛xa1 ♛c8
Necessary to prevent 18 ♛a8.
18 b5 ♘b8
Or 18...♘e7 19 ♘f6+ ♚h8 20 d4! breaking through the centre.
19 ♛a8 🏰e8 20 🏰a1 e4?!
This loses material, but a solid defence was hard to find, e.g. 20...c6 21 ♘c3 🖤b6 22 ♘e4 and the whole world is en pris.
21 de 🏰xe4 22 🏰a7 🏰xc4 23 ♚g2! 1-0
Now, for example, 23...c6 24 🏰xb7 wins a piece, whereas 23 🏰xb7? ♛h3! lets Black hold on.

Game 180: English

Kaufman-Kavalek
USA Ch, New York 1972

1 c4 e5 2 ♘c3 d6 3 ♘f3 🖤g4!? 4 d4 ♘d7
This is a sort of Old Indian Defence with ...🖤g4 thrown in to give increased control over d4; hence White's modest follow-up.
5 e3 ♘gf6 6 🖤e2 c6 7 h3 🖤h5 8 de?!
Reducing the central tension and allowing Black to establish a space

advantage. Byrne suggests 8 g4!? 🖤g6 9 ♘h4 or 8 ♘h4!?
8...de 9 0-0 e4! 10 ♘d2?!
Correct was 10 ♘d4.
10...🖤g6 11 b3?!
Allows Black's attacking manoeuvre but Byrne's 11 ♛c2 ♛e7 12 b4!, so that if 12...♛e5 13 c5, seems well answered by 12...a5!
11...♛c7 12 ♛c2 ♛e5 13 🏰d1 🖤d6 14 ♘f1 0-0 15 🖤b2 ♛e7 16 🏰d2 ♘e5 17 🏰ad1? (180)
Essential was 17 ♘g3.

180
B

17...♘f3+!! 18 gf ef 19 🖤d3 ♛e6! 20 ♘g3 ♛xh3 21 🖤f1 ♛h6! 22 🖤d3
Or 22 ♛xg6 hg 23 🏰xd6 ♘g4 24 🖤d3 ♛h2+ 25 ♚f1 ♛xf2 mate.
22...♘g4 23 ♘ce4 ♛h3! 0-1

Game 181: English

Korchnoi-Robatsch
Amsterdam 1972

1 c4 g6 2 e4 e5 3 ♘f3 d6 4 d4 ♘c6?!

Korchnoi goes all the way and gives this a ?; undoubtedly better is 4...♗g4!? and on 5 de ♗xf3 6 ♕xf3 de followed by ♘-c6-d4, or 5 d5 ♗h6!?

5 d5 ♘ce7 6 ♘c3 ♗g4 7 c5!?

So that 7...dc 8 ♕a4+ ♗d7 9 ♕b3 regains the pawn leaving Black weakened. Also good was 7 h3!? ♗xf3 8 ♕xf3 ♗h6(?) 9 ♗xh6 ♘xh6 10 ♕f6! intending 11 g4!

7...♗h6!? 8 cd cd 9 h3 ♗xf3 10 ♕xf3 ♗xc1 11 ♖xc1 a6 12 ♗d3 ♔f8! 13 b4!?

More dynamic than 13 0-0 when 13...g5!? is interesting. A matter of taste.

13...♔g7 14 ♕e3! ♘f6 15 0-0 ♘d7

Perhaps 15...♘h5!? is an improvement here, i.e. 16 g3 ♕d7 17 ♔h2 ♖hc8.

16 a4 ♕b6?

By 16...a5! 17 ♘b5 ♘c8 Black could semi-liquidate the Q-side and give his knight the handy c5 square. This ending is extremely favourable to White, as he now has a tactic.

17 ♕xb6 ♘xb6 18 a5 ♘d7 *(181)*

Or 18...♘bc8 19 ♘a4 and ♖c7.

181
W

19 ♘b5! ab 20 ♖c7 ♘f6?!

Best was 20...♘xd5 21 ed ♘f6 22 ♖xb7 ♘xd5 23 ♖xb5 when the a and b pawns should win.

21 ♖xe7 b6 22 ab ♖hb8

Also inadequate was 22...♖a4 23 b7 ♖xb4 24 ♖c1.

23 ♖a7! 1-0

The threat is 24 ♖fa1 ♖xa7 25 ba ♖a8 26 ♗xb5 and ♗c6.

Game 182: English Opening

Keene-Wockenfüss
Bad Lauterberg 1977

1 c4 e5 2 ♘c3 ♘f6 3 ♘f3 e4

Keene considers this move at best dubious.

4 ♘g5! b5!?

Better than 4...d5 5 cd ♗f5 6 ♘gxe4! and ♕a4+.

5 d3!? bc (5...ed!?) 6 de ♘c6 7 e3 ♗b4 8 ♗xc4 0-0 9 0-0 ♗xc3?!

Better was 9...h6; this inaccuracy develops White's Q-bishop quickly and allows a combination.

10 bc h6 *(182)*

182
W

11 f4!! hg 12 fg ♘h7

Or 12...♘xe4 13 g6 with forks at d5 in the offing; 13...♕h4 14 ♖f4!, or 13...♘d6 14 ♕h5!

13 g6 ♘g5

Not 13...♘f6 because of 14 ♖xf6! followed by ♕h5.

14 ♗a3! ♘e5

Or 14...d6? 15 ♗xf7+ ♘xf7 16 gf+ ♖xf7 17 ♖xf7 ♔xf7 18 ♕d5+ with two pawns and an attack.

15 ♗xf8 ♘xc4 16 gf+! ♔xf8

Forced. On 16...♘xf7 comes 17 ♖xf7! ♔xf7 19 ♕d5+ winning after 18...♔xf8 19 ♖f1+ ♔e7 20 ♕g5+! ♔e8 21 ♕g6+! ♔e7 22 ♖f7+, or 18...♔g6 19 ♖f1!, or 18...♔e8 19 ♕g8!

17 ♕h5 ♗b7 18 ♕h8+ ♔e7 19 ♕xg7 ♕f8 20 ♕f6 mate!

Game 183: English

Eising-Janetschek
Copenhagen 1977

1 c4 e5 2 ♘c3 ♘f6 3 ♘f3 ♘c6 4 e3 ♗b4 5 ♕c2 ♗xc3!?

This is like a reversed Sicilian. Also interesting is 5...0-0, waiting to see if White will oblige with a tempo-consuming 6 a3 (6 ♘d5!? - see game 184).

6 ♕xc3 ♕e7 7 ♗e2 0-0 8 0-0 a5! 9 d3 d5 10 ♖e1

White could try 10 cd here without hurting his chances.

10...e4!? 11 ♘d4 ♘b4!? 12 ♘c2 dc 13 dc c5! 14 ♘xb4?

A positional disaster (backward a-pawn) but White is in any event cramped and has trouble defending his king.

14...ab 15 ♕c2 ♘g4! 16 ♗f1? (183)

Into the mincer. Karner gives 16 h3? ♘xf2! and wins, e.g. 17 ♔xf2 ♕h4+ 18 ♔f1 (or 18 g3 ♕xh3 with the plan of ♖-a6-f6) 18...♕xh3! 19 gh ♕xh3+ 20 ♔f2 ♕h2+ 21 ♔f1 ♖a6. On 16 ♗xg4 ♗xg4 threats of ♖-a6-g6 and ♖-d8-d3 show that opposite coloured bishops favour the attacker.

183
B

16...b3! 17 ♕xb3

There was only 17 ♕e2 when 17 ...♖xa2 18 ♖b1 ♘e5 19 ♕d1 (19 f3 ♗f5) 19...♗g4 20 ♕xb3 ♘f3+! wins.

17...♕h4 0-1

Game 184: English

Brinck-Claussen–Jacobsen
Stockholm 1971/2

1 c4 e5 2 ♘c3 ♘f6 3 ♘f3 ♘c6 4 e3 ♗b4 5 ♕c2 0-0 6 ♘d5 ♖e8 7 ♘g5

Also fairly enterprising is 7 ♕f5!?
7...g6 8 ♘xb4?! ♘xb4 9 ♕b3 c5! 10
a3 ♘c6 11 ♕c2?!

This allows a forcing line. White
has completely misread the basic
character of the position. Necessary
was 11 d3.

**11...h6 12 ♘e4 ♘xe4 13 ♕xe4
♘d4! 14 ♕d3 *(184)***

On 14 ♕b1 ♘b3! 15 ♖a2 d5 is
very promising. Westerinen gives
14 ♗d3 d5! 15 ♕xd5 ♕xd5 16 cd
c4! with winning prospects.

14...d5! 15 ed ed+ 16 ♔d1

More precise than 16 ♗e2 dc 17
♕xc4 d3 when Black regains his
piece without losing the momen-
tum of his attack, i.e. 18 0-0 ♖xe2
19 ♕xc5 ♗f5! with a complete bind
on White's position.

16...b5! 17 cb

A very strong reply to 17 cd
would be 17...♕xd5 18 ♕xb5 ♗a6!
19 ♕a4 d3! with threats of ...♘c4,
...♕e5 and ...♖e4.

17...♗f5! 18 ♕g3 c4 19 ♗e2

The alternative is 19 d3 ♕a5! 20
♗d2 ♕a4+ 21 ♔c1 ♖ac8 strafing
him unmercifully.

19...♖xe2! 20 ♔xe2 ♕e7+ 0-1

Resistance ends after 21 ♔d1 ♖e8
22 ♕f3 ♗d3!

Game 185: English

Seirawan-Browne
Berkeley 1979

1 c4 e5 2 ♘c3 ♘c6 3 ♘f3 f5!? 4 d4
e4 5 ♘g5 h6 6 ♘h3 g5!? 7 f3

Fighting to justify his jaunt with
the knight. Browne gives 7 e3 ♘f6
8 ♗e2 ♗g7 9 ♘h5+ ♘xh5 10 ♕xh5+
♔f8 equal; the text threatens to
swap on e4, then play e3 and ♘f2.

**7...ef! 8 ef (8 gf!?) 8...♗g7 9 d5?!
(9 ♗e3 ♕e7? 10 ♘d5) 9...♕e7+!
10 ♔d2!?**

Since 10 ♕e2 (10 ♗e2 ♘d4) 10...
♕xe2+ favours Black slightly
because of his dominance of the
black squares, the junior world
champion play á la Steinitz.

10...♘d4 11 ♗d3 ♔d8!

And so does Browne! Now 12
♖e1?! ♕d6 attacks the h-pawn.

12 ♘g1!? b5! 13 ♘ge2

Or 13 ♘xb5 ♘xb5 14 cb ♗b7, or
13 cb a6 with a promising attack;
Black's king is much safer.

13...bc 14 ♗xc4 ♕c5! 15 ♔d3?

Best chance was 15 b3! ♗a6! 16
♗xa6 ♘xe2 17 ♔xe2! ♕xc3 18 ♖b1
♕a5 and Black's a little better.

15...♖b8 16 ♗e3?! *(185)*

Still 16 b3 was needed but now
16...♗a6 17 ♗xa6 ♘xe2 18 ♘xe2
♕xd5+ wins.

185
B

16...♛xc4+!! 17 ♔xc4 ♝a6+ 18 ♘b5 ♘xb5! 0-1

The threat was 19...♘a3+ 20 ♔c5 d6+ 21 ♔c6 ♘e7 mate and on 19 ♘d4 Browne gives the entertaining variation 19...♝xd4+ 20 ♔c3 ♘e2+ 21 ♔d2 ♖xb2+ 22 ♔e1 ♝c3+ 23 ♔f2 ♘f4+ 24 ♔g1 ♖xg2 mate!

Game 186: Réti

Adamski-Podgaets
Varna 1972

1 ♘f3 ♘f6 2 c4 g6 3 b3 ♝g7 4 ♝b2 0-0 5 g3 d6 6 d4 ♘bd7 7 ♛d2?!

This is horrible - why encourage ...♘e4; natural is 7 ♝g2 and 7...e5 8 de ♘g4 9 0-0 maintains a slight cramp.

7...c6 8 ♝g2 ♘e4! 9 ♛c2 d5 10 ♘c3 ♘df6 11 ♘d2?? (186)

A quite horrible mistake. White has already given away a tempo by misplacing his queen and he should castle. Having said that Black then has 11...♝f5 and the queen must move on - 12 ♘xe4 ♝xe4 13 ♛d2 ♘g4 leaves Black the initiative.

186
B

11...♘xf2! 12 ♔xf2 ♘g4+ 13 ♔f3

Or 13 ♔g1 ♝xd4+ 14 e3 ♝xe3+ 15 ♔f1 ♝f5 16 ♛d1 (16 ♛c1 dc) 16...♝c5 17 ♛f3 ♘e5 18 ♛d1 (18 ♛f4 ♘d3) 18...♝d3+ 19 ♘e2 (19 ♔e1 dc) 19...♘g4! wins; 13 ♔e1 ♘e3 14 ♛d3 ♝xd4!

13...♝xd4! 14 ♘d1

Minev gives 14 e4 ♘e3 15 ♛d3 ♝g4+ 16 ♔f2 dc winning.

14...♘e5+ 15 ♔f4 g5+ 16 ♔xg5+ ♛d6 17 ♖f1 ♔g7! 0-1

Game 187: Réti

Liebert-Tabor
Kecskemet 1970

1 ♘f3 ♘f6 2 g3 d6 3 d4 ♘bd7 4 ♝g2 e5 5 c4 ♝e7 6 ♘c3 c6 7 e4 ♛c7 8 0-0?! ♘f8!?

This differs from a King's Indian in two respects: Black's K-bishop is on e7, not g7, and White has castled but Black hasn't. As a result Black can conjure up a quick attack.

9 h3 ♘g6 10 ♝e3 h5! 11 ♛d2 ♝d7

12 b4 (vs. ...0-0-0) 12...♕c8! 13 ♘g5 h4 14 g4 *(187)*

14...♘xg4! 15 hg h3! 16 ♘xh3

On 16 ♗f3 f6 regains the piece and 16 ♗h1 h2+ 17 ♔g2 f6! 18 ♘f3 ♗xg4 19 ♘xh2 ♗h3+ 20 ♔g1 ♗xf1 21 ♘xf1 ♕g4+ wins, i.e. 22 ♗g2 ♘h4! or 22 ♘g3 ♖xh1+! 23 ♔xh1 ♕h3+ 24 ♔g1 ♘h4.

16...♗xg4 17 ♘g5 ♗xg5 18 ♘e2?!

Feeble. The critical line is 18 ♗xg5 ♗f3!! 19 ♕e3 (19 ♗xf3 ♕h3 20 ♖fc1 ♕xf3) 19...♖h1+! 20 ♗xh1 (20 ♔xh1 ♕h3+) 20...♕g4+ 21 ♔h2 ♕h5+! 22 ♔g3 ♘f4! 23 ♗xf4 ♕g4+ 24 ♔h2 ♕h4+ mating.

18...♗f3! 19 ♘g3

Or 19 ♗xf3 ♕h3, while if 19 ♗xg5 ♗xg2 wins.

19...♘h4 20 ♗xg5 ♘xg2 21 de ♕h3 0-1

Game 188: Réti

Spassov-P.Popov
Stara Zagora 1977

1 ♘f3 d5 2 c4 e6 3 g3 ♘f6 4 ♗g2

b6?!

Premature and involving weakened white squares.

5 0-0 ♗b7 6 ♘e5! ♘bd7 7 ♕a4 c5 8 ♘c3 ♕c7?! 9 cd! ♘xd5 (9...♕xe5 10 de) 10 ♘xd5 ♗xd5 (10...ed 11 d4! planning ♗f4) 11 e4 ♗b7 12 d4 f6 13 ♘f3!

Either the game opens up or White establishes his centre after this - exemplary Reti strategy. If now 13...♘xe4? 14 ♖e1 ♗d5 15 ♘g5! wins, e.g. 15...♗xg2 16 ♖xe6+ ♔d8 (16...♗e7 17 ♔xg2 fg 18 ♗xg5) 17 ♘f7+ ♔c8 18 ♔xg2.

13...♕c6 14 ♕d1! ♗e7

Of course not 14...♕xe4 because of 15 ♘h4.

15 ♖e1 0-0 16 ♗h3! e5

This was essential to prevent 17 d5!

17 d5 ♕c7 18 ♗e6+ ♔h8 19 ♘h4! ♖fd8 *(188)*

Against the threats of ♕h5, ♕g4; if 19...g6 20 ♘xg6+! hg 21 ♕g4 threatening ♗xd7, ♕xg6.

20 ♘g6+! hg 21 ♕g4 ♘f8 22 ♗f7!

Very pretty, and essential; on 22 ♕h4+ ♘h7 23 ♗f7 g5!, or 22 ♕h3+

♘h7 23 ♗f7 ♗c8! Black escapes.
22...♘h7 23 ♗xg6! 1-0
Forcing mate, i.e. 23...♔g8 24 ♕e6+ ♔h8 25 ♕h3, or 23...♗xd5 24 ed, or 23...♘f8 24 ♕h5+ ♔g8 25 ♗f7 mate.

Game 189: Réti

Bronstein-Alburt
Baku 1972

1 ♘f3 ♘f6 2 g3 b5!?
Spassky's variation, announcing vigorous counterplay on the Q-side and stopping c4.
3 ♗g2 ♗b7 4 0-0 c5 5 d3 e6 6 e4 d6
Interesting was 6...♗e7!? when 7 ♖e1 0-0 8 e5 ♘e8 followed by ...f6! exposes a weakness on f3. Unclear was 7 e5 ♘d5 8 c4!?
7 a4 b4 8 ♘bd2 ♘fd7?!
8...♘c6 was best here.
9 ♘c4 ♘c6 10 ♗g5!? ♕c7
Not 10...♗e7? 11 ♘xd6+, and 10 ...f6 offers a target for ♗h3 later.
11 ♘fd2 g6?!
Baranov suggests 11...♘de5 is correct, though 11...h6!? is also interesting.
12 ♗f4 ♘d4?!
A further inaccuracy; 12...e5!? was better.
13 c3 bc 14 bc ♘c6 15 a5! ♗a6? *(189)*
Allowing the decisive breakthrough. Either 15...e5 or 15...a6 was called for. Bronstein needs no further encouragement...

189
W

16 e5! d5
Or 16...de 17 ♘xe5! ♘bxe5 18 ♗xe5 ♘xe5 19 ♗xa8.
17 ♗xd5! ed 18 e6 ♘de5 19 ♘xe5 ♘xe5 20 ♗xe5! 1-0
After 20...♕xe5 21 ♕a4+ wins the queen.

Game 190: Réti

Hug-Korchnoi
Swiss Team Ch 1978

1 ♘f3 e6 2 g3 d5 3 ♗g2 c5 4 0-0 ♘c6 5 c4 dc! 6 ♕a4 ♗d7 7 ♕xc4 ♖c8! 8 ♘c3 ♘f6 9 d4?!
Seeing that 9...cd 10 ♘xd4 and Black knight moves are not dangerous; however, Black is now able to seize the initiative.
9 b5! 10 ♕d3
On 10 ♕xb5 cd Black is a little better and 10 ♘xb5? ♘a5! 11 ♕d3 c4 costs a piece.
10...cd 11 ♘xd4 ♘e5 12 ♕d1 ♕b6 13 ♗g5 ♗e7 14 ♖c1 0-0 15 ♘f3 ♘xf3+ 16 ♗xf3 ♖fd8 17 ♕b3?

Partos recommends 17 ♘e4 ♗c6 18 ♕e1 with equality.

17...b4 18 ♘e4 *(190a)*

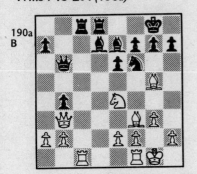

190a
B

18...♘xe4!! 19 ♗xe7 ♖xc1! (19... ♘d2? 20 ♗xd8) **20 ♖xc1**

Impossible was 20 ♗xd8 ♖xf1+ 21 ♔xf1 ♕xf2 mate.

20...♕xf2+ 21 ♔h1 ♖c8! 22 ♕d1

And not 22 ♖xc8+? ♗xc8 23 ♕d1 ♕xf3! 24 ef ♘f2+ winning a piece.

22...♖xc1 23 ♕xc1 ♗c6!! 24 ♗xb4? *(190b)*

Overlooking the threat - 24 ♕a1 was forced and losing, but 24 ♕g1 ♕xe2! 25 ♗xe2 ♘f2 mate, or 24 ♕b1 ♘d2 25 ♕g1 ♗xf3+ etc. with an easy ending weren't on.

190b
B

24...♕xe2!! 0-1

After 25 ♗xe2 ♘xg3+ 26 ♔g1 ♘xe2+ Black emerges a piece up. Superb play by Korchnoi.

Game 191: Réti

Sanguinetti-Donoso
Fortaleza 1975

1 ♘f3 ♘f6 2 c4 c6 3 ♘c3 d5 4 e3 e6 5 b3 ♘bd7 6 ♗b2 ♗e7

Quinteros marks this ?! and in turn recommends 6...♗d6.

7 d4 0-0 8 ♗d3 b6 9 0-0 ♗b7 10 ♕e2 ♖c8 11 ♖ad1!? ♕c7 12 ♘e5!?

Going for a Pillsbury attack set-up with f4, ♖f3 etc., and now 12... ♘xe5 13 de ♕xe5?? 14 ♘xd5. On 12 e4 de 13 ♘xe4 c5 Black is approaching equality.

12...dc 13 bc ♘xe5 14 de ♘e8?

The knight has no future here. 14 ...♘d7 was necessary.

15 ♕h5 g6

Better than 15...f5? when White has 16 ef ♘xf6 17 ♕h3 e5 18 ♗xh7+! ♘xh7 19 ♖d7.

16 ♕g4! ♕xe5? *(191)*

191
W

17 ♘d5! ♕d6

Or 17...♕xb2 18 ♘xe7+; 17...
♕g5 18 f4! ♕xg4 19 ♘xe7 mate.
18 ♗xg6!! hg 19 ♘f4 ♕b4 20
♘xg6! f5

On 20...♕xb2 21 ♘xe7+ ♔h8 22
♕h5+ ♔g7 23 ♕g5+ ♔h7 24 ♖d4
♕xd4 25 ed ♖c7 26 ♖e1 will win,
and 20...♗f6? 21 ♘e7+!
21 ♘xe7+ ♔f7 22 ♕g6+ ♔xe7 23
♕g5+ 1-0

There follows 23...♘f6 24 ♗xf6+
♖xf6 (24...♔e8 25 ♕g6+ ♖f7 26
♖d7! ♕f8 27 ♖fd1) 25 ♕g7+ ♖f7
26 ♖d7+! ♔xd7 27 ♕xf7+ and 28
♖d1+.

Game 192: Blümenfeld Counter Gambit

Spassov-Manolov
Primorsko 1975

1 ♘f3 ♘f6 2 c4 e6 3 d4 c5 4 d5
b5!? 5 ♗g5! ♕a5+

Minev gives 5...bc 6 e4 ♕a5+ 7
♗d2 ♕b6 8 ♘c3 with advantage to
White; Barden and Harding
recommend 5...ed 6 cd h6.
6 ♘bd2 bc?!

Black cannot afford to miss out
6...♘e4!
7 ♗xf6 gf 8 e4 f5!? 9 de

Or 9 ef ed!?
9...fxe4 10 ef+ ♔d8 11 ♗xc4! ♗b7

Not 11...ef 12 ♕xf3 with threats
of ♕xa8, ♕f6+xh8.
12 ♘g5 h6 *(192)*

13 ♘gxe4!

Poor is 13 ♘h3 d5, but 13 ♕h5
was a promising alternative.
13...♗xe4 14 ♕g4 d5 15 0-0!

And not 15 ♕g8 dc 16 ♕xh8 ♘d7
when the bishop installed at d3 will
favour Black. Now 15...dc 16
♕xe4 wins.
15...♕xd2 16 ♖ad1 h5

Any queen moves are met by 17
♕xe4.
17 ♕e6! ♕h6 18 ♕xe4 ♔c7 19
♕xd5 ♘c6

Or 19...♗d6 20 ♕xa8 ♘c6 21
♕e8/g8! wins. Black's in real
trouble now.
20 ♕d7+ ♔b6 21 ♖d3! ♘b4?! 22
♕b5+ 1-0

Game 193: King's Fianchetto

B.Jacobsen-Ljubojević
Groningen 1969/70

1 g3 e5 2 ♗g2 ♘c6 3 e4 ♗c5 4 ♘e2
♘f6 5 c3 d5 6 b4?!

All this stuff is having a bad effect on his white squares - no wonder the refutation comes out of the Morphy copy-book. Milič suggests 6 ed ♘xd5 7 0-0.

6...♗b6 7 ed ♘xd5 8 ♗a3?!

This is rather feeble. White must play 8 0-0 now so that he can meet 8...♗g5 with 9 d3 with some hope of eventually exploiting the h1-a8 diagonal.

8...♗g4! 9 0-0 (193)

9...♘f4!! 10 gf ♕d3! 11 ♖e1 0-0-0! 12 b5

White's position looks awfully silly. On 12 ♘c1 ♕g6! wins, so he has to try developing this way.

12...♘a5 13 ♗b4 ♘c4 14 a4 ef 15 a5

He puts his head into the lion's mouth, but 15 ♘xf4 ♕f5 16 ♕xg4 ♕xg4 17 ♗h3 ♕xg1 is illegal and on 16 ♗f3 here Milič gives 16...h5! and wins.

15...♗xf2+! 16 ♔xf2 ♘e3! 17 ♘a3

Other tries are also inadequate, i.e. 17 de ♕xe3+ or 17 ♕b3 ♘xg2 18 ♔xg2 ♖he8.

17...♘xd1+ 18 ♖axd1 f3 19 ♘c1 ♕f5 20 ♗h1 ♕f4! 0-1

Game 194: Double Fianchetto

Jim Plaskett is an aggressive well-prepared player who made an IM norm in this tournament.

Iskov-Plaskett
Ramsgate 1979

1 g3 f5 2 b3 e5 3 d4?!

Securing black square play at the cost of time and space.

3...ed 4 ♕xd4 ♘f6 5 ♗b2 (5 c4!? ♗b4+) 5...♗e7 6 ♗g2 (6 c4!?) 6...d5! 7 ♘h3 ♘c6 8 ♕d1 ♗e6 9 ♘f4 ♕d7 10 ♘xe6?!

Better was 10 e3 with the idea of c3, ♘a3-c2/b5 taking the sting out of Black's centre.

10...♕xe6 11 0-0 0-0-0! 12 e3 h5!

Straightforward and strong. Black clearly stands better.

13 ♘d2 h4 14 ♘f3 hg 15 hg ♘e4 16 ♕e2 ♖h5! 17 ♘e5?! (17 ♖fd1; 17 ♗xg7!?) 17...♖dh8 18 ♘xc6 (194)

Falling into the trap, but his defences were tottering.

18...♖h1+!! 19 ♗xh1 ♕h6! 20 ♘xe7+ ♔b8 21 ♔g2 ♘g5! 0-1

Game 195: Polish

Lindquist-Sorenfors
Corres 1975

1 b4 e5 2 ♗b2?!

Correct is 2 a3! The exchange of 'e' for 'b' pawn gives Black a promising attacking position down the central files.

2...♗xb4! 3 ♗xe5 ♘f6 4 c4 0-0 5 e3 d5!? 6 cd ♘xd5 7 ♘f3 ♖e8 8 ♗e2? *(195)*

Berglund gives 8 ♗b2 ♘f4 9 ♕a4 ♘a6! threatening ...♘c5, or 8 ♗c4? ♗g4 9 ♗b2 ♘xe3! 10 fe ♖xe3+ 11 ♔f2 ♖xf3+! 12 gf ♕h4+ 13 ♔g1 ♗h3 14 ♗f1 ♘c6 with an attack in both cases.

195
B

8...♖xe5! 9 ♗xe5 ♕f6 10 f4 ♘xe3 11 ♕b3 ♘xg2+ 12 ♔d1 ♘xf4 13 ♘xf7!?

Getting a pawn back, since 13 ♕xb4? ♕xe5 14 ♘c3 ♘xe2 wins without much trouble.

13...♕xf2 14 ♗c4 (14 ♕xb4 ♘xe2) 14...♗e6 15 ♗xe6 ♘xe6!? 16 ♖e1 ♘c6 17 ♕xe6 ♕xe6 18 ♖xe6 ♗d6! 19 h4?!

Losing the exchange, but in any case after 19 ♖e2 ♖f8 20 ♔c1 ♖f1+ 21 ♔b2 ♖h1 wins the pawn for an enjoyable ending since 22 ♘c3? runs into 22...♗a3+!

19...♗e5 20 ♘c3 ♖f8! 0-1

Either 21 ♔c1 ♖f1+ 22 ♔b2 ♖xa1 23 ♔xa1 ♗f7! or 21 ♖b1 ♖f1+ 22 ♔c2 ♘d4+! are hopeless.

Game 196: Polish

What else, between two Polish masters?

Dobosz-Bednarski
Esbjerg II 1979

1 b4 e5 2 ♗b2?! ♗xb4! 3 ♗xe5 ♘f6 4 ♘f3 0-0 5 e3 ♖e8 6 c4 d5 7 ♕b3

Instead 7 cd ♘xd5 transposes to game 195.

7...♘c6 8 ♗b2 d4! 9 ♗e2

White had to avoid 9 ♘xd4?? ♘xd4 10 ♕xb4 ♘c2+.

9...de 10 fe ♘e4 11 ♘c3?! *(196)*

Permitting horrible carnage, although a decent alternative was not easy to find.

196
B

11...♘xd2! 12 ♘xd2 ♖xe3 13 ♘f3
Or 13 ♘f1? ♖xe2+ 14 ♔xe2
♘d4+.
13...♗g4 14 ♔f2 ♗xf3! 15 ♗xf3
Here 15 ♔xe3 ♗c5+ leads to mate
or queen losses.
15...♕d2+ 16 ♔g3 ♗d6+ 17 ♔h3
♖xc3! 18 ♕xc3 ♕h6+ 19 ♔g4 f5+!
20 ♔xf5 ♕g6 mate.

Game 197: Nimzowitsch/ Larsen

Larsen-Eley
Hastings 1972/3

1 b3!? e5 2 ♗b2 ♘c6 3 e3 ♘f6 4
♗b5!? d6
Designated ?! by Bukić but more
natural than his suggested 4...
♕e7 (!?).
5 ♘e2 ♗d7?!
This seems pointless. One would
expect 5...♗e7 to complete his K-
side development or possibly 5...g6
intending an evental ...f5.
6 0-0 ♗e7 7 f4 e4 8 ♘g3 0-0 9 ♗xc6
bc
Fearing 9...♗xc6 10 ♘f5, although after 10...♗d7 11 ♘xe7+
♕xe7+ Black's lead in development
should enable him to counter the
pressure on the a1-h8 diagonal.
10 c4 d5 11 ♘c3 ♖e8 12 ♖c1 ♗g4
13 ♘ce2 ♘d7 14 h3 ♗xe2 15 ♕xe2
♘c5? *(197)*
Looks strong but now White can
force a win. 15...♗f6 was necessary
when White maintains a clear
positional advantage after 16 ♗xf6
♘xf6 17 cd ed 18 ♘f5.

197
W

16 ♕g4! g6
No good is 16...♗f6 17 ♗xf6
♕xf6 18 cd, or 16...♗f8 17 ♘h5!
17 f5! ♘d3
There's no defence, i.e. 17...♖f8
18 fg and wins; 18...hg 19 ♘f5!
♘d3 20 ♘xe7+ ♕xe7 21 ♗f6 and
22 ♕h4 or 18...fg 19 ♘f5! ♗f6 20
♗xf6 ♖xf6 21 cd.
18 fg hg
Not 18...fg? 19 ♕e6 mate!
19 ♖xf7! ♔xf7 20 ♖f1+ ♗f6 21
♗xf6 1-0
Neat; 21...♕xf6 22 ♕d7+! ♖e7
23 ♖xf6+ ♔xf6 24 ♕xc6+.

Game 198: Nimzowitsch/ Larsen

A well-known gem from the then
world champion, played in the
'Match of the Century' - USSR vs.
the World.

Larsen-Spassky
Belgrade 1970

1 b3 e5 2 ♗b2 ♘c6 3 c4 (3 e3) 3...

♘f6 4 ♘f3 (4 e3) 4...e4 5 ♘d4 ♗c5 6 ♘xc6 dc 7 e3 ♗f5!

That backward d-pawn looks horrible!

8 ♕c2 ♕e7 9 ♗e2 0-0-0 10 f4?

The decisive mistake; preferable was 10 ♗xf6 ♕xf6 11 ♘c3 - Spassky - or even 10 a3!?

10...♘g4!

With the threat of ...♕h4+.

11 g3 h5! (11...♖xd2!?) 12 h3 (198)

On 12 ♘c3 ♖xd2! decides matters i.e. 13 ♕xd2 ♗xe3 14 ♕d1 (14 ♕c2 ♗f2+ and 15...♘e3+ or 15...e3+) 14 ...♗f2+ 15 ♔f1 h4! wins, or 13 ♔xd2 ♗xe3+ 14 ♔d1 (14 ♔e1 ♗f2+ etc.) 14...♖d8+.

198
B

12...h4!!

Now if 13 ♗xg4 ♗xg4 14 hg hg 15 ♖g1 (15 ♖xh8 ♖xh8 leaves the king defenceless) 15...♖h1! as in the game.

13 hg hg 14 ♖g1 ♖h1!!

Sacrificing a rook for one tempo.

15 ♖xh1 g2 16 ♖f1

Or 16 ♖g1 ♕h4+ 17 ♔d1 ♕h1 18 ♕c3 ♕xg1+ 19 ♔c2 ♕f2 and wins.

16...♕h4+ 17 ♔d1 gf♕+ 0-1

Black mates, i.e. 18 ♗xf1 ♗xg4+ etc.

Game 199: Nimzowitsch/ Larsen

Ljubojevic-Kavalek
Manila 1973

1 b3 e5 2 ♗b2 d6 3 c4 ♘f6 4 ♘c3 g6 5 d4?! (5 e3) 5...ed 6 ♕xd4 ♘c6 7 ♕e3+?!

An artificial manoeuvre to create weakness in the Black camp which rebounds quickly. Ivkov suggests 7 ♕d2.

7...♗e6 8 ♘f3 ♗g7 9 ♘g5 0-0! 10 ♘xe6 fe 11 g3 (199)

Or 11 ♕xe6+ ♔h8 12 ♘d5 (12 e3 ♘d4!) 12...♘xd5 (12...♖e8? 13 ♕xf6!) 13 ♗xg7 ♔xg7 14 cd (14 ♕xd5 ♕f6) 14...♘d4 15 ♕e4 ♕f6 16 f3 ♖ae8 17 ♕d2 ♘xf3+ wins.

199
B

11...d5! 12 ♕xe6+

Here 12 ♗g2 ♔h8! with the double threat of ...d4 and ...♘g4, and if 13 ♕xe6 ♘d4 wins.

12...♔h8 13 ♘xd5 ♘xd5 14 ♗xg7+ ♔xg7 15 cd

Or 15 ♕xd5? ♕f6. It's amazing how safe Black's king is, and how unsafe White's.

15...♖e8! 16 ♕g4 ♕xd5 17 f3 ♘e5 18 ♖d1 ♘xf3+ 19 ♔f2 ♕xd1 20 ef

♛d2+ 21 ♔g1 ♖e1 22 ♕c4 ♖ae8
0-1

Game 200: Nimzowitsch/ Larsen

With this, the final game in the book, there is a twist in the tail. It raises the old question of whether chess can become 'played out'. I hope that the general message of this book is that, no, chess won't be played out for a while! But the alert reader should be able to 'solve' the diagram position without too much trouble...

Plachetka-Zinn
Dečin 1974

1 ♘f3 c5 2 b3 ♘c6 3 ♗b2 ♘f6 4 e3 d5

Not obstructing White's plan to control e5. Plachetka mentions 4... d6!? intending ...e5.

5 ♗b5 e6 6 ♘e5 ♕c7 7 0-0 ♗d6 8 ♗xc6+ bc 9 f4 0-0 10 ♖f3!?

! with an attack - Plachetka. True, it's dangerous but Black could defend (11...f6!?), and White's rook may be poorly placed at h3; possibly the quiet 10 d3 is better.

10...♘d7 11 ♖h3 g6? *(200)*

In the diagram position White's reply compelled instant resignation. For those who can't work it out, a hint; study the NIDQID Hybrid Opening!

Index of Players

The numbers next to players names refer to games. Numbers in bold indicate that the player was White; numbers in brackets refer to complete games in the notes to the numbered game.